BILL EDRICH

A BIOGRAPHY

by the same author

The Family Fortune –
A Saga of Sussex Cricket

A Chain of Spin Wizards

Hedley Verity

Johnny Wardle – Cricket Conjuror

Les Ames

Herbert Sutcliffe – Cricket Maestro

BILL EDRICH

A BIOGRAPHY

ALAN HILL

Foreword by
Denis Compton

ANDRE DEUTSCH

First published in Great Britain 1994
by André Deutsch Limited
106 Great Russell Street, London WC1B 3LJ

Copyright © 1994 Alan Hill

The author has asserted his moral rights

Cataloguing-in-publication data available
for this title from the British Library

ISBN 0 233 98868 8

Printed in Great Britain by
St Edmundsbury Press, Bury St Edmunds, Suffolk

by Denis Compton, CBE

They called us the Middlesex twins and that was right because our friendship, lasting over fifty years, was a very special one. We started as groundstaff boys and prospered together, taking pride in each other's achievements. I am especially proud that our names will be forever linked with the building of the Edrich and Compton stands at Lord's.

Bill was a remarkable chap; we were never jealous of each other and I cannot remember us ever having a cross word. We were just good chums. His courage as a batsman was second to none. It didn't matter how quick they bowled at him.

Alan Hill, in this first full-length biography of a great cricketer, has described Bill's encounter with Frank Tyson against Northamptonshire at Lord's in 1954. He was thirty-eight by this time, nearing the veteran stage, but his heroics, when he was struck a fearful blow by Frank, illustrated his fearlessness. He was entitled to extended sick leave, but the injury didn't stop him playing. He went up to Northampton a week later and scored a hundred against Tyson. Don Bradman, eighty-five last year, reckoned that Tyson, for a couple of years, was the fastest bowler he had ever seen, not excluding Harold Larwood; and he was certainly the quickest in my experience.

Make no mistake about it, Bill was a very brave man

and a tremendous fighter – in cricket and war. If I had to put my life on one man saving me, it would be Bill. Before and after the war Bill was a superb hooker of the ball off the back foot. Patsy Hendren, one of the all-time masters, taught us both this lesson in strokeplay in our apprentice days at Lord's. It was this ability to play off the back foot, a forgotten art these days, which demonstrated Bill's greatness as a batsman. The power he engendered in the hook shot was almost as vicious as when Patsy went to work. He was a wonderful player of off-spin, too, as Jim Laker often found to his cost. Bill used to strike the ball wide of mid-on. Nor was he afraid to hit over the top. He would guide the ball to exactly where he wanted it to go.

As a bowler, Bill was a bit of a slinger but, boy, he was pretty hasty and a bundle of energy. He had a good action, body and shoulders working in unison. And I can tell you that the slips used to stand well back to him! In 1938, against Australia at Lord's, Bill was very unlucky not to dismiss Don Bradman. He was bowling from the Pavilion End and got a ball to nip back and strike the Don on his pads. I was fielding at straightish mid-on, with a reasonable sight of the direction of the ball, and it looked to me as if it would hit halfway up the middle stump. I used to talk about the incident with Bradman in later years. The dear old Don would never admit that he was out. All he would say was: 'Yes, it must have been quite close!'

In his absorbing book Alan Hill lays proper emphasis on Bill's utter contempt for cheats in cricket. Bill, like Godfrey Evans, would never appeal for anything unless he thought the batsman was out. He adopted the same philosophy as a batsman. If he knew he had edged a catch, he didn't require the umpire to send him on his way to the pavilion.

Bill's death, in such tragic circumstances, was a

great personal loss. I know he enjoyed himself at the 1986 St George's Day lunch on the last day of his life. I would have loved to have been with him. I rarely missed this event but, as luck would have it, I couldn't be there. Bill, along with another good friend of mine, Douglas Bader, was a great patriot. It was an Englishman's day, a very special occasion. We were absolutely in our element on those occasions.

CONTENTS

ILLUSTRATIONS

16. a) Wreath for Bill Edrich's memorial service; b) Denis Compton opens the Compton and Edrich stands at Lord's, 1991

Cartoons in Text
Four cartoons from the *Natal Mercury* during the 'timeless' Test at Durban, on 8, 11, 14, 15 March 1939
(pages 62, 67, 70, 73)

Cartoon by Roy Ulyett, 'Battling Bill' from *The Greatest of my time* by Trevor Bailey
(page 147)

Edrich/Laker cartoon by Mahood from *Daily Mail*, April 1986
(page 223)

Acknowledgements for the photographs:
Edrich family archives: 1a, 2a, 2b, 3a, 3b, 3c, 4a, 4b, 6b, 7b, 9b, 14b, 14c, 15a, 15b, 15c, 16a
David Armstrong: 1b, 1c
D. M. Gaudoin: 2c
Sport & General Ltd: 7a, 8, 9a, 12b
Hulton-Deutsch: 10a, 10b, 10c, 12b
E. L. Hope: 5a
Imperial War Museum: 5b
Eastern Daily Press: 13a
C. G. Howard: 14a
Patrick Eagar: 16b

To Jasper and Justin
for their memories of Bill
a father they loved and admired

Author's Introduction

The anecdote of an old friend, as this project was nearing completion, presented a delightful image of the audacity and charm of Bill Edrich. 'You've chosen a smashing girl,' said the veteran Bill. It was intended as a sincere compliment to my friend's fiancée. Bill, the ageless romantic, was only mildly embarrassed to be told that a few days earlier he had expressed, in equally flattering terms, his admiration direct to the lady herself.

On another occasion, during the Scarborough Festival, his overflowing bonhomie was icily received at a reception at the Grand Hotel. The subject this time was Lady Leveson Gower, the wife of Sir Henry, known as 'Shrimp', and the long-standing organiser of the festival. Dennis Silk, the former Cambridge blue, Somerset cricketer and MCC president, recalled Edrich's salutation to his hostess. 'Bill was in his customary festive mood. He knelt before the austere Lady "Shrimp" and softly crooned: "Have I told you lately that I love you?" She was not amused by his serenade and lifted her head in disdain.'

Edrich, in his own estimation at least, was always a heart-throb; he danced his way into the lives of so many people. His spectacular life mingled the constant kindness and care of a true countryman with the bravado of a born crusader. The heroism, which gained him the

DFC in the second world war, brought him enduring respect as a formidable adversary at cricket. He was a patriot first and foremost. Playing for England and fighting for England, without blemish or shame, were his priorities. He steadfastly upheld these values.

Edrich, as I relate, first demonstrated his qualities of courage as a sixteen-year-old Norfolk debutant against All-India at Lakenham in 1932. The late Eric Edrich and his brothers and sister, Geoffrey, Brian and Ena, were splendid allies in evoking memories of this episode and other character-forming events of their childhood. I am deeply indebted to them and to D. M. Gaudoin, the present Headmaster at Bracondale School, for their help in the key opening passage of the book.

An auspicious beginning in first-class cricket had, as its highlight, the achievement of 1,000 runs before June in Edrich's second full season with Middlesex in 1938; but he used to say that none of his cricket exploits could ever approach the drama, endeavours and comradeship of his wartime campaign in the RAF. In describing his gallantry, and the low-level bombing raid which gained him the award of the DFC, I have been given access to family papers by his son, Justin. My thanks are also due to Air Marshal Sir Ivor Broom and to Ernie Hope, a member of Edrich's Blenheim crew throughout the campaign in 1941, both of whom were eloquent in praise of his daring leadership. Wing Commander Trevor Newman, at the RAF Personnel Management Centre at Innsworth, Gloucestershire, and the Ministry of Defence (Air Historical Branch) in London have also been most supportive with information.

Frank Tyson, a younger England colleague, has admiringly given evidence of a resilient and brave cricketer. His account of a duel with Edrich at Lord's in 1954 is placed next to the wartime chapter because it provides the starting-point for my reflections on a cricketer who did not seem to know the meaning of pain. Testimonies within this chapter also emphasise Edrich's impervious disregard for the formidable bouncers of Australian fast bowlers like Keith Miller and Ray Lindwall. Edrich, as his batting companion and friend, Denis Compton, relates, was at his best in a crisis. In addition, I retain my own vivid memory of Bill as a fighter in a seemingly lost cause when his aggression dumbfounded a Yorkshire crowd at Headingley in Bill Bowes' benefit match in 1947. His explosive strokeplay in Middlesex's second innings was in the death or glory category. It was an innings of remarkable power. As a boy with fierce Yorkshire loyalties, I had reluctantly to concede that I was watching an exciting batsman on the rampage.

Edrich was a man who inspired great affection, not least among the ladies who responded to his ebullient charm and whirlwind courtships. The interlude on his personality (Chapter 8) carries also impressions of the clouds of loneliness which lowered on a sensitive spirit. Jessy and Valerie Edrich, two of his surviving wives, have afforded glimpses of sadly curtailed relationships and yet retain fond memories of joyous times. The symptoms of his estrangement with the cricket hierarchy, which led to a three-year expulsion from Test cricket – he was uneasy with protocol and wary of those who primly objected to his exuberant lifestyle – are likewise outlined in the book; but it was a quarrel which should have been averted.

The legendary exploits of Edrich and Compton – and their respective gifts as batsmen – against the South Africans in 1947 occupy a special place in the book. My endeavours in recording these events were fortified and given a fresh impetus by the diligent researches of Jasper Edrich, Bill's elder son, in

Johannesburg. He has enlisted the testimonies of many of his father's South African rivals including Lindsay Tuckett, Jackie McGlew and Johnny Waite. Jasper, like his brother Justin, another enthusiastic collaborator, has clearly revelled in a journey of discovery, finding pleasure in tracing exploits beyond his memory. The former England Test player Willie Watson, now resident in South Africa, has also been most helpful to my research.

Edrich's career ended in an exultant late flowering as an inspirational leader of a band of happy young cricketers in Norfolk. Bill's zeal – and his devotion to the game – did not waver during this last sporting phase. These impressions were splendidly reinforced in conversations and correspondence with David Armstrong (the former Norfolk secretary); Jack Borrett; Bryan Stevens who, as the *Eastern Daily Press* cricket correspondent, admired and watched Edrich throughout his career; and other Norfolk contemporaries, Peter Powell, Nigel Moore and Tracey Moore.

As always, I must gratefully acknowledge the courteous assistance of the British Newspaper Library staff at Colindale, and of Stephen Green, the MCC curator at Lord's. Joe Hardstaff, the Middlesex CCC secretary, has placed me in contact with Edrich's county contemporaries. My thanks are also due to statisticians, David Kendix and Robert Briggs, for their detailed work on Edrich's career with England, Middlesex and Norfolk. Rallying voices during a challenging task have included my good friend, Don Rowan, who first suggested Edrich as a subject. An even more essential factor has been the support and encouragement of my wife, Betty. She has helped to lighten the course, becoming in the process, almost as enthralled as myself in the pursuit of an irrepressible man.

Denis Compton, who has kindly provided the Foreword to the book, has called upon his memories of a close and illustrious companion with Middlesex and England. Helping to supplement his impressions were other contemporaries at Lord's – George Mann, Jack Robertson, John Dewes, Peter Parfitt, Alan Moss, John Murray and Harry Sharp. Marking the goodwill, loyalty and affection which Edrich inspired as a cricketer and a man have been the contributions of many England and other colleagues and opponents: Alfred Gover, Trevor Bailey, Godfrey Evans, Alec Bedser, Peter May, Bob Appleyard, Roy Tattersall and Hubert Doggart. All, without exception, have attested to Edrich's gallantry and cherished the joys of his friendship.

It has been instructive in my appraisal of a multi-faceted man to listen to and gauge the views of other observers, including E. W. 'Jim' Swanton, Donald Carr, Doug Insole, Geoffrey Howard, Jack Belton, Tom Pearce, Philip Snow, Christopher Martin-Jenkins, Michael Denison, Ben and David Brocklehurst and the late Brian Johnston. Colin Webb, Edrich's former business manager, has praised the achievements of his colleague as a financial consultant during the later years; and Sir Donald Bradman, Arthur Morris, Keith Miller, Ray Lindwall, and the late Bill O'Reilly among Bill's Australian rivals have presented their tributes.

Two significant opinions, one from a post-war England captain and admiring pupil, the other from a noted cricket writer, underline the shining qualities of Bill Edrich. Peter May observed: 'I had the greatest possible regard for Bill's pugnacity. He was a marvellous player to have in your side.' Alan Ross, an astute commentator, wrote in his book *Australia 55*: 'His character and concentration are worth the easier strokes of his batting rivals. His stature grows in a crisis while theirs diminish.'

ALAN HILL
Lindfield, Sussex
December 1993

CHAPTER 1

Challenging the Goliaths

'If he has nerves, he controls them admirably, and his confidence is amazing in one of his age.' – *Eastern Daily Press*

The emblem of courage was paraded by Bill Edrich at an early age. As a sixteen-year-old Norwich schoolboy, he passed his first test on a tented field at Lakenham. The occasion was his Norfolk debut against All-India. 'He was only a little fellow, his face just peering over the top of the stumps,' recalled a long-standing friend. Young Billy gripped his bat just as stubbornly as he drew back the strings of his catapult in farmyard escapades at home. The race of his pounding heart matched the lengthening strides of the tall and menacing Mohammad Nissar, one of the fastest bowlers of his time. Nissar headed the tourists' bowling averages in this season. His alarming swing sorely troubled the pride of England's batsmen. One of them, Wally Hammond, on the Indians' first representative visit to this country in 1946, paid tribute to his magnificent control.

Among the crowd of 3,000 on this June day in 1932 was a large, vocal and proud contingent of black and white blazered Bracondale schoolboys, who had been given a day's holiday to support their fellow pupil. Watching the proceedings with equal intensity were members of the Edrich family. There was a jangle of

1

apprehension and, perhaps, a prayer for his survival as they awaited the outcome of a seemingly one-sided contest.

'I think we all trembled with fear. There was our little cherub facing this enormous dark man,' remembered Brian, Billy's younger brother.

Norfolk, to general astonishment, had bowled out India for 101 in less than three hours. Caution was indeed crucial on a wicket off which the ball came at varying heights, but the home bowlers did deserve special commendation for reducing the normally free-scoring Indian batsmen to warranted sedateness. The dismissal of the visitors for their second lowest total at this stage of the tour was, however, the signal for a ferocious response by Nissar and his new-ball partner, Nazir Ali. Norfolk lost five wickets for 21 runs before Edrich came to the crease.

Billy, as he later recalled, aspired only to avoid the indignity of a duck. 'I hung on to my bat like grim death as Nissar approached on his long bounding run. I set my teeth so hard that they hurt, and my brain kept repeating that I must not get out without scoring.'

Edrich demonstrated for the first time the defiance which was to become his trademark in the illustrious years ahead. Nissar took six wickets for 14 runs, and Norfolk were dismissed for 49; but by this time Edrich had won his laurels. In forty minutes he scored 20, sharing a partnership of 25 runs with Desmond Rought-Rought. No-one else reached double figures and the next highest score was eight by Basil Rought-Rought. Edrich was finally caught low down by the wicket-keeper off Nissar and not a run was added after his dismissal.

The *Eastern Daily Press* reported: 'It was a severe examination for a boy of sixteen. His nerve was un-shaken by the rapid fall of wickets, and if anyone expected him to display timidity facing bowlers flushed with success they were probably amazed and delighted by the splendid note of aggression in his batting.' The local correspondent enthused: 'His manpower shots were cheered by his delighted schoolfellows at the ringside. His legside play was particularly good. He took a ball from Nazir Ali, banged it to the square-leg boundary, and repeated the shot off the next ball.'

It was a county debut carrying the assurance and resolution of a seasoned county player. There was another rearguard action in the second innings. Edrich and Thistleton-Smith were associated in a partnership of 40 runs – Norfolk's best stand of the match – to cherish in a defeat without shame. All-India, immensely aided by another eight wickets from Nissar, did not seal their victory by 128 runs until ten minutes before time on the second and final day. Edrich's accomplishments at Lakenham also included an economical bowling spell of eight overs, conceding only 11 runs, and the wicket of Nazir Ali.

The happy exuberance of young Billy in the field flourished again when he took a skied catch with the coolness of a veteran. 'Nayudu hit a ball high enough for the boy to get cold feet before it fell,' reported the *Eastern Daily Press*. 'But whatever else young Edrich may lack he is not without confidence.'

Holding an excited court at Lakenham from the seat of his old Humber car was grandfather Harry, the doyen of the Edrich clan. It was Harry's custom on days of cricket achievement by his family to punch the car horn insistently with his stick. His gestures of elation did irritate other spectators, but the medley of discordant fanfares, merging with and drowned by rapturous applause, was more forgiveable on young Billy's triumphant day.

Harry Edrich, the bluff and kind yeoman farmer,

must be accorded legendary status. He was a fierce disciplinarian and could play the role of the tyrant, especially where the vanity of his daughters was concerned. None of them was allowed to wear make-up. He did, though, possess a disarming charisma and was acknowledged as an astute and wily businessman in the Norfolk farming community. Harry and his wife, Elizabeth, married in 1889 and brought up a family of thirteen children, nine sons and four daughters. They founded a cricketing dynasty with few parallels. Before the turn of the century Harry was locally renowned as an all-rounder, a vigorous hitter and a lively bowler. His active cricket career ended in his mid-forties when he was struck down with poliomyelitis and paralysed from the hips down. The disability did not quench his love of the game which continued unabated until his death, at the age of eighty-four, in 1942. Harry put his trust in his sons and grandsons, and never failed forcibly to remind them of their inheritance. The club he founded at Lingwood, a tiny village on the edge of the Norfolk Broads, was his grandson Billy's cricket cradle. Billy was born in a quaint little farmhouse close by the church.

'We had a grand start – we lived in a flat county,' was the aptly sporting recollection of Billy Edrich in his years of cricket fame. Born in March 1916, Billy was raised in the invigorating marshlands between Great Yarmouth and Norwich. The stirring tang of the sea and the whispering whirr of the windmills were the smells and sounds of his childhood. More significantly, he rejoiced in the prevailing cricket fanaticism. His father, Bill senior, played for Norfolk Club and Ground, only one rung below county status. The demands of farming did not permit further advancement, but his pioneering spirit never deserted him as the family fortunes prospered and waned. He showed a remarkable resilience in seizing opportunities to overcome the hurdles of a precarious livelihood between the wars.

At each of his Norfolk farming posts – from Lingwood to Cantley and Upton and then, after a short sojourn in Yorkshire, back to Norfolk and a living at Heacham – he found time to pursue his own cricket as well as communicate his fervour for the game to his four young sons. The ripples of his sporting devotions spilled over into a flood. The spreading branches of the extended family of later generations intermingled to unite an all-Edrich eleven capable of competing with the best. The name of Edrich was to become synonymous with cricket throughout the county and beyond.

Old Bill was a cricket visionary. As an eighteen-year-old in 1908, he made one of his early appearances for Blofield. He founded teams at Cantley and Upton, hitherto without cricket before his arrival. He demonstrated that perseverance can win rewards, not excepting one personal milestone which eluded him until middle age – his maiden century was recorded at Londesborough Park in the Yorkshire Wolds in 1934. Old Bill was forty-three and this belated honour was celebrated, to quote his own words, 'by a grand drop of scotch from an uncle'. His career extended beyond the second world war. In 1946, he joined Lillingstone Dayrell and reformed the team which won the Buckinghamshire and District League three years later. In 1953 he returned to Norfolk and played for Ingham until his sixty-eighth year. It had been a long and wonderful innings, but Old Bill reluctantly conceded it was time to retire. It was not a question of flagging enthusiasm; his mobility was impaired by arthritis.

The remembrances of Old Bill's sons give substance to his allegiance to cricket. 'Build on a good defence,' was the lesson he taught them on the practice wickets at their homes at Cantley and Upton. 'Wait for the loose ball, and when it comes, make sure you hit it for four.' The combination of the correct stance and the straight, watchful bat was a drill supervised with the precision of a parade-ground sergeant. Another lesson strictly enforced was sporting good manners. 'When you hit a catch, however faintly, you must walk,' the boys were told. Cricket honesty among the Edriches was paramount; and from this time on, defeat, when it came, was accepted with reasonable grace.

The disciplines bequeathed by Old Bill gave his sons the best possible start on their journeys into first-class cricket. Eric, the eldest and a wicket-keeper batsman, followed Billy into the Norfolk eleven. At the advanced age of thirty-two, he stepped up briefly into first-class cricket with Lancashire after the war. The promotion was not misplaced, as Yorkshire found to their cost when he scored a century against them in a Roses match at Leeds in 1948. Geoffrey, the third-born and another Lancashire recruit, believed that Eric might have prospered as hugely as Billy had he joined his brother at Lord's in the mid-1930s, but Eric's agile hands were needed on the farm in those recessionary times. The last of the Edrich sons, Brian (a left-hander at the insistence of his father) was potentially a cricketer of equal status. Brian joined the Kent ground staff as a sixteen-year-old in 1939. The intervention of the war, and service in the Royal Air Force, deprived him of a vital cricket apprenticeship. Brian rejoined Kent after the war and later moved to Glamorgan before taking up the post of coach at St Edmund's College, Oxford.

Eric Edrich summoned up an idyllic picture of the boyhood years spent at the imposing three-winged Cantley Manor set in grounds of seven hundred acres. His father employed a team of thirty men, working round the clock on the long summer days, harnessing and grooming the horses in the stables, and ministering to the needs of the extensive range of bullocks, pigs and other livestock. The domestic duties were carried out by four alert young maids, all recruited from one family in the village, and accommodated at one end of the house. There were bells in all the rooms to summon the girls to work, waiting on table during the lavish family dinners, or shyly serving refreshments during the village dances in the ballroom at Cantley. They also had to act as unyielding umpires as the boys pleaded for one more innings before bedtime. 'It was a lovely old farm,' remembered Eric. 'There were peaches around the walls; all kinds of fruits in the vast orchards; and three large glasshouses for growing tomatoes.' Every tree, and there were many of them, was climbed, especially by Billy, ever the ringleader and an adventurous rascal who would then laughingly tumble down. 'My word, he was quite a lad, but he never seemed to hurt himself,' remarked Eric.

It was a prosperous interlude for the Edrich family. The boys, nourished by good food and the outdoors life, proudly watched their muscles harden as they helped with the farmyard tasks. 'We were really well fed,' recalled Eric. 'Dad got his beef on Sunday. I'm not exaggerating when I say it was 20 lb. or more. Uncle George, before he got married, used to come for lunch. There were lots of relations and friends, really quite a crowd of us.'

The Edrich boys, at first with airguns, all became good shots. Shooting was a necessary accomplishment and it was a mark of pride to be invited on expeditions in the fields of neighbouring farms. Eric and Billy were enrolled at an early age. Their brief was to keep the rat population within reasonable limits in the farm stacks. A careful strategy was involved in this pursuit. They

7

were directed by their father to vary the routes and approach their quarries from different angles. 'We used to go out ratting at night time, with acetylene lamps to light the way,' said Eric. 'On a good night we might shoot as many as a dozen rats.'

Farming reaped the priceless gifts of strength and vibrant health; but there was always time for cricket. The joys of Christmas included new bats, never over-sized so as not to restrict the shots of the boys, and a shared football. Bill senior, the tireless tutor, who always spared the time to put the boys through their paces, never failed to stress the importance of true wickets in the making of a cricketer. The pitch on the lawn at Cantley was lovingly tended, cut and rolled before the day's play. At their next home at Upton the narrow asphalt path leading up to the kitchen door, upon which the wicket was marked in chalk, was the practice area. Here again the sure surface allowed swift, confident footwork, forward and back in the time-honoured manner. Batting defence was not entirely certain: the bombardment of the door panels with a hard ball inevitably entailed weekly carpentry. Play was never abandoned because of rain; it simply meant moving to another concrete wicket in the barn.

In 1913 Bill senior had married a pretty Cumberland girl named Edith Mattocks whose parents had moved to East Anglia at the turn of the century. The journey to more profitable pastures, so it was said, involved the hiring of trains to transport their furniture, livestock and farming equipment to Norfolk. Edith Edrich was fiery, courageous and charming, all characteristics which surfaced again in her son, Billy. All who knew her are glowing in their praise of a 'wonderful woman'. She was totally besotted with her sporting sons. In an article written during their years of fame, she remembered them as children as 'lusty little fellows'. She attributed their vigour to the legacy of the excellent physique of their ancestors. The Edriches were renowned for their longevity. Billy's great-grandmother Harriet lived until she was ninety-eight; his grandfather and grandmother reached their eighties; and his parents both embraced comfort and dignity as nonagenarians.

The resources of energy and stamina of another generation were the gain of a well-stocked table. 'The boys were brought up on good plain food,' wrote Edith. 'Porridge for breakfast and bacon and eggs (when they were old enough). For lunch there was Yorkshire pudding, gravy and plenty of vegetables; milk puddings and suet puddings with golden syrup in the winter and lots of fruit, fresh, or in puddings in the summer, with cream only occasionally. For tea they had home-made bread and butter and lots of salads with the Norfolk shortcake. Supper was often Grapenuts, with sugar and plenty of milk. They always had at least twelve hours' sleep at night.'

Ena, always known as Dinah after a popular song of the period, was the last-born in 1924, and the subject of groans among the boys. 'She won't be any good – she won't be able to play cricket,' they all said. Ena, the butt of much affectionate fun, could not match the sporting prowess of her Aunt Alice. Alice, or Cis as she was called, was a fast bowler and a fine bat, who captained the Norfolk ladies' team and later coached cricket after emigrating to New Zealand. Ena, for her part, could not escape the tug of sport. She overcame the reservations of her brothers as a scampering fielder and tousled goalkeeper at football. She could never be 'the nice little girl my mother wanted', amid the rough and tumble of her childhood.

The Edrich household was a patriarchal one but

Ena maintained that the women were not second-class citizens. 'They did take a back seat but they wielded a tremendous influence in the family.' Eric Edrich remembered how his mother 'used to rear five hundred turkeys a year to help make a little pocket money. She was brilliant in the dairies; she used to sell butter and eggs at Norwich market, and all our men were given their milk free.' The proceeds of the market sales enabled her parents, Ena believed, to meet school fees in later difficult times.

It is the sense of camaraderie and warmth in a friendly domain which lingers in the memories of the Edrich children. 'Mother would play the piano and there were boisterous sing-songs at the end of the day,' recalled Ena. At other evening times the decks of cards – bridge and whist – were shuffled on the fireside table. Bad hands might then give way to rowdiness and a change to other highly competitive sessions of billiards and table tennis.

Edith Edrich also played a key role in the sporting grooming of the boys. 'We were always reasonably attired, not necessarily immaculate on occasions because the money did not run to it,' added Brian Edrich. 'Ma knitted all our cricket pullovers, made sure they were clean; and if there were any holes, they were darned.' The accent was on pride in their appearance on the cricket field. The ritual on Friday nights was the whitening of boots and pads. 'Everything was spotless,' recalled Ena.

Billy Edrich won his colours at Bracondale School, Norwich, when he was thirteen, and such was the dominance of his all-round cricket that he was appointed captain in the following year. His first major distinction was recorded against Norwich High School on 11 June 1930, when he took ten wickets, all clean bowled, for 18 runs in 49 balls. For another schoolboy

10

of that time, Bryan Stevens, the former *Eastern Daily Press* cricket correspondent, Edrich's performance is engraved in his memory: 'a furious sprint to the bowling crease, the ball catapulting from the hand, and Edrich himself following through at full pelt'.

Stevens played his first game with Edrich in a Norfolk Club and Ground match at Great Yarmouth in 1934. Jack Nichols, the county professional and coach, who played a major part in Edrich's development at Bracondale, was in charge of the team. Stevens had expected to keep wicket, but Nichols himself took over the gloves. 'I was bitterly disappointed,' said Stevens. 'But I had cause later to concede the wisdom of his decision. Playing with Bill over the next few seasons, I soon discovered the meaning of really fast bowling. It was surprising how he generated such pace considering his not very long but swiftly accelerating run-up and a rather curious slinging action.' Edrich's follow-through, Stevens added, was almost as fast as the ball!

In 1930 Edrich provided further evidence of his blossoming talents when he hit his first century, 121 out of 168 for 6 declared, against Diss Secondary School. He then proceeded to take eight wickets for 20 runs. 'After it all,' recalled Bill, 'I ate the tea of a lifetime, all cream buns and lemonade and ices'. By the following summer, although still one of the smallest boys in the school eleven, he was indisputably the maestro. He topped the batting and bowling averages. His 477 runs in all matches placed him more than 300 runs ahead of his nearest rival. In the bowling lists his tally of 71 wickets (at an average of less than five runs apiece) showed the size of his contributions to the school's success. Against the City of Norwich School Bill scored 149 not out, including two sixes and 22 fours, in an hour and three-quarters. The next highest score was five by his last-wicket partner.

Edrich's growing influence at Bracondale can also be seen in the results of the team. From 1926, his first year, to 1931 the School XI won 23 games out of 35, drew three and lost only nine. In each of the 1929 and 1931 seasons they suffered only one defeat. At the age of fifteen, despite his eligibility as a junior colt, Edrich represented Norfolk seniors at Lakenham. He was the outstanding player in the match. 'Edrich belongs to the class of all-round cricketers whom it is impossible to efface,' commented the *Eastern Daily Press*. Praising Edrich's responsible 57 in an innings lasting two hours, the writer added: 'He has a great variety of strokes, his wristwork and footwork are good, and his style is quite correct. He also hits the ball very hard.' The trial among his elders set Edrich against boys from Eton, Rugby, Uppingham and Marlborough. Bill was put on to bowl with a gale behind him. He hurtled in to take four wickets for one run in four overs before his captain signalled that he should take his sweater as an act of grace to the rest of the batsmen and to the other colts waiting for their chance to make an impression.

Edrich's sporting riches at Bracondale were not confined to cricket. He also excelled at tennis, swimming and athletics. In addition, an early verdict on Edrich as the football captain and a sprightly left-wing, was that he promised to make his mark in Norfolk soccer. A note in the *Bracondalian*, the school magazine, described him as 'a finished player, with excellent ball control', adding, not surprisingly, 'most of the openings were made by him'. In the 1930–31 season Bracondale won 12 out of 19 games and scored 100 goals.

In 1933, Edrich's last year there, he averaged 60 with the bat and took 59 wickets at an average of 3.50 runs each. 'So good was Edrich,' reported the *Bracondalian*, 'that he tended to be more than the mainstay of the cricket and football elevens – he was almost half the side. Many years must pass before we can hope to see his equal . . . The rest of the team, for the most part, played the roles of enthusiastic supporters, supplying applause but neither runs nor wickets'.

Edrich, as at home on the farm, polished his craft as a batsman on a concrete wicket at Bracondale specially laid for all-weather practice at the instigation of the sports master, Frederick Scott. 'Hard-wicket cricket is like chess – there is no element of chance in it, and only those who perfect themselves survive,' maintained Edrich in later years. 'I owe much to Mr Scott's insistence on a concrete wicket, as well as to his kindly coaching.'

Another of Bill's early mentors was Jack Nichols. Jack took a boyish delight, when the coast was clear, in delivering balls for dispatch by his pupils into the gooseberry bushes in the headmaster's garden. Bill recalled the variety of monster red dessert gooseberries whose succulence, he said, was not equalled in his experience. 'The batsman who made a long hit by custom fetched his own ball – and tasted these good fruits.'

The Bracondale scavengers had to be unerring strikers of the ball on the leg side before they could take their pick of the gooseberries. 'Jack combined the innocence of a dove with the cunning of a serpent,' said Bill. 'He bowled every batsman his due, and it took the absolute best of your batting to hit him into those enticing bushes.' There was also a practical side to these interludes. Edrich, along with other Bracondale boys coached by Nichols, developed power in his hook shots. So while the fruit-picking mercenaries begged their coach to bowl them a 'gooseberry' they would, as adults, be well-fitted to take up the challenge of the steepling bouncers in club and county cricket.

Lindwall and Miller, Bill's future Australian rivals, soon learned to become sparing with their 'gooseberries'. The high standards of sportsmanship and conduct set by Edrich were applauded by his masters at Bracondale. In an article carrying the title 'The Sporting Spirit', and published in the *Bracondalian* in 1951, he acknowledged his debt to the school. If it now reads tritely as an unfashionable statement, it still conveys an admirable sentiment. It was a sample of the patriotic fervour which illuminated his each and every deed. Edrich described how the British schoolboy 'learned how to win modestly and lose gracefully; to press home an advantage and to fight back from a bad position.' He added: 'Later on these qualities will influence everything he does; he will be respected and will respect others having the same qualities.' As President of the Bracondale Old Boys' Union in 1947, Edrich delivered another token of his regard and that of his family to the school. He instituted the annual award of the Edrich bat to be presented to the outstanding all round cricketer at Bracondale.

Norfolk were the Minor Counties championship leaders in 1933. Edrich, now regularly batting at no. 3, was awarded his county cap by his captain, Michael Falcon. It followed his 55 not out, including ten fours, which helped to seal a prized victory over Buckinghamshire. It was Norfolk's first success over their redoubtable rivals for five years. Edrich and Rodney Rought-Rought, sharing ten wickets, had first routed the reigning champions. The *Eastern Daily Press* saluted Edrich's batting: 'The boy's innings was worthy of an old campaigner. If he has nerves, he controls them admirably, and his confidence is amazing in one of his age. Driving, hooking and cutting, he made his runs in a most attractive manner. Quite early in his innings, he was struck over the heart by a rising ball, but he always faced the fast bowling unflinchingly, and his defence was excellent.'

The steadfast batsmanship did not yield when the touring West Indians, with the feared Martindale and Griffith in their ranks, visited Lakenham in August. The grandeur of a double-century by George Headley was a batting feast to savour on a summer's day of Caribbean heat. Headley was unbeaten on 257, despite his droll sally at lunch that he was not feeling too well! His diminished health did not prevent him from sharing a second-wicket partnership of 186 runs with Roach. The West Indians, on their glorious rampage, scored 496 before stumps were drawn. Norfolk, in reply, batted doggedly to force a draw. Edrich scored 35 and, in tandem with Basil Rought-Rought, added 93 for the second wicket in two hours and ten minutes. 'The justifiable patience which he and his partner displayed constituted a fine example of defensive play,' commented the *Eastern Daily Press*.

Bill Edrich, as a gifted son of Norfolk, glittered as a prodigy on the brink of fame in the 1930s. His prominence foretold a future at the highest level. After one of his centuries, a Herefordshire bowler, who had been obliged to do most of his bowling at Edrich, remarked: 'It was quite a treat to begin an over with someone else at the wicket.' Yet, as David Armstrong, the former Norfolk secretary who is now Secretary of the Minor Counties Association, relates, Edrich's achievements were no less startling than those of David Walker, who began his Norfolk career in 1931. Walker, who was killed in the second world war, was one of five university blues in the county team. He played for four seasons in the Uppingham XI, from 1929 to 1932; and in his last school season he scored prolifically, making 625 runs at an average of 78.12. Going up to Oxford, Walker gained his blue as a Freshman, and in his third year he captained the university side. In his curtailed Norfolk career, extending over only nine seasons, he scored nearly 4,000 runs at an astonishing average of 63.46. He equalled the record of G. A. Stevens in achieving two double-centuries for the county.

Tristan Ballance, a fine slow left-arm bowler, was another recruit from Uppingham and Oxford, along with a fellow Oxford blue, M. R. Barton. Michael Barton, who captained Surrey after the war, partnered Edrich in another outstanding exploit against the South Africans in 1935. The brothers, Desmond and Rodney Rought-Rought, Suffolk-born all-rounders, also won blues at Cambridge. Along with their elder brother, Basil, they were a notable force in Norfolk cricket.

Norfolk's elder statesman was another Cambridge blue, Norwich-born Michael Falcon. He was regarded by many good judges as possessing England credentials had he appeared more often in first-class cricket. Falcon gave more than a hint of his potential as a member of Archie Maclaren's eleven which spectacularly defeated the hitherto unbeaten Australians at Eastbourne in 1921.

Falcon's talents, from his debut as a Harrow schoolboy for Norfolk in 1906, were assigned to furthering the progress of his native county. He was an influential captain from 1912 to 1946, and among those who profited from the guardianship were the Edrich brothers. Falcon endorsed the first-class claims of Bill and he was also instrumental in guiding Eric and Geoffrey to Old Trafford.

In 1933, Bill Edrich was tussling with the conflicting calls of cricket and teaching. At Bracondale in July he had gained seven credits in his matriculation examination. He could, almost certainly, have progressed to gain a place at Cambridge. The dilemma was partially resolved by the necessity to earn a living. This was not because he would have lacked parental support although it would have meant an urgent review of their financial resources. Eric Edrich believed that Bill's priority would have been cricket whatever the circumstances. 'He was a brainy boy but he was so wrapped up in the game that I doubt if he ever intended to go into teaching.'

There were many long, anxious family debates on Bill's future. Venturing into the precarious climate of first-class cricket was fraught with peril. The clouds of uncertainty were lifted, at least for Bill, by the intervention of Jack Nichols, his patient Bracondale coach, and Michael Falcon. Nichols had long prophesied that Edrich would gain renown: 'That boy will play for England,' he had told Bill's parents. Falcon was at first reluctant to endorse Edrich as a candidate and so burden him with the hazards of professional cricket. It was a gamble, even for a boy as prodigiously talented as Edrich; but Falcon was won over by Bill's earnest protestations. He decided that the best course, if it could be arranged, would be to set up a trial at Lord's. He contacted William Findlay, the MCC secretary, and delivered his considered view that Edrich was of the right calibre ultimately to fill one of the places soon to be vacated by Hendren and Hearne. The outcome was that Edrich received an invitation to report for a trial in April 1934.

It was, as Eric Edrich remembered, an appointment that should have been postponed. Bill had left Bracondale at Christmas in the preceding year to join his family at work on the Yorkshire farm. Two days before the Lord's trial, while unyoking a big Suffolk horse from a farm cart, he jammed his fingers in the chain on the shafts. His ravaged hand was split clean across the right palm between the first finger and thumb roots. There was only time before the trial for emergency treatment. Edith Edrich, as always, was Bill's nurse and comforting supporter, but her ministrations could not disguise her concern.

Eric Edrich recalled the panic in the family. 'Dad told Bill: "I think you ought to cancel the appointment and go another time." ' Bill, although crestfallen by the accident, was determined to proceed with the trial. 'I'm not going to let slip this chance. I shan't tell them what has happened.'

It was with considerable misgiving that he was put on the train at York for the fateful journey to London. At Lord's, recalled Bill, 'my hands seemed all thumbs and my buttons fastened with twisted wire; but at last I was into my flannels and walking, bat under arm, to the nets.' Edrich was introduced by George Fenner, the chief coach, to Ronnie Aird, the MCC Assistant Secretary. Aird looked on as Fenner bowled a few balls at the triallist. 'My hand was stiff and awkward, but as soon as I felt the ball on the bat I knew I was all right. I was nervous, but I had a sudden conviction that I could do it,' said Edrich.

Both Aird and Fenner were quietly impressed with his resolution. Bill was told that he would be engaged on the second-class ground staff. There was, without doubt, one other matter which assured the rugged farmer's boy of a future at Lord's. As he took off his batting gloves, the right one was drenched with blood. The hastily repaired hand had split open again. Bill pressed his handkerchief over the wound, but it did not escape the notice of George Fenner. If anyone was going to make good, it was this indomitable lad. Fenner, at this moment, knew they had discovered an extraordinary competitor.

Fenner's words, after he had listened to the explanation of the injury, must have enhanced Bill's state of bliss. There was a chuckle of satisfaction in his response. 'I really must tell Mr Aird all about this,' he told the happy boy.

CHAPTER 2

Starting at the Nursery End

'There is no mistaking the class of Edrich, Compton and Hutton. They are the three discoveries of a generation.' – *The Cricketer*

The Middlesex juniors were appropriately housed at the Nursery End at Lord's, so called because it was once a market garden. Their off-duty perch was on the roof of the ivy-clad Clock Tower overlooking the practice ground. Bill Edrich, newly-enrolled as a member of the second-class staff in 1934, was one of this eager contingent. The boys, who tugged on the ropes of the monster roller, were later to make as deep an impression on lighter feet between the wickets, as did the impact of this strenuous haul on the hallowed turf.

'It was not a bad little team,' recalled Jack Robertson, one of the hard-worked recruits. The roll-call of young labourers also included Harry Sharp, Laurie Gray, and the brothers, Les and Denis Compton. Their apprenticeship was a brusque awakening to the realities facing cricket fledglings. As Edrich remembered, it was not a glamorous beginning. A privilege had been conferred from the moment they passed through the Grace Gates. They had, though, been invested with responsibilities as an élite group of candidates; and in such august surroundings – and autocratic times – it was important not to blot their copybooks. They all had to submit to unaccustomed disciplines; and many a silent curse must have been uttered as they gathered their mops, for the third or fourth time in a week, to cleanse the seats of the droppings of the colony of pigeons at Lord's. The benches had to glisten to the satisfaction of the head groundsman, Harry White.

The boys earned between three and four pounds a week, their basic wages augmented by a commission on the sales of scorecards at Test and county matches. Takings were always pooled. On rare occasions, with members indulgent after dining well, or pleasured by an innings by Hammond, they could count riches of £5 each. The strict regime was tempered by other rewards in the nets. The boys, as part of their training and cricket education, were required to bowl to MCC members. Denis Compton recalled the cunning of his elders, the experienced professionals, who would unerringly single out those city gentlemen more generous with their wealth. The juniors generally had to be content with thrifty members, and they soon learned how to avoid the miserly donors.

The seasoned campaigners were not, however, averse to passing on their wisdom in these matters. 'The old pros at Lord's knew the big tippers,' said Compton. 'Dear old Jim Powell, a leg-spinner who played a few matches for Middlesex between the wars, was one of our guides. He used to tell us youngsters: "This member here, he'll be good for your bowling – and pocket. You take him out to the nets." At other times, we might bowl for two hours and only get a shilling; but it was all good experience.' One of Compton's best patrons was Sir Charles Aubrey Smith, the former Sussex and England captain and later an actor and doyen of the English film community in Hollywood.

21

Sir Aubrey, then in his seventies, invariably asked for 'young Compton' when he came to Lord's. 'I did bowl a reasonable length, which was quite good practice for the old boy,' said Denis. 'He was my best tipper – half-a-crown for an hour – which I thought was pretty good.'

The friendship of Compton and Edrich, the intriguing combination of town and country, blossomed from the start. 'Bill was a remarkable chap. We never had a cross word in over fifty years,' recalled Denis. 'There was never any jealousy between us. We were just good chums.' The first of their batting partnerships occurred as MCC ground staff boys against Beaumont College. Someone had neglected to inform the MCC captain of their strengths as batsmen. Another version of the story is that Bill and Denis teasingly claimed that they were just bowlers. At all events, for the only time in their joint careers, they propped up the order at nos. 10 and 11. The MCC lost wickets so rapidly that the prospect loomed of an humiliating defeat at the hands of the college boys. Post-mortems at Lord's were averted by an anxious last-wicket stand. 'Denis glanced at me and I at him,' said Edrich. 'There was only one thing to do to avoid uncomfortable inquiries. We scored 60 together, and just scrambled home.'

While Edrich won high commendation among the farming folk of Norfolk, Compton, the London schoolboy, beat the path to fame in the streets of Hendon. It is instructive to juxtapose their two youthful exploits, each warmly praised and separated by only a few weeks in 1932. Edrich's batting defiance against All-India at Lakenham was followed by the fourteen-year-old Compton's century for London Elementary Schools against Mr C. F. Tufnell's XI at Lord's in September. Compton, as captain, scored 114 to steer his team to victory. He shared a century partnership with Arthur

McIntyre, a South London schoolboy, who was destined to keep wicket for Surrey and England. McIntyre never failed to remind Denis that he ran him out on that occasion. Desmond Eagar, a future Oxford blue and Hampshire captain, was in the opposition ranks. 'It almost depressed me at the time to think anyone could be so good as Denis at the same age as myself,' he said. Pelham Warner, who was to champion Bill Edrich as enthusiastically as Compton, watched the innings at Lord's in September. The decision that Denis should join the MCC staff, preceding his future partner by just one year, was undoubtedly taken that day. He arrived in April 1933.

Compton made his Middlesex debut, going in last, against Sussex in the traditional Whitsuntide match at Lord's in 1936. He scored 14 to help gain a first-innings lead. His dismissal, lbw to Jim Parks (senior), aroused the anger of Gubby Allen. The subject of Allen's indignation was Bill Reeves, the umpire and a roguish cricket wit. 'Young Compton wasn't out, and well you know it,' said Allen. Reeves replied: 'I know he wasn't, sir. But I was dying to spend a penny, and so I gave him out.' The unwarranted dismissal was a needless mishap, funny in retrospect; but it was only the mildest disturbance in an astonishing advance.

Three weeks after his first county appearance Compton hit his first hundred, against Northants at Northampton; the ensuing accession to a proper place in the order acknowledged his precocity. By the end of a curtailed season he had moved up two grades to first-class status on the Lord's staff and was awarded his county cap. His aggregate of 1,000 runs, lifted him to second place in the averages to Hendren among the regular Middlesex players. Had Gubby Allen, the England captain, been prepared to thrust his young pupil into the Test cauldron in Australia,

Compton very probably would have gained inclusion in the MCC team in the following winter. There were many supporters urging his selection. Les Ames, speaking before his death in 1990, also thought that Edrich was a fitting candidate. Edrich, in 1936, was not yet qualified for Middlesex. His pedigree was sound but he had no experience of first-class cricket. Both he and Compton – and Leonard Hutton – might have confounded Australia on this tour. But it would have required a remarkable faith in their talents and an uncommon enterprise by the England selectors to have picked them at this early stage.

The days of acclaim for Edrich, two years older than Compton, were not far off. His skills, when not required by MCC, flourished on the fields of Norfolk. In five seasons leading up to his Middlesex qualification Edrich played in 46 Minor Counties matches and scored 1,886 runs at an average of 30.91. In addition, he obtained 117 wickets at the modest cost of 18.05 runs each. The promise of his early success against All-India was amply fulfilled.

In 1935 Edrich achieved an aggregate of 488 runs for Norfolk. His peak performance immediately followed his top score of 152 for his home county against Hertfordshire at Broxbourne. It was another notable landmark, 111 against the touring South Africans at Lakenham. The thermometer on this July day soared into the eighties – the hottest day of the year in Norwich – and the quality of the county's batting rose with the temperature. Tents, large and small, ringed the field; and the carnival atmosphere was enlivened by a crowd of 5,000, the highest attendance recorded at Lakenham. They spilled beyond the boundaries and severely taxed the vigilance of the stewards. The Norfolk total of 325, bolstered by a furiously wagging tail, surpassed the figures previously obtained by any of the first-class counties against the unbeaten South Africans. After a wearisome night rail journey from Nottingham, the tourists were kept in the field until twenty-three minutes to six.

The South Africans included seven of the side which had gained an historic first Test victory in England at Lord's a few days earlier. Within their ranks were Bob Crisp, later to be reckoned by Edrich as one of his finest bowling rivals, and Sandy Bell. Norfolk lost two wickets for 34 runs against this new-ball attack, but then followed a stand lasting two hours between Edrich and Michael Barton, and the addition of 146 runs. Edrich joined a select band of cricketers who had scored centuries against the South Africans at this stage of the tour. The others were Norman Mitchell-Innes, for Oxford University; Cyril Smart (Glamorgan); Bob Wyatt, for England in the first Test at Nottingham; and Joe Hardstaff and George Gunn for their own county in the match at Trent Bridge.

'Edrich was the real hero of the day,' reported the *Eastern Daily Press* correspondent from Lakenham. 'He has now the confidence, skill and variety of strokes of a batsman of ripe experience. His innings, which extended over two hours and forty minutes, bore the hallmark of first-class. He has all the shots of a major batsman, and he played them with ease and certainty.' Edrich, driving sweetly and hooking ferociously, exacted a toll of eleven boundaries in his century. He corrected the shaking of knowing heads among those pessimists resigned to poverty after the early reverses. After his innings there were congratulations from Michael Falcon and his old coach, Jack Nichols. From another man, Ben Ling, a local auctioneer and former amateur batsman, there was a reminder of the time when they had opened together for East Norfolk. 'Oh, blast you,

25

boy, you'll be the death of me,' he had told young Bill, as they scampered between the wickets. At Lakenham, Ling, beaming with pleasure, said: 'Running them to death again, Bill'!

A serious ankle injury prevented Edrich from achieving equal renown on the football field. The injury was sustained in a heavy tackle against Swansea soon after he had won a regular place in the Tottenham first team in the 1936–37 season. It was so troublesome that he concluded, after several months of enforced idleness, that the hazards of soccer might threaten his cricket aspirations. Tottenham, at this time, were a Second Division team, and their great years lay ahead. Edrich, though, was ushered into a formidable company, all of whom displayed a kindly attitude towards him. The Spurs team in those days included, at centre half, Arthur Rowe, who was to become an influential manager at White Hart Lane; the England internationals, Hunt and Alsford; and two other internationals, Hall and Evans, one of the most outstanding left-wing alliances.

The introduction to the London club was gained through a chance meeting between Edrich's brother, Eric, and his father and the Tottenham chief scout in an Heacham hotel in Norfolk. 'My lad wants something to do in the winter,' said Bill senior, mindful of the fact that his son would welcome the extra money. Old Bill, the exemplar of enthusiasm, clearly provided a glowing testimonial, for a trial was arranged at Northfleet, the Spurs' nursery club, in September 1934. The plaudits must have dwelt upon the quickness and strength of the junior Bill as a left-winger. Eric Edrich, who partnered Bill on the left wing at Bracondale School, recalled that his brother possessed a fearsome shot with either foot. As a boy, at practice on the farm lawn, Bill had once driven the ball so hard that his father, keeping a leisurely goal, had had hastily to withdraw his pipe, or it might have disappeared down his throat.

Young Bill was first put through his high-stepping paces in a Tottenham Reserves game against Brighton and Hove Albion. 'It was my lucky day,' he recalled. 'My passes dropped at the feet they were meant for. I could spin round opponents who tried to intercept me. I felt right up on my toes. I scored a hat-trick, and walked off the field delighted and content.' The sequel was not, as he pardonably imagined, a swift promotion to the first team, but a season of goal-scoring at the Northfleet nursery. Bill said he expended enough energy to drive a train. His opportunism produced a yield of 30 goals; the nets, as he struck their inviting targets, billowed upwards like balloons caught on a sudden gust of wind.

Before the start of the 1935–36 season Edrich was contesting for an extended run alongside the luminaries at White Hart Lane. The wish was not granted but he did make his debut in the match against Blackpool. He deputised on the left wing for the Welsh international, Willie Evans, and played a key role in Tottenham's 3–1 victory. 'On his first appearance in the premier eleven, Edrich proved a polished winger,' commented an observer. 'The quick feet of youth were guided by a coolness and confidence which would have done credit to a veteran.'

The praise was not misplaced, as Edrich assisted in all three of Tottenham's goals. Fifteen minutes before the interval, his precise corner swung high into the goalmouth, and Morrison's header put the home side in the lead. Ten minutes later his arm was held aloft again. He had outpaced the Blackpool defence and his low, scudding centre was deflected by Cardwell past his own goalkeeper. Wallace, the wrong-footed 'keeper, could not be blamed for this reverse; and he

27

was also without fault as Tottenham added a third goal late in the second half. Edrich, neatly served by his England international partner, Willie Hall, unleashed a fierce drive. Wallace did well to parry the shot but the ball broke loose, and Duncan, following up, had the simplest of chances to give his team an unassailable lead. Edrich, 'the bright young star' of the newspaper reports, had had his moment of football glory. Evans, the Welsh ace, sensibly regained his fitness to deny his irrepressible deputy further opportunities in that season.

Edrich, in his brief flirtation with professional soccer, gave a glimpse of his prowess and appended his name to the list of other Middlesex footballer-cricketers – Hendren, Hulme, Robins, Durston and Les and Denis Compton. Unlike Denis, who persisted almost disastrously (his damaged knee causing a vitrual apoplexy in cricket circles) with Arsenal in combining the two games, Edrich wisely chose to concentrate on cricket. He had been given a warning of the dangers of doubling up as a sportsman in his last injury-curtailed season at Tottenham. The Spurs manager, Bill Tresidder, expressed his regret at Edrich's decision. 'Bill could have been one of the best outside-lefts in the country,' he said.

Back at Lord's, Edrich had to suffer the disappointment of a delayed qualification for Middlesex. Before he returned to football at the end of the 1935 season, he was summoned to the office of the MCC secretary, William Findlay. Edrich, to his astonishment, was told that his qualification would not take effect until October 1936. Findlay said the registration forms were not submitted by the Norfolk secretary until the autumn of 1934, five months after Edrich had joined the MCC staff. The announcement, not to be disputed in those autocratic days, meant that Edrich's entry into Middlesex cricket would be postponed until 1937. A bewildered Bill privately thought that this unexpected misunderstanding deserved investigation; but, as on other more crucial occasions, he had to be philosophical about the turn in his fortunes.

It is, however, interesting to reflect on Edrich's determination to underline his credentials in 1936. The advance of Denis Compton in that season dominated the headlines; but Bill's own performances, admittedly in less competitive MCC matches, outshone those of Compton. Edrich had only nine innings but they included three centuries against Surrey and Oxford University at Lord's, and Kent in the Folkestone festival. He scored 440 runs, with an average of 55, and was nominally second in the first-class averages to Wally Hammond. Bill derived enormous benefit from the comforting presence of Patsy Hendren, then aged forty-seven, one of the greatest of England's batsmen, in the MCC team. Hendren's experience and understanding, as Denis Compton also testified, constituted a major factor in Edrich's success.

T. C. F. Prittie wrote of Hendren in *Cricket North and South*: 'He brought a cockney wit and a spirit of comedy to the sobriety and refinement of the Lord's atmosphere. His grin, when he made a century, was of genuine delight, and there was a quirk in his batting, a gesture, a grimace, a comical relief, and a sudden thumping pugnacity.' Edrich paid his own tribute to a wise mentor. 'The shrewdness of the old campaigner gave us something new to learn every day; his monkeyish humour laughed disaster off the field with victory at its heels. To us all he was a model of willing and faithful service, good temper and huge endeavour.'

Bill and Denis profited hugely from Hendren's counsel. 'Don't worry about the name of the bowler,' he told

BILL EDRICH

them. 'Just try to see the maker's name on the ball.'
Edrich, who was to become an adept and courageous
hooker in his own right, remembered the teachings of
the master. 'Watch my feet,' said Patsy. 'Get right back
when you hook. Give yourself room and a little more
time.' Both his pupils recalled how Hendren would
position himself in line, body behind the ball, and
then resoundingly strike the ball to square leg, or even
mid-wicket. 'The greatest thing I learned from Patsy,'
said Edrich, 'was to play my shots in the direction in
which the ball was swinging or turning, and play with
the tide.' Another lesson, as Compton has related, was
an insistence on playing off the back foot to exceptional
pace, the hallmark of all great batsmen. Denis and Bill,
in their memorable years together, were almost invariably on the back foot before the ball was bowled. 'It
is a fallacy that you cannot hit a half-volley off the
back foot just as well as off the front foot,' declared
Compton.

Edrich, now as a first-class professional in 1936,
strove mightily in service with the veteran Hendren.
He had to stifle his eagerness to win the strike. 'I was
lucky to receive more than two balls an over in a long
stand,' he recalled. 'Look, son,' Hendren would say,
'I'm getting the runs. Just be content to watch me.'
Hendren and Edrich shared a third-wicket stand of
296 for the MCC against Surrey at Lord's. Edrich hit
his first century of the summer, and 51 not out in the
second innings. Bill Bowes, capped by Yorkshire but
fulfilling this engagement as a member of the MCC
staff, took seven wickets in the match. Surrey were
beaten by seven wickets. Their toiling bowlers were
confronted by Hendren in his most audacious mood.
He scored 202, out of 297, in three hours of awesome
strokeplay. Edrich, as his captivated partner, recalled
the innings. 'More than twice my age, he was so nimble

he made me marvel; he crashed into his century like a band playing martial music, and went on to his double-century, so that I could only envy and admire.'

Six weeks later, against Oxford University, Edrich again batted with Hendren; but this time he was equally dominant. Norman Mitchell-Innes, the Oxford captain, mindful of the problems of a drying pitch after a thunderstorm, put MCC in to bat. It looked a winning venture as four wickets, including that of Compton, went down for 74 runs. The initiative was stolen by the resource of Hendren and Edrich. The *Wisden* report on Edrich's innings of 114 declared that he 'hit magnificently all round the wicket'. Another writer, in *The Times*, enthused about the 'excellence of his strokes', which, he said, 'were astonishing for a youth of 20, and even more remarkable was the seasoned judgement and maturity of his style.' Hendren (98) and Edrich rescued the MCC with a stand of 141 runs in 85 minutes. The recovery enabled their slow bowlers to gain the ascendancy. Compton made amends for his batting failure with two wickets in an over in the Oxford first innings; and another Middlesex man, fast bowler, Jim Smith, took seven wickets in the second innings, as the MCC won by an innings and 123 runs.

There was the garland of another century by Edrich against Kent at Folkestone in September. He followed up a first innings duck, bowled by Watt, with 112; and his joy was undiminished by the winning run-spree of the Kent trio of Ames, Todd and Valentine. Edrich completed an outstanding season by dismissing one of his batting idols, Frank Woolley, caught by his former Norfolk colleague, David Walker, at slip.

Edrich began his association with Middlesex, which was to extend over twenty-two years, in impressive form in 1937. This was Patsy Hendren's last season;

31

and his exit from the Lord's stage so soon after the retirement of his long-standing ally, Jack Hearne, was charged with emotion. The focus was now thrust on their successors, Edrich and Compton. 'The genuine regret at the passing of two great England and Middlesex players is tempered by the arrival of two of the most promising young cricketers of the decade,' commented one national newspaper. 'Of the two, Edrich is rather more matured after his years of continuous progress in Minor Counties cricket. He seems destined for a most successful career.'

Wisden, discussing the merits of the two players, thought Edrich was the 'more consistent, if not perhaps as attractive to watch, and more reliable.' In his first season Edrich quickly established himself at no. 3 in the Middlesex order; and, as one observer said, 'he set the pavilion critics the pretty problem of deciding whether he or Compton was the better batsman.' It was not a problem which ever concerned Bill or Denis. 'We greeted each other's success as if it was our own,' said Compton. 'If I scored a hundred, or was having a good time with the bat and Bill wasn't, he said: "That's marvellous, Denis. You were terrific." It was just the same with me. I was so pleased when he was doing well.'

Another writer in *The Cricketer* also presented an appreciation of Leonard Hutton. 'There is no mistaking the class of Edrich, Compton and Hutton. They are the three discoveries of a generation. Edrich, at twenty-one, may very well prove to be as good as Charles Barnett. Compton, barely nineteen, though not yet as mature as Edrich and Hutton, plainly has the Test match mark upon him. All three can take a turn with the ball, and their fielding is exhilarating.'

The distinctive virtues of Hutton, now emerging from the shadow of his mentor, Herbert Sutcliffe, were rewarded by his selection for the first Test against

New Zealand at Lord's in 1937. Hutton's aggregate of 2,888 runs placed him, marginally inferior on average, next to another batsman of growing accomplishment, Joe Hardstaff. Hutton, Hardstaff, Edrich and Compton were on the threshold of greatness in the years leading up to the war. They are regarded as an England batting quartet with few if any parallels; and it is one of cricket's regrets that this thrilling combination was not allowed to prosper in the early 1940s.

Edrich and Compton vied with each other in achievement in 1937. Compton made his England debut at The Oval. Edrich, on merit, might have been spared a faltering debut in Test cricket against Australia a year later had he been given a less severe baptism against New Zealand. His delayed Middlesex qualification had cost him the benefit of a proving season in first-class cricket, and it led, perhaps, to impetuosity and a feeling that he needed to make up for lost time.

As Edrich, in his imperious youth, drove his way to over 2,000 runs in his first season with Middlesex, concern was expressed that he should not shoulder too great a burden as a bowler. The well-meaning protectors had yet to recognise the zeal of the Norfolk boy and the stamina which enabled him to dovetail the 'genuinely fast bowling' with the bright adventure of his batting. Edrich's talents as an all-rounder before the war were to prove his salvation in retaining the faith of the Test selectors.

Edrich failed by only three runs to score a century for MCC against Surrey; but his first championship hundred, with Hendren as his companion, was achieved in rousing and heroic fashion against Lancashire in June 1937. 'The second day's play was dominated by Edrich, who played magnificently during a stay of four hours and forty minutes,' reported *The Cricketer*. 'He straight-drove brilliantly any ball the slightest degree overpitched, and he had a most effective half-cut, half-chop for the short ball on the offside.' Another writer recalled how Edrich 'scored at a progressively greater rate as his mastery over a hostile and spirited Lancashire attack grew steadily more pronounced.' Edrich displayed the gift of barely perceptible acceleration, which enables major players gradually to assert their authority in unpropitious circumstances.

Edrich's 175 was more than half the runs scored by his team, and made on a rapidly deteriorating wicket at Lord's. 'Now and then the ball would spitfire up head high,' he recalled. 'At other times one would shoot along the ground like a snake.' The care and calm of his vigil against the Lancashire attack was interrupted by the strident command of his captain, Walter Robins, whose message to improve the rate of scoring was relayed by the blithe and unorthodox Jim Smith. Smith proceeded to clarify the information in inimitable style. His rumbustious approach had no connection with the batting manual. One of his soaring pulls cleft the skies above the Grandstand and the ball disappeared over 'Father Time'. Edrich said: 'That was a nice one.' Big Jim was not content with the trajectory of his shot. He replied: 'It would have been, if only I had middled it properly.'

Middlesex were set a target of 174 on a wicket soft on top and hard underneath. They lost six wickets for 35 runs. Phillipson and Pollard, as the principal aggressors, revelled in prime conditions for bowling, and marshalled a venomous accuracy on the badly worn pitch. Edrich's valour in the crisis was conducted with negligible support. Only two other batsmen, Robins and Smith, reached double figures. 'With wickets falling around him like ninepins,' commented one writer, 'Edrich made a great singlehanded attempt to win the game for his side.' Robins and Sims helped him add 74 runs; then Jim Smith struck 20 runs in one over from Pollard before falling to a catch by Lister off Pollard. Laurie Gray, the last man, who had been unable to bowl in the Lancashire second innings, came in to bat with his hand in a splint. He was run out, attempting to give Edrich the bowling. Lancashire were the victors by 22 runs. Edrich was unbeaten. His 73 was a cameo of unrewarded doggedness.

There were two other centuries for Edrich, both against Somerset, in 1937; and he did not mind missing another, by four runs, because he had been afforded the pleasure of sharing the stage with Patsy Hendren in the maestro's farewell against Surrey at Lord's. Their stand realised 182 runs for the third wicket. Middlesex were runners-up to Yorkshire in a fierce struggle for honours. As the *News Chronicle* put it on that emotional day, this was a 'trifling matter compared with the fact that Pat Hendren was playing in his last championship match'. Errol Holmes, the Surrey captain, assembled his players around Hendren on his arrival at the crease. He led them in three cheers for the old warrior, a measure of affection to supplement a thunderous roar of acclaim from the packed crowd. Just on the stroke of three Hendren completed his fifth century of the season, and the 170th of a distinguished career, which had begun as long ago as 1907. 'This time the delighted spectators not only rose to their feet but one of their number, happily inspired, led the gathering in the singing of "For he's a jolly good fellow",' reported a witness of the scene. 'Not since the departure of Hobbs at The Oval could one remember a game being held up so long in honour of a popular favourite.'

Edrich, as his helpmate for the last time, rejoiced in one of 'their nicest partnerships'. 'Patsy was right on top of his form, so that everyone wondered why such a batsman dreamed of retiring.' Afterwards, said Bill, 'he told us that he had been anxious to give the customers a good show for his farewell.'

The spotlight on the newly-capped Edrich did not waver in the last months of 1937, but another sign of the growing appreciation of his talents came with his selection for the tour of India in the winter. This was undertaken under the sponsorship and captaincy of Lord Tennyson. Lionel Tennyson, grandson of the Poet Laureate and Hampshire captain for fifteen years, is best known for his courage against the all-conquering Australians in the third Test at Leeds in 1921. In Australia's first innings Tennyson attempted to stop a fierce drive by Macartney and he split the web between his left thumb and finger so badly that it had to be stitched.

England were in dire straits, having already lost Jack Hobbs, a victim of appendicitis. The severely handicapped Tennyson decided, on a last-minute impulse, to take his innings. His thumb and forefinger were tightly strapped together and it seemed highly unlikely he would survive very long against the searing pace of Gregory and McDonald. Tennyson disregarded his injury and proceeded to throw caution to the winds. In eighty minutes of superb attacking cricket, batting largely with one hand, he scored 63, including ten fours, out of 106. Two of the most feared bowlers in cricket history were put to rout. Tennyson finally perished to a slip catch off McDonald, and he departed the Headingley field a national hero. Many years later he recalled the innings: 'Always liked the fast stuff,' he told a friend. 'It comes on to the bat so damned sweet.'

Edrich's own lifestyle was closely to parallel that of Tennyson, who was regarded by those who met him as a latter-day Regency buck. Phil Mead, another of

Hampshire's favourite sporting sons, said: 'The skipper was a lovely man, just a big boy, really'. The Hampshire professionals in those days were obliged to meet the costs of their own food and accommodation. Mead recalled: 'Often, when we were going up north for a game, the skipper would say: "Come along and have dinner with me, Mead – oh, hang it, ask all the chaps." He'd give us all dinner, champagne as well – he was like that, and he never grew up.'

Tennyson, at forty-seven, was embarking on his last serious cricket venture in India in 1937–38. His team was regarded as the strongest to visit the sub-continent up to that time. Edrich was joined on his first trip abroad by Norman Yardley, with whom he was to establish a long-standing association. They were both sociable men. Yardley shared another quality with Edrich. He was never known to say anything unpleasant about anybody. 'Norman was as good at friendship as he was at games,' remembered Bill. Their companions in India included another Yorkshireman, Paul Gibb; George Pope and Stan Worthington, from Derbyshire; Arthur Wellard (Somerset); Ian Peebles (Middlesex); Peter Smith (Essex); Neil McCorkell (Hampshire); Joe Hardstaff (Notts); and the Sussex pair, Jim Parks and Jim Langridge. All of them, with the exception of Pope, McCorkell and Smith, were England players in the 1930s. Alfred Gover, the Surrey and England fast bowler, was another member of the party. Edrich stood high in his estimation: 'Bill was an integral part of Tennyson's team,' he recalled.

Edrich headed the batting averages in India, with 876 runs at an average of 46.10. In his first three innings he scored 244 runs for once out. Hardstaff shared the honours with him. They both scored over 1,000 runs in all matches on the tour. Tennyson's team were afflicted by misfortune: injuries and sickness took their toll; and although they won three of the five unofficial Tests, they lost five of the 24 games. India were captained by the elegant Vijay Merchant and within their ranks were six of the team which took part in the first post-war series in England in 1946.

Edrich renewed his rivalry in India with the mighty Mohammad Nissar, with whom he had nervously tussled as a schoolboy at Lakenham. Nissar and his partner, Amar Singh, still carried the menace which had bewildered England's batsmen in two Tests at Lord's in 1932 and 1936. Jim Swanton considered that Amar Singh – 'tall and slim, but broad in the shoulders, long in the back and loose in the wrist' – possessed the ideal requirements for a bowler of pace. 'His speed from a short run was fast-medium, and he had a command of swing and cut and life off the pitch that brought comparison with Maurice Tate in his prime.' Amar Singh and Nissar were supported by Lala Amarnath, bowling his neat little inswingers and off-cutters. At their side, purveying his left-arm spin, was the twenty-one-year-old Vinoo Mankad. Mankad was the gifted protégé of Bert Wensley, the former Sussex professional, who was then coaching in India.

Alf Gover said that Edrich, even at that early stage in his career, refused to be cowed by the hostility of Nissar. The impression of Edrich's confidence as a boy at Lakenham might have been retained by the big Indian bowler. 'He daren't drop 'em short at Bill on those placid wickets,' recalled Gover. 'Bill would have hooked him out of sight.'

Edrich, opening the innings against Sind at Karachi, carried his bat to score 140. He was associated with Tennyson in a tall-scoring sixth-wicket stand. Edrich had reached his half-century when his captain strode out to join him. 'Tennyson's score rattled after mine towards the century,' recalled Bill. 'Presently he had overtaken me with the aid of two gigantic sixes and 13 fours, and soon our scores stood level at 92 apiece.' The temperature was over 100° Fahrenheit. Tennyson was a large man in physique as well as personality. At that time his weight had advanced to nearly seventeen stone. Edrich, as the younger man, believed that his stamina would outlast that of his captain. He had the temerity to ask Tennyson, by now furiously mopping his brow in the heat, whether he thought the century might elude him. They each wagered a pound on the outcome of their personal duel. 'He looked wet through and done for, but he cracked up the remaining runs and won the bet,' said Edrich.

During the first 'Test' at Lahore an earthquake caused consternation among the spectators and startled glances among the English fieldsmen. Edrich, deep in concentration, or perhaps recovering from earlier festivities, was only mildly distracted. He was on patrol in the outfield, fielding at fine leg to the bowling of Gover. The lamenting wails and cries of the crowd were, he thought, a form of Indian barracking. At the end of the over he casually asked for an explanation of this weird cacophony. He was told, to his astonishment, that what he had heard were real cries of terror. The brief earthquake had caused serious damage to the Punjabi Club and other buildings in the city. The disturbance, as can be judged, did not affect Edrich. He hit two half-centuries in the match, and shared a partnership of 132 runs with Yardley, as the tourists won by nine wickets.

India, with Mankad in enterprising form as a batsman, glimpsed victory in the next representative match at Bombay. Only two batsmen managed over 50 in a low-scoring game. The immaculate Mankad paced his innings of 88 superbly to check the supremacy of Gover and Wellard. Edrich's unbeaten 86 on a wearing wicket produced the winning counter and Tennyson's XI emerged as victors by six wickets. Centuries by Mushtaq Ali and Amarnath provided the platform for the Indian revival at Calcutta. Amar Singh and Nissar shared 12 wickets in the match and India won by 93 runs. They levelled the series with a conclusive innings victory at Madras – the first innings defeat suffered by a touring side in India.

Mankad, seizing his chance once again, hit an unbeaten 113 out of a total of 263. Then rain intervened and the tourists collapsed twice against Amar Singh. The Indian bowler, with measured accuracy, took 11 wickets in the match. He maintained his compelling form with a haul of nine wickets in the deciding match at Bombay. Edrich, with another half-century, came to the rescue after the tourists had lost four wickets for 85 runs. Worthington was his partner in a hard-hitting stand; Wellard and Pope pushed home the advantage with bat and ball; and victory was achieved by 156 runs.

Bill Edrich delighted in the exotic sights and sounds of India; the opulent hospitality and lavish banquets; and the excitement of a ceremonial panther shoot arranged in their honour. On his first overseas tour, he had, as a role model, his captain, Lionel Tennyson. As a Guards Officer, trencherman and outrageous gambler – at the races and cricket – Tennyson had led a spectacular life. In his autobiography he related: 'A succession of lovely ladies held first place in my heart and towards them all, in turn, I was ever generous.' Edrich's own exuberant charm, as a romantic buccaneer, was to win over other hearts too.

CHAPTER 3

Plunder in Maytime

'Bill's 1,000 runs came as a mixed blessing to him. When things ran against him he had to endure those suggestions of a lack of temperament that can be more than a little offensive.' – *E. W. Swanton*

The target of 1,000 runs before June in 1938 was an enticing bait and Bill Edrich, like an unwary fish, slipped into dangerous depths in order to grasp it. He was seeking to join the illustrious trio of W. G. Grace, Wally Hammond and Charles Hallows, the only three English batsmen to have performed this feat in the month of May. A fourth player, Tom Hayward, had achieved the aggregate before the beginning of June 1900, but his total included runs made in April, similarly recorded by Don Bradman on his first English tour in 1930.

The magnet of the prize was, as one writer reflected, the primary cause of a later temporary eclipse, but in a glorious spring the temper of Edrich's cricket crackled with the menace of thunder. At twenty-two he was a rampant young batsman, who threatened to dislodge all others in his swaggering parade. One MCC member, watching Edrich voraciously reeling in 1,000 runs, all scored at Lord's before the beginning of June, observed: 'This is sheer murder without attenuating mercy towards the bowlers'.

Edrich, pursued by a flurry of ecstatic headlines, sought to obey his credo of a straight bat and a modest mind. As he approached the target, he tried to escape the charge of stunt, which is inevitably attached to achievements of this kind. He pragmatically expressed his intentions. 'I just hope that I can pick the right ball to hit and then hit it,' he said. The vigour and accuracy of this exercise was demonstrated in his start to the season. There was no hint of fickle fortune as he began with centuries for the MCC against redoubtable opponents, Surrey, and then Yorkshire, the reigning champions. He increased his challenge with a resolute 182 for Middlesex in a thrilling encounter with Gloucestershire. The match produced an aggregate of 1,443 runs, a record for a championship match at Lord's.

The pattern of this contest should be enshrined in cricket charters. It was designed for adventurous instincts. The centuries of Hammond and Neale were schooled in this mode; and Edrich and Compton, in the Middlesex reply, vied with each other in their batting thrusts. In the three hours and a quarter before Compton's dismissal, they added 304 runs for the third wicket. Their absolute command while they held the stage permitted scant hopes of any interruption. Within their sights was the English county third-wicket record of 375 of their predecessors, Hendren and Hearne, for Middlesex against Hampshire at Southampton fifteen years earlier. Sinfield and Goddard wheeled away solemnly and exclusively throughout the onslaught on a perfect wicket. Their joint marathon of 100 overs in the day was a feat as challenging, if not as profitable, as those of their two opponents.

Edrich recalled the droll humour of Goddard and the optimism of his appeals, irrespective of the direction or height of the ball. 'Tom was a beautiful bowler, propelling the ball from an enormous spinning finger, shaped like a sinewy hook.' Goddard glowered with disapproval when one appeal for lbw against Edrich was turned down in the match at Lord's. 'Jesus Christ,' said Tom, 'you lucky devil, Bill.' Edrich remembered that he was four yards up the wicket when the ball smacked against his pad.

The extent of Goddard's endurance and his off-spinning skills were revealed once he had broken the partnership. Middlesex were instantly perplexed and in thrall to his mystery. Goddard mentally checked his analysis, and clicked his fingers to gain compensation for his labours. His seven wickets, including five in his ultimate mastery, yielded a tie on the first innings. Middlesex were set an imposing target of 244 runs in two hours and a quarter on the last day. Edrich, with 71, was the enterprising master. 'From the start,' wrote the *Daily Telegraph* correspondent, 'he was a batsman who takes the initiative out of the bowlers' hands and into his own. He was constantly reproaching those who had been critical of his ability really to attack.'

Edrich drove and cut Barnett and Hammond for boundaries; and the introduction of Sinfield and Goddard only served to emphasise the boldness of his stroke-play. A mighty pulled drive off Sinfield sealed his half-century – 52 out of a total of 75 in 35 minutes. He went on hitting, cutting delectably and driving furiously until he was narrowly run out by a fast and accurate return to the wicket. Flutters of anxiety nearly undermined Middlesex in their race against the clock after his departure. W. H. Webster and Robins, both searching for quick runs, were caught in the deep. Seven wickets had fallen for 224 before Jim Smith resolved the issue in luxuriant style. The field was not big enough to contain his mountainous, spiralling sixes; and Middlesex won by three wickets.

Edrich, always the unselfish cricketer, was elated by the team spirit which produced this triumph. He could, though, hardly disdain other great expectations and the surge of excitement which greeted his deeds. In six completed innings he had scored 592 runs. Ten days later he was pulling smoothly towards the crest of a cricketing Everest. Bolstering his aggregate was a double-century against Nottinghamshire and the combined and still feared forces of Larwood and Voce. 'Saturday at Lord's belonged to Edrich,' enthused the *Daily Telegraph*. 'His mastery was complete. He made only one false hit, did not give a chance, and his 36 fours went all round the map from fine-leg to past the slips, with the straight drive and the hook as, perhaps, the finest glories.'

The high endeavours of the day followed the dismissals of Brown and Webster. Edrich stood on tiptoe in dominance. He began with Compton in a briefly flowering partnership which produced 72 runs in fifty minutes; he then shared in three-figure stands with J. H. Human and Allen. One of his hooks, off Larwood, pitched inside the boundary and then tore through a copy of *The Times* newspaper held by a spectator in the stand. Reading at such a time was hardly the proper attitude of a cricket partisan; but it was remedied a few days later in a letter to Edrich. 'I would like you to know that, if I did have to have all my teeth extracted at once, that is the way I wanted it done. Well played, sir.' Edrich's 245 spearheaded another Middlesex victory and it left him only 19 short of his 1,000 runs. All but 21 of them had been recorded in May. His nearest rival was Don Bradman, who had then scored 876 runs, but 258 of these were the product of one innings in April.

Extravagant romances do not always have happy endings. Edrich, by his own admission, lost his nerve (and verve) on the brink of success. 'A new and

a) Bill Edrich, making his debut for Norfolk at sixteen, goes out to face the All-India attack, 1932.

b) the Norfolk and Indian teams.

c) the tented cricket ground at Lakenham, Norfolk CCC's headquarters.

a) Bill Edrich senior, father and strict cricket coach, and young Bill's mother Edith "besotted with her sporting sons".

b) Cantley Manor in the Norfolk farmlands.

c) Bracondale School XI, 1931. Bill Edrich, third from left, middle row.

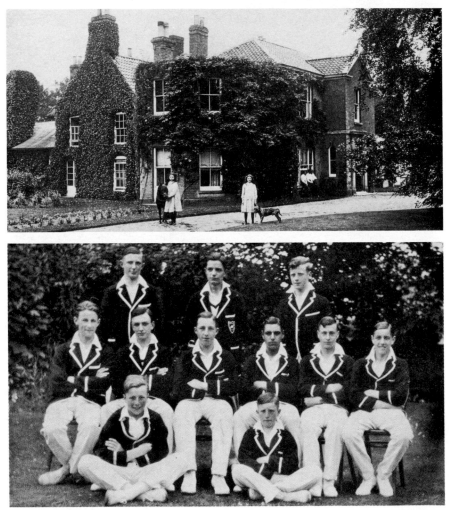

a) Edrich, twenty, going out to bat with veteran Patsy Hendren for Middlesex against Oxford University at Lord's, 1936.

b) Edrich, the earnest young sportsman.

c) Sir Pelham Warner always took an interest in Bill's career.

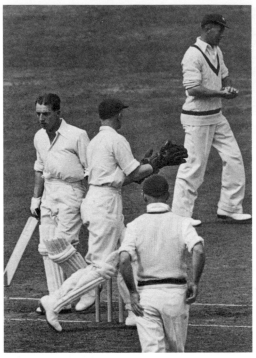

a) Edrich, lbw b. O'Reilly, 12, another in a string of Test failures, in the Oval Test of 1938.

b) in South Africa 1938-39 : seated left to right, Les Ames, Doug Wright, Edrich, Reg Perks, and Norman Yardley.

a) A rare picture of Edrich in RAF uniform as best man to E.L. Hope.

b) Squadron Leader Edrich was awarded the DFC for his leadership in a daylight attack on the Cologne power stations in August 1941. This picture shows one aircraft which has dropped its bombs, and two others in the distance passing through flak.

a) Portrait of Edrich the cricketer in action, *Picture Post*, 16 August 1947.

b) the four Edrich brothers who all played first-class cricket : Eric (Lancs),Bill (Middx), Geoffrey (Lancs), and Brian (Kent).

a) Edrich the bowler, seen as a slinger, but the slips stood well back to him ! (1947).

b) Middlesex, 1947 : *front row*, Edrich, George Mann, Robins (captain), Sims, Denis Compton; *back row*, Bedford, Thompson, Gray, Leslie Compton, Robertson, Brown, Young.

Edrich and Compton, the 'Middlesex Twins', going out to bat after lunch at Lord's, May 1947. Already they have made 80 runs between them.

pawkier Edrich now trod the record-maker's road,' commented T. C. F. Prittie. 'He deserted his natural methods, applying himself to the uncongenial and inappropriate task of wearing down opposing bowlers and letting runs come of their own accord.' Edrich, indeed, would have flunked the examination but for the later co-operation and generosity of Bradman. He had lost the invincible feeling and his unease was compounded in the next match. He was out for a duck, caught and bowled by Bob Crisp, his earlier South African rival, in the one innings at his disposal against Worcestershire. This dismissal meant that he had only one more chance to reach the target.

Middlesex's next opponents were the Australians, and within their ranks was the wily and great Bill O'Reilly, who was to prove Edrich's *bête noire* in the forthcoming Tests. Middlesex, on a rain-affected wicket and in an abbreviated match, headed the tourists on the first innings. Edrich's contribution was only nine runs. 'O'Reilly found the turf to his liking and he looked very unpleasant,' commented the *Daily Telegraph* correspondent. 'He bowled his googly most spitefully, and it was this ball which whipped back to bowl Edrich and rob him of what appeared to be his last chance of completing his 1,000.'

The Australians cleared their deficit; and Bradman, his own 1,000 achieved on the previous day at Southampton, declared to allow Edrich the opportunity to score the elusive ten runs. Edrich expressed his gratitude to the Australian captain for his gesture in granting a reprieve to a 'miserable youngster'. 'His action gave me the confidence to knock up the runs, for I felt I just could not let him down,' he said.

Bradman, in a recent letter, referred to the episode. 'A slight question mark did hang over Bill's performance. It was a little contrived in that I closed the Australian innings against Middlesex for the sole purpose of giving Edrich the chance to achieve this milestone.' It was not in his character to present Edrich with the runs. 'We tried our best to get him out – but the opportunity was a gift.' Edrich, with Compton sent in as his rallying opening partner, duly reached his objective. In scoring 1,010 runs, with an average of 84.16, in just fifteen innings before June, Edrich became the fifth Englishman to achieve a notable feat.

Edrich thrice scored over 2,000 runs in each of the seasons in his curtailed pre-war career. He was to become, as T. C. F. Prittie wrote, 'the most argued over man in the cricketing world . . . certainly he was the most violently and adversely criticised in the whole history of the game.' His reputation was still untarnished in the early weeks of the 1938 season; he had already given notice of his England claims as the leading batsman on Tennyson's tour of India in the preceding winter. Those who were to veer wildly and indiscriminately from praise to criticism showed little appreciation of the burden placed on Edrich. Prittie contrasted the tardy beginnings in first-class cricket of Hobbs and Hammond with that of Edrich. He pointed out that the Middlesex man was, statistically, the superior performer in his early days. Hobbs had first played for Surrey in 1905; he became a Test cricketer three years later at the age of twenty-five. Hammond played his first full season in 1923. In 1928, then aged twenty-six, he was batting at no. 3 for England. Edrich, at twenty-one, was given one short year to reach the same standard. He was, Prittie argued in a telling footnote, expected to show himself to be a far greater prodigy than two of the most successful of England's Test batsmen.

Temperamental and technical shortcomings were

among the accusations as Edrich failed abysmally in his first Test series against Australia. R. C. Robertson-Glasgow wrote later: 'He has talent; or more truly, he started with a number of talents and increased them to riches. He rose, half fell, and then rose again, to a place higher and less slippery.' Other observers, like William Pollock, a feature writer for the *Daily Express*, were patronising and almost sneering in their judgements. 'Edrich's quality is obvious,' wrote Pollock, 'but his quantity is next to nothing.' The preliminary figures of 67 runs in six innings against Australia did plunge Edrich deep into a hateful nightmare. It was akin to the plight of Graeme Hick in recent times. Hick's record of 173 runs in his first eight Test matches against the West Indies and Pakistan was a consequence of his immobility against the searing pace and accuracy of Ambrose and Waqar Younis. The source of the crisis for Edrich, in his own embattled time, was the conquering spin of Bill O'Reilly, one of the greatest bowlers in cricket history. O'Reilly took Edrich's wicket six times in 1938: thrice in the Tests, once against Middlesex, and twice more in a representative match at Blackpool at the end of August.

Before this spectacular decline Edrich had taken 113 runs off the Australian attack; and this appeared to confirm his Test qualifications. The buoyancy of his batting in May assured him of selection for the first Test at Trent Bridge. The ensuing surfeit of runs, including seven centuries at Nottingham, made his own failure even harder to bear. He was the disappointed onlooker as Hutton, Barnett and Compton all scored hundreds and Paynter perkily ran to a double-century. Eric Edrich was among the family clan present at Nottingham to witness an eagerly awaited Test debut. The joys of a magnificent opening partnership of 219 runs, 169 of them before lunch, between Hutton and Barnett, were dispelled by Edrich's quick departure: 'It was wearing to sit so long with my pads on in my first Test,' recalled Bill. 'When my turn came at last I was screwed up a bit too tight.' He scored only five; one bold boundary off O'Reilly held fleeting promise; but he was then confounded by the Australian's quicker ball. It spun disconcertingly off the middle of his bat, on to his foot, from which it cannoned back on to the wicket. 'The poor old boy had been tucked up in the pavilion. He had had to wait a long time to bat,' said Eric Edrich. 'Bill wasn't a nervous boy; but, of course, you'd much rather go in at the start of an innings, following the roller. It's really the only place to bat.' The elder Edrich added that it is in the nature of things that another breakthrough often follows a big partnership. 'It was just unfortunate. Bill did have a bad time against Australia. He was very down by the time of the Leeds Test. He wondered if he was going to make it.'

Misfortune was the strong underlying factor in Edrich's reverses throughout the rest of the series. The extremes of form were too wide to be convincing in a cricketer of his class. He recalled: 'I experienced a chapter of dismissals that convinced me that gremlins were nesting in my cricket bag.' At Lord's, in the second Test, he failed to score. He was overcome by McCormick bowling at his fastest and in his most threatening phase of the tour. Hutton and Barnett were both caught at short-leg; in twenty-five deliveries McCormick took three wickets for 15 runs. Edrich was the second of this trio of victims in the first half-hour of the day. After one essay at a hook, he tried another and cut the ball down on to his stumps. 'Edrich must remember that to attempt to hook a fast bowler – and especially at Lord's – until one is thoroughly set is to invite disaster,' was the rebuke of one writer.

In the second innings Edrich was dismissed for 10, caught by McCabe at backward square-leg off McCormick. The wicket was fiery after rain and should have induced caution. Edrich, then as always, was not prepared to be intimidated by the bouncing ball. Once again he ventured a hook. It was a tremendous strike. The ball hurtled towards McCabe, who was late in judging its flight. He was, though, alert enough, as the ball thudded into his chest, to clutch it with frantic hands. 'Experience is a rare teacher,' said a charitable writer. 'The exuberance and joyousness of youth must not be judged too severely.'

Charity was in short supply as the criticism mounted during Edrich's summer of Test torment. At Leeds, where O'Reilly overwhelmed England, he was dismissed by a brute of a googly in one innings; and was then stumped by Ben Barnett off Fleetwood-Smith in the disastrous second innings. Amid the disarray he shared an opening partnership of 60 runs with Charles Barnett. It was the most productive stand of the match. Edrich was second top scorer with 28, and he acquitted himself well on a worn and dusty pitch. England were bowled out for 123, O'Reilly and Fleetwood-Smith sharing nine wickets, and Australia also struggled before wresting victory by five wickets. At The Oval Edrich was too low in morale to take advantage of a ludicrously innocuous opening attack of McCabe and Waite, one of the weakest to represent Australia. England, with Hutton compiling his record score of 364, amassed 903 for 7 declared. Edrich was the disillusioned bystander, one of O'Reilly's three scalps in a marathon spell of 85 overs.

Edrich, in his topsy-turvy season, was thought to have been over-praised. He was attacked unmercifully in the press. His judgement was considered not mature enough to deal with Australian bowlers on the warpath.

He was slow on his feet and not proof against fast bowling; his backplay was unsound and his bat was not always straight. There was no end to the catalogue of deficiencies. Even his hook shot was held up to ridicule. A stroke, which had yielded a harvest of runs and unqualified praise, was now condemned as wanton recklessness. It was a tour de force, which was permissible on the county circuit, but not in Test cricket. Edrich was an all too easy prey for the snipers. 'Every critic whose primary preoccupation was pleasing his public became wise after the event,' commented one of the more objective writers. Edrich, it was decreed, did not have the Test match temperament.

The vexed debate also centred on the omission of Charles Barnett at The Oval. Barnett, without doubt, deserved to be retained after his rousing century at Trent Bridge. He had been ranked behind Hammond and Leyland on Gubby Allen's tour of Australia in 1936–37. Gloucestershire supporters did have cause to be aggrieved. There was understandable resentment that Edrich should hold his place when Hutton, an absentee at Leeds, returned to the team after injury. There was also, perhaps even more pertinently, the matter of a provincial prejudice against Lord's, which had grown to the sourness of an abscess. 'Censure,' said Dean Swift, 'is the tax a man pays for being eminent.' Edrich, to add to his discomfort, paid a surcharge for being on the Lord's staff.

Jim Swanton latterly drew attention to the affinity which prevailed between Hammond, the England captain, and Edrich. 'Wally was mad about Bill,' he said. It did seem a kind of madness to persevere with Edrich. In the circumstances, it was an act of remarkable faith. Hammond's prestige as a cricketer was undoubtedly a major factor in guiding Edrich through a difficult time. He does, though, deserve immense credit for this patronage. Edrich, as an undaunted man, very likely would still have prevailed in his aspirations; but his ruffled plumage was allowed time to glow again.

Swanton also believed that Hugh Bartlett of Sussex and Norman Yardley of Yorkshire, who both won places on the following tour of South Africa, might have more strongly exercised the selectors' minds in 1938. Bartlett, adjudged suspect against fast bowling, was a cheerful and flamboyant cricketer. He was an engaging friend and the flow of his shots courted equal popularity. He thrillingly struck 157, reaching the fastest century of the season in only 57 minutes, against the Australians at Hove. He was equally conspicuous for the Gentlemen in their victory by 133 runs over the Players at Lord's. Bartlett's 175 not out was the second highest in the fixture since C. B. Fry's unbeaten 232 in 1903. He hit four sixes and 24 fours in a tremendous display of batting power.

The admirable qualities of Bartlett and Yardley, both middle-order batsmen, would not have solved the problem of a replacement opening batsman against Australia. Paynter could have been elevated to the position to accommodate one or other of them down the order. The veteran Sutcliffe, still an outstanding player, might have been restored to the team; and Arthur Fagg and John Langridge, both in fine form, were other candidates jostling for favour. Fagg had been stricken by rheumatic fever during the earlier tour of Australia. The illness had kept him out of first-class cricket in 1937. His assets in 1938 included two double-centuries for Kent in one match against Essex. He was strongly tipped to open with Hutton at The Oval. Many years later he remained bitter about his exclusion and Edrich's retention. John Langridge, generally regarded as one of the best openers never to represent England, would have erred on the side of modesty in expressing his claims. Langridge was massively resistant; he never quite erased his image as a dour accumulator; but lesser players have been capped. In addition, he was an expert slip fieldsman. Edrich might have been spared his trauma by relegation to a lower position (as did happen in the series in South Africa); but there is room for doubt whether it would have been any more productive than the similar decision taken by the selectors in demoting Graeme Hick against Pakistan in 1992.

As an ironic counterpoint to the fevers of Test cricket, Edrich maintained an unflurried march on the county scene in 1938. He scored another century against Gloucestershire at Bristol; 159 against Warwickshire at Edgbaston; and, in company with Jack Robertson, was just five runs short of another hundred against Sussex at Hove. Middlesex, largely due to his assured batting, responded to the task of scoring 300 runs and won by three wickets.

There was, in addition, a glimpse of the resilience which was to become a byword in his cricket. It occurred in the interval between the abandoned Test at Old Trafford and the next match at Leeds. Edrich and Hutton were the Players' opening partners against the Gentlemen at Lord's. Farnes, omitted from the Test team at Manchester, delivered his answer with an explosive display of fast bowling. He took eight wickets for 43 runs in 21 overs; and the Players slumped to 218 all out. Edrich recalled that Farnes, operating from the Pavilion End, bowled as fast as any other bowler he had previously encountered. 'His first ball jumped off the completely dead pitch and flew outside my off stump head high, from only just short of a length. The next ball, pitched at the same length on the leg stump, jumped like a lightning bolt straight at my eyes.'

Edrich attempted a defensive stroke while turning his head and lifting his hands to shield his face. He was not quick enough to avoid the ball and was knocked out. Soothing hands came to his aid and he managed to gulp down a reviving glass of water. Despite his spinning head, he was prepared to continue his innings until it was gently revealed to him that he was out in cricket as well as physical terms. The ball had flicked his glove on to the side of his face and thence into the hands of J. W. A. Stephenson fielding at backward point. Edrich said the appeal was delayed while they were picking him up; but, as the umpire reluctantly confirmed the decision, they were quite in order to claim his wicket once he was on his feet and ready to bat again! Edrich's vision had cleared before the second innings. He could not deny the Gentlemen their conclusive victory; but he was in defiant mood. 'His 78 (the top score of the innings) was a superb effort,' commented the *Daily Telegraph*. 'It was proof of his courage and determination as well as his skill. He had spent the previous day in bed, nursing his wounds; and his success gave the greatest satisfaction.'

Edrich's recuperative powers, shown on this and other occasions, were a testimony to his astonishing strength. He was small in stature but big in heart. The satisfaction of his recovery against the Gentlemen was probably surpassed by another more rewarding innings against Yorkshire at Lord's. It produced the stimulus for a cherished victory by Middlesex over their opponents, even though it was unavailing in the context of the fierce battle for the championship. Yorkshire, it is true, were handicapped by injuries to key players when Robins put them in on a wicket made violent by overnight rain. Hutton sustained a broken finger; Gibb was struck on the head by a short-pitched delivery; and Leyland's thumb was fractured. Excepting Leyland, who briefly batted before another blow on his thumb caused him to retire, the others did not appear in Yorkshire's second innings. Edrich was in his element in the conditions, with the odds pitted against him. He cheerfully accepted an onerous defensive task. He was top scorer with 53, grafting grittily against the combined and formidable forces of Bowes, Smailes and Verity for nearly four hours.

In September Edrich returned home to Norfolk. He was glad to be back among old friends at the end of a frustrating season. His appearance at Blofield marked the start of a long-running saga of games featuring the all-Edrich eleven. The match against a Norfolk XI captained by Michael Falcon was the idea of the local rector. He astutely recognised that 'young Billy', their local celebrity, would be the magnet to draw the crowds and raise much-needed funds for the village recreation ground. The match assumed national proportions. A BBC radio unit travelled to Blofield to cover the game and this aroused further excitement. Their presence reflected the appeal to the public imagination of a family challenging the county. Bill, as captain, assembled for the first time a team comprising his father, brothers, Eric, Geoffrey and Brian, three cousins and three uncles. Three other Edriches were available as reserves. Among the spectators was eighty-year-old Harry Edrich, holding a sprightly court and proud to welcome home his favourite grandson.

A small army of enthusiasts braved the incessant drizzle, sheltered by umbrellas, raincoats and car rugs, in the hope of watching Edrich at his entertaining best. Bill, accompanied by his father, walked out to begin the innings. Armed with the new ball was George Pilch, a direct descendant of the famed Fuller Pilch. 'All was prepared,' recalled Bill. 'As the great man who had represented his family in the Tests against Australia, I was given the honour of taking the first ball.' Edrich, to his embarrassment and gasps of astonishment from the expectant crowd, glided the ball straight into the hands of Rodney Rought-Rought at slip. He had managed to get out before the start of the broadcast. Radio listeners, to add to Bill's confusion, were told how he had succumbed first ball on his homecoming. The applause which had greeted him had scarcely died away before he was returning to the pavilion. It was left to brother Eric to make amends and uphold the family tradition. Eric opened his shoulders to hit out lustily before the rains descended in earnest to lower the curtain on an historic encounter.

The conviviality of the lunch at Blofield, presided over by James Colman, the Lord Lieutenant of Norfolk, did much to reduce Bill's blushes after his unexpected dismissal. Back at Lord's England's Test selectors risked another outburst of hostility by selecting Edrich, against all expectations, for the forthcoming tour of South Africa; and Bill, among his Norfolk friends, enjoyed their renewed congratulations. Here, at least, there was a conviction that he would at last make runs in a far distant country.

CHAPTER 4

Reprieve at Durban

'Edrich played the innings of his life. Justification came just in front of the bailiff.' – A. G. Moyes.

Edrich's eviction might, and perhaps should have been enforced by the indulgent selectors, and Bill himself was close to joining the dispossessed after his much derided selection for the winter tour of 1938–39. In five Test innings in South Africa he scored just 21 runs; and, in the words of one writer, 'his batting failures had passed into the currency of music-hall jokes'.

The post-mortems in cricket talk will always dwell on the enigma of Edrich in those distressing days. It was a *cause célèbre*; but with hindsight we can applaud the percipience of Edrich's champions, not least that of Wally Hammond, the England captain. Edrich's unproductive apprenticeship must have weighed heavily on the minds of other suspicious and disregarded aspirants. He was ridiculed as Hammond's pet. One cartoon of the period depicted a huge set of stumps, a tiny figure with a minute bat in front of them, a duck perched on the bails, and a giant umpire's finger pointing skywards.

Edrich himself was deeply worried that he could not make an impact as a Test batsman. He was at the nadir of his cricketing life. How he must have wished to be able to recall the sunny idyll of his boyhood, and his uninhibited strokeplay against the touring South Africans at Lakenham in 1935. The charmless scrapes and tentative prods on the veld buffeted his self-esteem. He floundered like a novice. 'It gave me serious worry,' he recalled, 'as to whether or not I had passed the summit of a short and unsuccessful career, and would be one of the numerous players who begin brilliantly and then fade out.'

The depression was reinforced by the unreality of his dismissals, abject and inevitable, during the early weeks of the tour. In England, in the previous summer, Edrich had forgivably lost his battles against the taunting spin of O'Reilly and Fleetwood-Smith. There was little excuse this time. He had been outmanoeuvred by a modest South African attack. What is more, his record was even worse than against Australia. All the protestations of his captain could not calm his jangled nerves.

Jim Swanton, who was behind the microphone to relay the first live cricket broadcasts back to England, has reflected upon Edrich's plight. 'Bill really ought not to have been in the side after the first three Tests. Gibb, batting in place of the injured Hutton, had made his position secure with 93 and 106 in the first Test at Johannesburg. Either Yardley (picked for this first Test) or Bartlett should have played in the final Test, if not the fourth.' George Mann, the post-war Middlesex and England captain, took a more lenient view. 'It was a dismal beginning for a player of Bill's class. The selectors were heavily criticised at the time, but they had the courage and good intelligence to persevere with him.' Another county rival, Doug Insole, believed that Edrich was a good enough player, who was able to make contributions other than with the bat, for people with judgement to say that he was bound to make the grade.

It is, perhaps, also appropriate to consider just how much Edrich was affected by the absence of Denis Compton, who missed the tour because of his soccer duties with Arsenal. Their devotion as cricket comrades was disrupted in South Africa; and certainly Edrich benefited from their rapport, even when he was making runs rather than Denis. Compton has inveighed on fluctuating fortunes in cricket. 'It is amazing how quickly you can tumble from being so full of confidence – and on top of the world – to lose form and wonder where the next runs are coming from.'

Another of Edrich's great friends, Leonard Hutton, also had his problems in South Africa. His confidence, as he once explained, was severely shaken by a blow on the head during the match against Transvaal in December. After his record-breaking feat at The Oval in 1938, Hutton did not once reach three figures in the Tests. His and Edrich's averages in South Africa were remarkably similar. Hutton scored 265 runs, with an average of 44.16; Edrich's aggregate was 240 runs at an average of 40. Away from the Test scene they both prospered with serene batsmanship. Edrich's tally of 914 runs, at an average of 60.93, placed him third behind Paynter and Hutton in all first-class matches on the tour.

The figures tellingly demonstrate how his turmoil in the Tests was at variance with his form in the provincial matches. Edrich scored centuries against Griqualand West and Rhodesia at Kimberley and Salisbury, and 98 against Natal at Durban. These included two double-century opening partnerships with Hutton at Durban and on the mat at Kimberley, where Edrich was commended for a 'delightful exhibition of strokeplay'. He could not, however, control the tremors of anxiety in a feeble start to the Test programme. Opening the England innings at Johannesburg, Edrich scored four and 10. In the second innings he survived two chances – in the slips and a stumping – before scrambling to double figures.

The second Test at Cape Town was dominated by Hammond and Ames, who both scored centuries and shared a record fourth-wicket stand of 197 runs in England-South Africa Tests. England's total of 559 was also their highest against South Africa. Edrich, relegated in the order, was bowled by Gordon without scoring. He was, perhaps fortuitously, permitted only one innings in the next two Tests at Durban and Johannesburg. Paynter, with a magnificent double-century and Farnes with seven wickets, piloted England to an innings victory at Durban. Edrich did not bat in this Test; and, heading the tailenders at no. 7, he scored only six in the fourth Test at Johannesburg.

The first signs of his impending recovery were witnessed in the match against Natal at Pietermaritzburg, on the eve of the final Test at the end of February. The holiday atmosphere at the Alexandra Park Oval helped to lift his spirits. Edrich, commented the *Natal Mercury*, 'must have felt that fate was no longer in a frowning mood'. An England place still beckoned, with doubts lingering over Paynter's fitness. Edrich stepped into the fray, after Hutton had struck a short ball to the boundary but then allowed the bat to slip in his hand and fall on to the wicket. Edrich was, at first, grim in defence. Brilliant fielding baulked his progress; and his discretion was intensified by the dismissals of Gibb and Hammond. Gibb fell to a well-judged running catch by Nourse; Hammond to a juggling catch by Rose in the slips. Only 70 runs were scored in the 90 minutes before lunch.

The arrival of Ames, in merry and audacious mood, broke the spell of attrition. Edrich reached his half-century soon after the interval; and now, feeling more secure, set out more vigorously after runs. A group of invited local college boys had the treat of watching the spectacular batting of the MCC batsmen. Between lunch and tea, in two hours' play, the score was advanced by 195 runs. The second 100 of the innings came up in only 64 minutes. During the stand of 114 runs for the fourth wicket Ames twice smote enormous sixes off the bowling of Eric Dalton. He did not quite time another mighty hit and was caught by Wade at deep mid-on. He had scored 62 in just over an hour.

Doug Wright was now Edrich's ally in his welcome batting revel. He watched a relaxed Edrich unleash a pounding straight drive, and rejoiced with him in the fulfilment of a splendid century. The spate of boundaries, as the tiring bowlers succumbed to strain, did mean less work for the fieldsmen. It had become a forlorn quest to check the exultant batsmen; they now cantered gently to the distant points of the field to collect the balls thrown in by the spectators. All that was missing in an uproarious carnival was the serenade of a brass band. Edrich, thumping the ball heartily, galloped to his 150. It included 24 fours and one six. 'There was nothing merciful about his work,' reported the *Natal Mercury*. 'Edrich has had sufficient bad luck on this tour to enjoy punishing the bowlers. No sadistic schoolmaster, flourishing his cane, could have had greater satisfaction than the little Middlesex man was giving himself.'

Bob Crisp, who held a watching brief at Pietermaritzburg, thought that Edrich's best innings of the tour had the fervour of his Maytime exploits in 1938. On a day of broiling heat he considered it was a mercy that Hutton had broken his wicket and that Paynter had been unable to play. The steamy warmth had compelled Gibb to send for a towel not long after he had taken stride. Dalton could hardly hold the ball because the sweat kept running down his arms and into his hand. 'Edrich,' said Crisp in his amusing commentary, 'made a noise like a splash every time he hit the ball. If he had run up and down the wicket much longer, it would have been a gluepot by six o'clock.'

There was, however, more serious business looming. By virtue of his innings against Natal, Edrich had done just enough to retain his place for the final Test at Durban. It was thought then that it would be played to a finish. He must have looked wistfully at the newly-planted saplings, celebrating the century achievements of Paynter and Hammond in the earlier Test, on the mounds above the Kingsmead ground. Hammond lost the toss at Durban after winning it in eight previous Tests. Edrich had more time to brood on his batting, as South Africa compiled 530, their highest total in Test cricket. Verity marshalled his precise resources to bowl 55 eight-ball overs and six balls and take two wickets for 97 runs. It was the longest innings in Tests between the two countries, lasting thirteen hours.

England began their reply late on the third day; on the fourth they scored 231 for six wickets. The headlines hailed the imminence of an England defeat. Hutton was run out; Hammond stumped off Dalton; and Paynter, after batting for four hours and twenty minutes for 62, was lbw to Langton. The snailpace rate of scoring prompted one cartoonist to caption his drawing for the day: 'This Timeless Pest'. He added, with delicious irony: 'When South Africa had dismissed Hutton, Hammond and Paynter it seemed that England's policy of appeasement would have to be abandoned'.

The score was 169 for four when Edrich came to the wicket. His opponent was Arthur Langton, the best of the South African bowlers. Langton was brisk and purposeful as he attacked the newcomer. 'Here

THIS TIMELESS PEST—

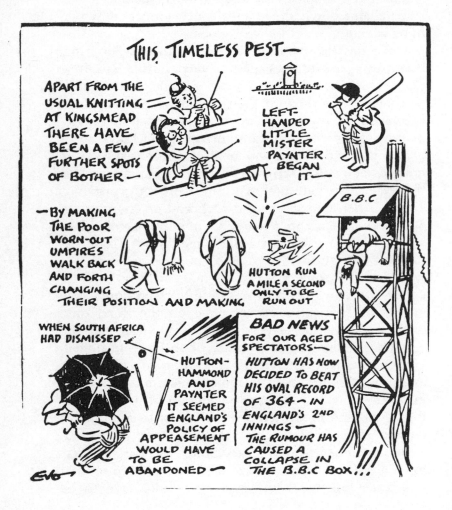

APART FROM THE USUAL KNITTING AT KINGSMEAD THERE HAVE BEEN A FEW FURTHER SPOTS OF BOTHER —

LEFT-HANDED LITTLE MISTER PAYNTER BEGAN IT —

— BY MAKING THE POOR WORN-OUT UMPIRES WALK BACK AND FORTH CHANGING THEIR POSITION AND MAKING

HUTTON RUN A MILE A SECOND ONLY TO BE RUN OUT

B.B.C

WHEN SOUTH AFRICA HAD DISMISSED

HUTTON-HAMMOND AND PAYNTER IT SEEMED ENGLAND'S POLICY OF APPEASEMENT WOULD HAVE TO BE ABANDONED —

BAD NEWS FOR OUR AGED SPECTATORS — HUTTON HAS NOW DECIDED TO BEAT HIS OVAL RECORD OF 364 — IN ENGLAND'S 2ND INNINGS — THE RUMOUR HAS CAUSED A COLLAPSE IN THE B.B.C BOX!!!

EVO

was Edrich's chance,' reported the *Natal Mercury*. 'A century from him would justify everything. But his evil fortune pursued him. He made a single and then a slow ball from Langton found him too far forward, and he spooned up an easy catch to Eric Rowan at silly mid-on.' Ralph Barker wrote: 'Edrich, normally the most composed of cricketers, was miserably tense. A black shadow seemed to hang behind the bowler's arm. Just when a determined innings was needed to keep England in the game, Edrich failed again.' England were all out on the fifth morning for 316, 214 runs in arrears. Everyone did better than Edrich. Ames scored 84, and even Farnes and Wright had twenties to their credit.

Alan Melville, the South African captain, did not enforce the follow-on. He preferred to drive home his advantage in the expectation of a deteriorating wicket and profit for his bowlers in England's second innings. The South African Cricket Board were now resigned to the longueurs of an interminable match. They tried to entice those spectators, who had not been compelled to return to work, by reducing admission prices. Bookings for the stands were suspended, and holders of tickets for the official stand were notified that they would be admitted on the presentation of their ticket stubs.

The *Natal Mercury*, in a circulation drive, offered a prize of five guineas to a reader who could correctly, or nearly guess the ultimate duration of the playing time of the match. The players themselves had now concluded that the affair was a joke. One South African batsman, Ken Viljoen, later laughingly remarked that he and his colleagues would be afraid to ask for leave in future in case their employers referred to the game. It did merit one description which considered the slowly unfolding events 'as tedious as a twice-told tale, vexing the dull ear of a drowsy man'.

Bill Edrich was wide awake as he contemplated the course of the match. His next innings was invested with immense significance. Another failure would undoubtedly have plunged him into oblivion. Throughout the sixth day of the match South Africa remorselessly built up a seemingly unassailable lead. When they were finally out shortly before the close for 481, England required 696 for victory. It was a target beyond comprehension. Only once in the fourth innings of a Test match had a side made 400, and even then it had been a losing total. Only five times in first-class cricket had a side made more than 500 in the last innings, and no side had ever made 600. Among the previous highest Test match targets had been the 708 required by England at The Oval in 1934; Australia's 742 at Brisbane in 1928–29; and West Indies' 836 in the 1929–30 series. All had been unavailing quests as had the 702 needed by Australia to save the follow-on at The Oval in 1938. The demoralising effect of such a task had been demonstrated on that occasion.

Edrich's own state of mind had fallen even lower. In an attempt to regain form, he had subjected himself to a strict regime of early nights, strictly rationed drink and smoking. It had proved a futile exercise for such a sociable man. He had been a party-goer from his early days as a cricketer. In India, even under the captaincy of Lionel Tennyson, he had been warned to restrain his bohemian jollities. He had been told that it would be an act of discourtesy to his hosts to drink before, rather than during, major functions. More seriously, he had discovered that the unaccustomed sedate lifestyle, instead of helping him, had actually increased his nervousness. The pretence was dropped and it had an invigorating sequel.

In the knowledge, as Denis Compton has said, that matters could hardly get any worse, Edrich drank freely on the night before his marathon innings at Durban. He was the guest at a party given by Dr H. G. Owen-Smith, the former Oxford and South African all-rounder, with whom he had played for Middlesex. It had lasted until the early hours of the morning, and it was a champagne tonic for Edrich's flagging spirits. He forgot all his worries amid the camaraderie of the party. Eric Edrich related that his brother, not for the last time, enjoyed the intervals of relaxation before big cricket events. 'They had to put Bill to bed that morning in Durban,' he said. Edrich was smiling when they shook him awake to play the innings to save his Test career.

Hammond now produced a masterly stroke of leadership. Edrich was called upon to take the offensive and head the England challenge. He was promoted above Paynter, England's leading batsman in the series. 'I'm going to put you in first-wicket down, Bill,' said Hammond. 'This is your last chance in the series. You can make runs, if you try. Don't be afraid to go for the runs, if you get the opportunity.' Hammond was all too aware of the importance of the occasion for Edrich. His own pride and reputation were also at stake in this last gamble. The next words produced a leap in Edrich's heart. They were calculated to bolster the morale of a beleaguered batsman. 'If you can get a couple of hundred, we might stand a chance,' declared Hammond.

Jim Swanton has dwelt upon the extraordinary lasting powers of the Kingsmead wicket at Durban. It did contribute to the course of the game. One of the playing regulations in the series empowered the groundsman to roll before a day's play began if there had been any rain and if he thought this would improve the pitch. Accordingly before the third, the fourth, the sixth, and the ninth days, Vic Robbins, the curator, as he was called, used the heavy roller. 'This chap was out there at 5.30 in the morning. In effect, the rolling made a new cake which the tropical sun had dried out by the start of play. The wicket became easier and easier.'

South Africa, according to Swanton, had begun the match with a lightweight attack. In the trying conditions, as the game moved stealthily on, their stamina and resolve dwindled. The perspiring bowlers included Norman Gordon, who, Leonard Hutton believed, would have been seen to advantage in England had not the war intervened. His new-ball partners were Newson, playing in his only Test, and Arthur Langton, who went lame in England's second innings and had to bowl his 56 overs at half pace. The subsidiary roles were occupied by leg-spinners, Bruce Mitchell and Eric Dalton, both primarily batsmen. 'Far from being impossible,' reflected Swanton on England's objective, 'you felt it was just a question of when it would be reached.'

The verdict does not take into account the psychological factors inherent in England's – and, especially, in Edrich's – mission. On the seventh day – Friday, 10 March – England scored 253 for one wicket, the prized one of Hutton, bowled by Mitchell. At that stage, with only 76 runs on the board, South Africa had strongly scented victory. They were even more gleeful when, to their surprise, Edrich came in ahead of Paynter and Hammond. Their barely concealed laughter was speedily stifled. 'Edrich showed no signs of nerves at all,' commented the *Natal Mercury*. 'The first ball from Mitchell he struck with venom for four and then, in the next over, he drove another gloriously to the fence.' The two shots affirmed that his belligerence was restored.

Paul Gibb, in his usual obdurate sheet-anchor role, stood firm as Edrich moved with almost indecent haste

to his half-century. It contained eight fours and was the fastest fifty of the match. 'Edrich was the master of himself and the bowlers alike, and he continued in this vein throughout the day,' wrote one observer. Ralph Barker, in his account, said the tea interval had a calming effect on Edrich's ferocity. There was a realisation that he should graft and aim for a really big score. South Africa took the new ball – the tenth of the game – but it did nothing to deflect Edrich in his burgeoning command. 'Now Gibb was forgotten, ploughing his way along,' continued the *Natal Mercury* correspondent. 'Edrich won his way into the nineties and everybody wanted to see him get a hundred.'

Edrich moved unhurriedly to this milestone. Three singles took him to 97, then he straight drove for two runs, and finally he scampered the run which took him to his first Test century. He had batted for thirteen minutes over three hours and hit 12 fours. 'There is a pleasing vigour about this little man, which takes the eye, and he was given an enormous reception,' reported Norman Preston in *Wisden*. He also recalled the scene of acclamation. 'High up on the pavilion balcony shouts of triumph came from his comrades.' 'It was', added the *Natal Mercury*, 'a glorious and courageous start on a task that might well have appalled the stoutest-hearted band of cricketers to have visited this country.'

Rain on the eighth day, the second Saturday of the match, provided a welcome respite; but it also led to quivers of concern that time was running out. It was announced, strangely in view of the later decision, that alternative transport arrangements had been made in order to complete the match. In the event of the game being uncompleted by the Tuesday evening, play would continue on the Wednesday morning. The England players had been provisionally booked on the express train leaving Durban for Cape Town in the afternoon.

The optimistic theories of local partisans, examining the wicket before the resumption on Monday, held forth on the fact that, though the surface was dry, the body of the wicket must hold moisture after weekend rain, and concluded that it would break up in the afternoon. Their hopes of trouble for England's batsmen proved unfounded. Gibb, who had won his place only because of his fellow Yorkshireman Hutton's earlier injury, scored a century, his second of the series. It was the slowest by an England batsman, lasting seven and a half hours. The innings was grimly conceived, but it was in keeping with the cause. At lunch the score was 331 for 1, Edrich having completed his 150; by the time Gibb was bowled by Dalton the pair had added 280, then the highest partnership in matches between the two countries.

Edrich, riding the crest of confidence, went on to his double-century. It had occupied six hours and 35 minutes and included 23 boundaries. He could now afford to be indulgent about two escapes in the slips, which would have caused palpitations at the start of the innings. The uncertainties were behind him. He was still battling on at the tea interval when England rested on 440 for 2. The aggregate of runs had, at this stage, surpassed the 1,753 scored by Australia and England at Adelaide in the 1920–21 series. The eventual tally of 1,981 runs exceeded the previous highest of 1,815 scored by West Indies and England at Kingston in 1929–30.

The lowering clouds did not dim England's expectations on the resumption. There was now the prospect of an unexpected success. The margin had been reduced to 250 runs when Edrich made a fatal mistake. He played a tired shot against Langton, and Gordon, close

to the wicket, took a good catch.

Edrich had made handsome amends for his previous failures. His 219, compiled in a deep personal crisis, had almost delivered victory into England's grasp. If this was a Test of endurance for players and spectators, it was doubly so for Edrich in his critical vigil at Durban. Amid the clamour over the oppressively somnolent wicket, one interested observer back in England expressed his relief and delight: Edrich's joy was sealed by a congratulatory telegram from his friend and partner, Denis Compton.

England required exactly 200 runs before the fiasco of the last day. By lunch the end was in sight. Hammond reached his third century of the series and his twenty-first in Test cricket to equal the record of Bradman. The first indications of the impending storm came with a rustle among spectators as they put on raincoats and hoisted umbrellas. Hammond and Paynter belatedly started to bustle for runs. Two showers brought brief delays. 'Here was disappointment,' reported the *Natal Mercury*. 'Devoted enthusiasts, who had been there day after lengthy day, had settled themselves for the finish. Now the weather, which had played for England up to this point, was going to rob them of a well-deserved triumph.'

The closing stages of the match were recalled by Jim Swanton. Just after lunch, following a broadcasting session, he had received at telephone call from a listener with English sympathies. 'Buck up, England,' urged the enthusiast. Swanton was asked to relay a message to Hammond that the downpour had begun at Isipingo, a coastal resort fourteen miles south of Durban. The information was passed on by the MCC manager, Flight-Lieutenant Jack Holmes, the Sussex captain. Holmes, using the pretext of a replacement glove, stressed the urgency of quick runs to Hammond.

71

The subsequent flurry of strokes came too late. Only 46 runs were needed when Hammond surrendered his wicket in his haste to beat the rain. He danced down the wicket to punish Dalton and was stumped by Grieveson. For a little while longer play continued under the dark, forbidding skies. Tea was taken amid dwindling hopes that the rains would relent. Just as the players started to clatter down the stairs for the last time, heavy showers swept across the field to send them back again.

'By the sheer cussedness of things, the game was just then in an intensely interesting stage,' wrote William Pollock. 'The players were suddenly keyed up, the spectators agog over the drama that might unfold before the final curtain.'

The marathon at Durban had toppled over into frustration and farce. It was abandoned without a result. A 'timeless' Test, after all, had a limit. England, with five wickets in hand, were just 42 runs short of victory when the thunderstorm peremptorily closed the proceedings. The match was intriguingly poised before the abandonment. Either side could still have won; but it would have required an extraordinary somersault in fortunes for South Africa to snatch victory. England's sixth-wicket pair, Ames and Valentine, both renowned strikers, would surely have made a swift and winning thrust.

The South African Board of Control and the two captains conferred before issuing a statement that the game had to be called off. There had clearly been second thoughts on the proposed extension until lunchtime on the Wednesday. The reason given was that the England team had to catch the 8.05 train on Tuesday night in order to reach Cape Town – a distance of around 1,000 miles – in time to sail home on the *Athlone Castle* on the following Friday. A flight

NO GAME WAS EVER YET WORTH A RAP
 FOR A RATIONAL MAN TO PLAY
INTO WHICH NO ACCIDENT, NO MISHAP,
 COULD POSSIBLY FIND ITS WAY.
           A.L.Cordon in "YE WEARY WAYFARER"

was considered impracticable. English cricketers were then thought too precious to be entrusted to the care of an aeroplane. Hugh Bartlett, one of the MCC party, was disbelieving at the waste of England's endeavours. 'The sailing could not be postponed. We had to get back because of contracts with our counties. It was a terrible labour in vain for eleven chaps who had strived so hard to win a Test match.'

The duration of the match exceeded the previous longest between England and the West Indies at Kingston, Jamaica, in April 1930. Les Ames, one of the frustrated batsmen at Durban, had taken part in the earlier supposedly timeless and fruitless encounter. On that occasion West Indies had been set an even more ludicrous target of 836 runs before another washout.

Bill Edrich would have been pleased (his family have expressed their disappointment most strenuously in recent times) if the blessing of his cricket resurrection had been crowned with an England victory at Durban. It was a bizarre match yielding an avalanche of records, which will never be equalled. For those players without futures in peril the cessation of play was a thankful release. The *Natal Mercury* cartoonist, paraphrasing the words of a romantic song, provided a wry epitaph to the saga. He marked the end in jocular terms. 'When I grow too old to dream, I'll have this Test to remember,' he told his readers. Edrich, as the irrepressible troubadour, had an ear for a haunting lyric. There were, happily, to be other cherished cricket moments; but it expressed, if not in the manner intended, his thoughts after the epic feat at Durban.

Edrich was named as one of *Wisden*'s Five Cricketers of the Year in 1939. The honour was, not surprisingly, tempered by the verdict that he could not complain at lack of opportunity. 'No other cricketer has been persevered with in the face of continued non-success as a batsman.' Edrich, despite his revival, was required to serve a season of penance. Hutton had three different opening partners – Gimblett, Fagg and Keeton – and Compton and Hardstaff were recalled in the last pre-war series against the West Indies. Edrich was ignored. Yet in championship games he scored seven centuries. In the last six weeks of 1939 he scored 1,300 runs, and played some of the best cricket of his life. Six years of war – and bravery of another kind against the odds – were to ensue before he could confirm his cricket stature as an essential bulwark at England's helm.

CHAPTER 5

Wakes on the Water

'The exploits of our daylight bombers can be likened to the Charge of the Light Brigade at Balaclava.' – *Winston Churchill*

The attack on Cologne on 12 August 1941 was the first daylight raid deep into the German industrial heartland. The force of 54 Blenheim bombers was denied a fighter escort because the 250 miles across enemy territory was beyond their range. It was one of the most spectacular low-level assaults of the summer and a landmark in the British counter-offensive. The objectives were the power stations of Knapsack and Quadrath, both of major strategic importance to the German war industries in the Ruhr.

Bill Edrich led a section of 107 Squadron on the mission. He had been upgraded from Pilot Officer to Acting Squadron Leader in the space of nineteen days, an indication of the heavy losses among the Blenheim crews. None of his cricket achievements, he commented later, could ever approach the drama, endeavours and comradeship of his wartime campaign. It was an expression of an unashamed romantic who carried the torch of patriotism throughout his life. 'In four months in 1941 I experienced the heights and depths of emotions – supreme elation, like the effects of good wine, and profound remorse at losing so many fine friends,' he said.

An extract from one Fighter Intelligence report after a raid on the Cherbourg docks presented an eloquent image of the low-flying quests. 'The sea-coloured camouflage on the top surface of the Blenheims was so effective that the first we saw of them as they flew out from the target was their wakes on the water.' The perils of these daylight attacks, judged to be among the most dangerous of the war, claimed casualties on an horrendous scale. Brian Edrich, who also served in the Royal Air Force, described the skills required by his brother and fellow pilots. The low-level raids on enemy convoys in the North Sea and English Channel were carried out often at mast height, between 10 feet and 20 feet. The convoys were escorted by flak (anti-aircraft) ships, which could zero in on the bombers with their heavy and light guns. 'The Blenheims attacked the ships by coming straight at them, just lifting over the top, and then releasing their bombs into the sides of the vessels. At the speed they came in – around 250 mph – they were fairly easy targets,' explained the younger Edrich. The hazards were heightened by the lack of manoeuvrability of the slow and cumbersome Blenheim bombers, which had been developed from civilian aircraft. Evasion tactics had to be learned by bitter experience. Once over the first few trips pilots had a better chance of survival. Sadly, many did not progress so far and were killed in their initial operations.

Bill Edrich was never deflated by apparently insuperable odds, in war, or in cricket. 'Billy boy, we'd follow you anywhere,' was the compliment of one Canadian flier. His loyalty was endorsed by another man, Ernie Hope, a Lancastrian. Hope was Edrich's wireless operator and rear-gunner. He was a friend and associate from their days at the RAF operational training unit at Upwood in Cambridgeshire. Hope regarded Edrich as an inspirational figure. 'Bill was a great man and he flew his aircraft in the same cavalier spirit as he played his cricket,' he said. Edrich was Hope's best man at his wedding in June 1942.

Edrich had always wanted to fly; he felt that he was best qualified to undergo training for aircrew; and that this would be the fullest contribution he could make in the war. At Christmas in 1939 he was still awaiting call-up at home with his family in Norfolk. He did have to exercise a little subterfuge to gain his wings. A friend had told him that the quickest route into aircrew was to join the RAF Physical Training Branch and then remuster. He was posted to Uxbridge, where one of his instructors was his Middlesex captain, Walter Robins. It was a lucky reunion and there was a friendly game of cricket to seal it. After the match Robins asked Edrich to let him know if he had any requests. 'Yes,' said Bill, 'I want a transfer to aircrew.' Within forty-eight hours he was enrolled in the first of a series of courses. Twelve months later, after flying training at Cranwell, at the end of which he was commissioned, and operational training on Blenheims at Upwood, Edrich was posted to No. 2 Group, Bomber Command. On 21 May 1941 he reported to 107 Squadron at Little Massingham in Norfolk.

His flair for flying and mastery of another craft earned the respect and admiration of all who knew him. His own later description of the Blenheim adventures exemplifies the zest of his crusade. 'Flattened low on the water, tucked in as close as I dared to the leader, I felt an exhilaration that swamped all other emotions. Low flying did not bother me. I loved it. It gave me an illusion of speed and security. Two hundred knots may not be much by "sound barrier" standards; but with the sea racing by 30 feet below it seems incredibly fast.'

'There's the target – dead ahead,' called out Edrich's

navigator, Vic Phipps, a Londoner. They were approaching the power station at Knapsack in the bright sunlight of 12 August. The Blenheim force to Cologne had hedgehopped all the way across Holland to the Ruhr. The bombers had soared over the flat countryside, pulling over the tall trees and church spires. They were given an ecstatic welcome by Dutch farmworkers looking upwards to see RAF roundels on the aircraft flying low over their fields for the first time. 'It was great to watch them waving joyously to us as we sped over,' said Edrich. Harvesting was in progress, as the corn ripened in the glorious weather. The landscape and the activity were reminders of other happier times on the farmlands of his own native Norfolk.

Edrich recalled how they had practised the attack many times over a disused power station at St Neots in Bedfordshire. It had worked like clockwork then and they had achieved their dummy run in less than three seconds. The weeks of practice now had to be just as precisely translated into success on the real target. They were each carrying four 250-lb. bombs, with eleven-second fuses, to allow the three boxes of six aircraft to follow each other through the target area at the lowest possible height; and for the last aircraft to steer clear by the time the first bombs exploded.

The tall chimneys of the power station stood out ominously, forcing the Blenheims up to around 400 feet. There was some light flak bursting around them; but otherwise they were unopposed. They had achieved complete surprise. The core of the station was in flames. Ernie Hope reported many direct hits and photographs taken by rear-facing cameras later confirmed the finding. Plumes of smoke billowed into the air as they returned to close formation for the journey home. Edrich had expected a riposte from lurking German fighters. In the event, the worst moments came as they ran into a heavy thunderstorm, which broke up the formation as they neared the Scheldt estuary. It was followed by an even greater hazard of huge flocks of ducks and geese rising from their nesting grounds. 'Birds seemed to be shooting past us in all directions, and it was easily the most frightening part of the whole trip,' said Edrich.

Twelve of the 54 Blenheim bombers failed to return from the mission to Cologne. 'It had been a thrilling trip to take part in, and although we had achieved a large measure of success, it was a heavy price to pay,' commented Edrich. Two days later the leaders of the formations and sections were summoned to receive the personal congratulations of the Chief of the Air Staff, Sir Charles Portal. The leaders of the three formations of 18 were each awarded the DSO. Edrich, along with other leaders of the boxes of six aircraft, won the DFC.

Extracts from the recommendations for his award read: 'This officer had the difficult task of bringing his formation in to attack the main power station immediately after the leading box had attacked. This needed fine judgement as it was imperative that the target should be bombed from as low an altitude as possible. He had to delay his attack in order to avoid his formation being destroyed by explosions from the delay action bombs of the previous boxes. This required coolness and courage . . . Squadron Leader Edrich led his formation in at exactly the right height and time, all aircraft dropping the bombs in the centre of the target area. By carrying out his orders with the greatest exactitude and determination, he must be given credit for a large part of the success of the attack.'

Air Marshal Sir Ivor Broom was a member of 114 Squadron at the parent station at West Raynham, close to Edrich's base at Massingham. Sir Ivor was also engaged in the attack on Cologne and has since said that such events tend to create a life-long bond. 'Bill's dynamic and cheerful leadership imparted tremendous confidence in those who followed him. The immediate award of the DFC brought great pleasure to his many Royal Air Force friends who so admired and loved him.'

Bryan Stevens, Bill's old Norfolk cricket friend, remembered the tremendous ovation received by the newly-honoured Edrich at Lord's a few weeks later. Edrich was a member of a Lord's XI opposed to an Army team. Stevens was then serving in the Royal Corps of Signals and stationed in Whitehall prior to being posted to the Middle East. By careful negotiation with his colleagues, he was able to arrange time off to coincide with cricket occasions in London. 'There was a big crowd, approaching 10,000, and we had a great day's cricket. Bill was soon in the picture, dismissing the first Army batsman with a good slip catch, and then taking a couple of wickets.'

Stevens recalled: 'The crowd rose to Bill when he came out to bat. He was cheered all the way out to the wicket'. The salutations were rudely halted by a certain Army sergeant running at full tilt to take a catch in front of the pavilion. Edrich had scored only four. 'Bill was brilliantly caught by Sergeant-Instructor Denis Compton.' Compton had already scored a century; his alertness deprived the spectators of another batting feast.

'Germany must be forced to move her fighters westwards,' exhorted Winston Churchill in a speech at Massingham in June 1941. The visit of the Prime Minister closely preceded Edrich's first operational flight. Churchill told the assembled aircrews that the German intervention in the Middle East was turning the war against Britain in that theatre. He reminded his audience that 43,000 civilians had been killed in air raids over Britain in the previous twelve months, and that

81

his promise that the RAF would retaliate by day and night had not yet been fulfilled. 'Our purpose must be to relieve pressure on other fronts,' said Churchill. 'I'm relying on you.'

The eve-of-the-battle appeal from the Prime Minister bolstered morale; but, sitting in the cockpit of his Blenheim on the following morning, Edrich knew that he was just another freshman pilot on the threshold of a new experience. It was a journey into the unknown. His task was to attack a heavily defended enemy convoy moving from Hamburg down the Dutch coast to Rotterdam. It was a sensational episode; an example of adrenalin-charged opportunism and consummate flying skills. As a signal demonstration of courage and coolness, it must rank among Edrich's bravest deeds. He was, though, lucky to survive the operation.

The formation of Blenheims headed for their quarry, dropping down to below 100 feet over the sea. Their approach was obstructed by a veil of cloud. 'We were enmeshed in this cotton-wool cloud, flying entirely on instruments,' said Edrich. 'I had no experience of cloud formation flying. I was frightened. Several times I nearly gave up. But for twenty minutes, I hung on, concentrating more fiercely than ever before in my life.'

Suddenly the clouds thinned and soon the convoy appeared in their sights. Two big merchant ships stood out from all the others, one in the centre of the convoy and the other near the rear. Edrich bore down on the latter ship, jinking and rolling to distract the defending gunners. They were now flying through an intense barrage. 'I experienced an extraordinary feeling of claustrophobia, trapped in the goldfish bowl of the cockpit,' wrote Edrich in a personal account in the family's papers. 'I felt that if any of these rising balls of light hit the windscreen my world would disappear in some abrupt feat of legerdemain.' He pressed his own gun button, letting the tracer hose all over the ship. The superstructure was floating up towards him at an alarming rate. He gave the order to release their four bombs in swift succession. He then held on until he was sure they had gone. 'The deck of the merchant ship filled my windscreen. I felt certain we must hit her,' continued Edrich. 'I pulled back viciously on the stick and, with a prayer of thankfulness, we zoomed upwards, just in time to clear the masts. As we turned, we looked back at the ship. She was labouring in flames.'

The extent of the near calamity under enemy fire was revealed when they landed at Massingham. A huge segment of the aircraft rudder had been shot away in the attack. Edrich said: 'The Blenheim had taken a lot of punishment. I was learning to have great faith in my aircraft. I was never quite so happy in any other machine.'

Bill Edrich senior, in another anecdote, related that his son had already carried out an early morning raid on Westerland, the fighter airfield on the island of Sylt. At ten o'clock, soon after his return, a report had been received that the German convoy was in the North Sea. The pilot who should have gone was unavailable, so Edrich volunteered to lead the new attack. It was to prove a remarkable day, even for a man of his stamina.

Anthony Richards, who was the 107 Squadron adjutant at Massingham, provided an account of the hectic round of activity. Richards shared quarters with the Administration Officer, Squadron Leader 'Tubby' Clayton. They were housed in a requisitioned cottage in the village. During their time at Massingham, Colonel Birbeck, the local squire, had constantly tried to arrange a cricket match with the squadron. He possessed his own private cricket ground in delightful surroundings. Operations and the toll of casualties had caused repeated postponements. Arrangements had now been finalised for the match to be played on this Saturday in June. 'Every member of the team is detailed to report to me by ten o'clock, so I know I've got the so-and-so's this time,' remarked Clayton. 'We can't disappoint the Colonel again.'

By ten-thirty ten members of the team had satisfactorily reported. Another had failed to do so. He was Bill Edrich. Clayton was furious. 'Why the hell isn't he here?' He looked up the name of the missing airman again. 'But he's a keen cricketer. Everyone says so, at any rate. Supposed to know something about it, too.' Richards replied that their colleague was away on an operation. 'It's a box of three. They're after shipping.' 'I hope he doesn't get killed,' said Clayton. 'He'll absolutely put paid to my side. After all the trouble I've had. What a nuisance these people are.'

At half-past twelve two surviving crews returned. The third Blenheim had been shot down over the Channel on the way back. The box had been attacked by Messerschmitt fighters for ten minutes. Edrich was badly shaken. He removed his tattered England sweater, which he had worn for his first Test match three years before. He never failed to wear it while flying – it was his lucky mascot – and drank a reviving beer.

'At half-past two,' continued Richards, 'Bill was batting first-wicket-down for the squadron side. He made some eighty-odd runs in under half an hour. One cricket ball was irretrievably lost over the elm trees. He then proceeded to run himself out purposely, to let the rest have a chance, else he'd still have been batting, and then consumed a vast cup of tea.'

Edrich had had a busy day: a sortie before breakfast;

an enemy vessel destroyed by nine o'clock; and a desperate air battle over the Channel by eleven o'clock. He
had earned his pot of beer by mid-day, as a refresher
for cricket and the riot of runs before three o'clock in
the afternoon. There was another pleasing assignation
to complete the day. Bill had a rendezvous with a
handsome village girl that evening.

In later times, Denis Compton, in reference to
Edrich's driving, would tell his friend: 'Just remember,
Bill, you're not flying your aeroplane.' Bill drove a
succession of cars just as furiously as he flew his
Blenheims. He affected his more nervous passengers
in much the same manner as he scattered the wits of a
chimney sweep on one flying jaunt during the war. The
Edrich family by this time had moved to Lillingstone
Dayrell in Buckinghamshire. One of Bill's customary
actions, on his safe return from an operation, was to
dip his wings in salute to his family. His elder brother,
Eric, said: 'Bill would swoop low over the meadows. He
gave the village quite a display.' Brian Edrich believed
that Bill regarded the 'shoot-ups' as the best practice
for his shipping strikes. 'The people in our village would
rush out and say: "Bill's here". There was a small valley
leading up to our house. Bill would circle round and
you could actually look down on him and watch the
plane zoom up to the houses.'

On one occasion, to Edrich's immense relief, a
suicidal mission to Brest to attack the German war-
ship *Prinz Eugen* was halted soon after take-off. An
elated Bill returned home from the airfield at Portreath
in Cornwall. He signalled his arrival with an aerobatics
extravaganza. To Amos Clark, the village chimney
sweep, this presented an imminent threat of disintegrating chimneys; he was poised on a ladder, working
on one of them. There was no warning, just an eerie
rush of air as Bill's aircraft careered over the roof-

tops. The terrified Amos vowed he would never go up a chimney again. 'Blast these young devils, always playing about,' he said.

Edrich's devilry was misplaced in this location; but it was a symptom of an attitude which was to persist in other years. The daily death-defying operations were to have a profound influence on his future lifestyle. Emerging unscathed from a terrible conflict gave him a perspective at odds with others who thought him reckless and incorrigible in his misbehaviour. He was pursued by the charge of juvenilia in some quarters, but Edrich's outlook was to count every day a bonus and one to be enjoyed after the trauma of war. As an explanation, he could point to a near-disastrous confrontation with the superior fire-power of the German fighters.

Returning from one attack, his Blenheims were intercepted by a group of Messerschmitts. It was an unequal contest; a series of direct hits had left the Blenheims badly mauled; their guns were either jammed, or out of ammunition. Evasion was their only hope. 'Mercifully, three of the 109s had given up the chase, but a fourth was coming in for the kill,' recalled Edrich. 'The German pilot was approaching from the port rear, and we could not shake him off. Reassured by the absence of answering fire, he came in closer and closer. We were sitting ducks. Yet still he did not fire.'

The gravity of the situation lingered in Edrich's mind for a long time afterwards. They were completely helpless and he must have felt that these were to be his last moments. 'As he overtook us, he banked above me, and I looked straight up into his face. His look of exasperation was unmistakable. He too had run out of ammunition. With a shrug of his shoulders, he turned away.' David Brocklehurst, a friend of later years, was given another version of the escape. Edrich said that the German pilot had flown around him twice and, then, flying alongside, they had waved at each other. The German raised his thumb to concede his failure and flew off home. A glance at Bill's severely damaged aircraft, spinning desperately in the skies, convinced him that his enemy would soon plunge into the seas and oblivion.

It was in the nature of a miracle that all but two of the Blenheims were able to limp back to their base at Driffield. The faces of the ground crew were almost as grim as the returning airmen. 'We thought you'd had it, sir,' one man told Edrich. Another thought he was looking at a ghost.

The sadness at the loss of cherished companions had a special poignancy in one fatality towards the end of Edrich's tour of duty. It was an important low-level strike on the harbour at Rotterdam. Edrich was specifically ordered not to fly; but he was extremely worried that his inexperienced deputy and close friend, Dick Shuttleworth, was to lead on so dangerous an operation. He was also concerned about the concept of the operation. It was a repeat of an earlier successful raid. Edrich believed that this time the Germans would mount a vigilant guard. They would be waiting to gain their revenge against the marauding Blenheims. He expressed his fears at the station headquarters, making a strong plea that, if the attack was to proceed, he should be allowed to lead the mission. His request was refused.

Edrich's worst fears were confirmed. Only two of the Blenheims returned; and among the four pilots shot down was Dick Shuttleworth. Shuttleworth's wife was staying at a local hotel. Edrich was asked to convey the news. He said it was one of the saddest nights of his life. 'Dick's wife was very brave.' He drove her to the home of her father-in-law at Wroxham, near Norwich.

At two o'clock in the morning he rang the doorbell of the house. The parents instantly knew what had happened. Bill watched as Dick's father poured out two large whiskies. 'You probably need this,' he said, 'as much as I do.'

Next day Edrich discovered why he had not been allowed to take part in the attack on Rotterdam. He had been posted to the No. 2 Group Headquarters. His tour of operations was over. He had earned his rest. Apart from one week's leave, he had been flying for virtually the entire summer, and he was one of the few airmen to survive.

In 1943 Edrich was one of eight RAF officers sent on a course, lasting sixteen weeks, to the Army Staff College at Camberley, having been pronounced unfit for flying duties. He was subsequently employed on RAF Group operations at Wallingford in Berkshire. His round-the-clock duties were to help in the preparations for D-Day and the invasion of Europe.

As the plans took shape and the invasion went ahead on 6 June 1944, Edrich was able to relax once again at cricket. One of these interludes, during the time of the German flying bombs, carried dangers at odds with this peaceful activity. He was thrust again into the firing line in a match between the RAF and the Army at Lord's. The players had heard several bursts in London while the match was in progress. One or two of the sinister bombs had seemed to pass over their heads. Then they heard the sound of an engine, very loud, that stopped abruptly overhead. The missile was invisible in the low clouds above Lord's.

Edrich related: 'Bob Wyatt was about to begin his bowling run to the batsman, Jack Robertson, and both seemed to hesitate a little as the engine stopped. Then out of the clouds just above us, travelling downwards at terrific speed, we saw the bomb in its shallow dive.

We all flung ourselves down to the ground instantly.' The flying bomb missed the playing area, but the explosion shattered the windows of the pavilion. It knocked down adjacent houses in St John's Wood and caused casualties within two to three hundred yards north of the ground. Amid the ringing of ambulance bells, Wyatt scrambled to his feet. He found the ball still firmly grasped in his fingers and continued his run to the wicket. Robertson, equally undeterred, took strike again. He raised his bat and struck the ball for six. 'If Hitler had seen them,' said Edrich, 'I think it would have broken his heart.'

Brian Edrich has reflected on the endurance of the bold Blenheim boys as they sought to arrest the German offensive in the cruel summer days of 1941. 'It was a tough and ugly war for Bill, as it was for so many other brave men.' Brian and his sister, Ena, remembered how their brother struggled to regain his spirits at the end of his Blenheim tour. 'Bill came over to see us all at our Buckinghamshire home,' said Ena. 'He had been on a lot of raids. He looked extraordinarily tired.' It was completely out of character for the extrovert Bill to refuse any invitation. He would normally have accepted with alacrity a summons to go on an outing. Ena had suggested an afternoon's swimming at nearby Stowe. 'Bill just wanted to relax in the garden. He was totally depleted and had no energy left.'

More than fifty years on, the memories of a valiant summer have not faded for Edrich's friend and comrade, Ernie Hope. Hope, living in retirement in Australia, presented his testimony in one of the finest tributes that can be paid to any man. 'I shall always feel that I can thank Bill for the fact that I am still alive.'

CHAPTER 6

Engulfed by a Typhoon

'Bill was a fine batsman in a golden age, and of all the players I have seen and played against none showed greater courage.' – *Sir Donald Bradman*

The spreading bloodstain on the wicket at Lord's conveyed an atmosphere of horror. It was caused by a ball of unforeseen velocity whose recipient later remarked: 'Frank was just a little quicker than I thought he was'. The thrust which overthrew but did not vanquish a brave cricketer was delivered by a bowler who was shortly to wreck the defences of his Australian rivals with the ferocity of a typhoon.

The protagonists at Lord's on the July evening in 1954 were Bill Edrich, at thirty-eight the veteran master of bumper duels, and the Northamptonshire fast bowler, Frank Tyson, fourteen years his junior and glowing with menace and power. It was a heavensent opportunity for Tyson, then in his first full season in county cricket, to impress the watching selectors. Tyson's growing reputation had preceded him before this first outing at Lord's. It would not be true to say that white flags draped the Middlesex balcony; but there was no mistaking the blinking unease of the batsmen waiting to face the searing pace of the young Lancastrian.

One heart did not flutter among the apprehensive assembly. Edrich had triumphed in the heat of the battle against Australia's Lindwall and Miller. 'He had a small man's aggression, never terrorised by bouncers, only inspired by them,' wrote one observer. Neville Cardus enthused: 'He does not understand the meaning of compromise with overpowering odds. He seems able by willpower to laugh, or to ignore ordinary mortal wounds.' Edrich, said Tyson, was the man who displayed to him, at Lord's, the indomitability of the human spirit.

Northamptonshire had batted first on the rain-affected first day and were all out for 409, just before the close of the second day. Tyson recalled: 'The Lord's pitch was lively in those days, with the ball lifting off the ridge and moving up and down the hill.' The situation of the Middlesex openers, Jack Robertson and Harry Sharp, was also imperilled by the dwindling light. The first casualty was the wicket-keeper, Keith Andrew, who was to gain selection, along with Tyson, for the tour of Australia in the following winter. 'Keith insisted on standing up to the left-handed medium-pace of Bob Clarke,' said Tyson. 'For his pains he was struck under the chin by a lifting ball, which gashed him and sprinkled the crease area with blood which we soaked up with sawdust – but not before he had caught Robertson behind off Clarke.'

Four balls now remained to be bowled in the last over of the day. Edrich strode jauntily to the wicket. His demeanour reflected his purpose to quell the newcomer. As he took guard, he noted the retreating wicket-keeper and slips, all well beyond conversational distance. Tyson, vigorously rubbing the ball, was a barely discernible silhouette at the start of his long, pounding run. 'I had heard of Bill's reputation as a hooker,' related Tyson, 'and I decided to test him out with a bouncer. He accepted the challenge willingly but had only moved minimally across the pitch to the offside, when my very fast bumper caught him square on the cheek, and broke it. He went down in a welter of blood and was carted off to hospital.'

There was now the gruesome spectacle of a cricket pitch with blood-streaked patches of sawdust at both ends. Denis Compton should have been next man in. He had not anticipated having to bat that evening and was in the bath when Edrich was struck down. Peter Delisle, the nineteen-year-old West Indian and Oxford undergraduate, had the unenviable task of filling the breach. 'I swear he was green when he came to the wicket,' said Tyson. From the comfort of the bar, Compton, by now changed and intensely interested, looked down on the new bowling discovery. 'This bloke will be fast in Australia next winter,' he said.

To general astonishment, Edrich reappeared on the following morning, determined to resume his innings. Frank Lee, one of the umpires, was among those disconcerted by Edrich's intention. Bill, his pipe jutting out from his swollen mouth, had exchanged a few cursory words with Lee on the state of the wicket before the start of play. He was heedless of his own condition. Denis Compton, as acting captain, firmly insisted that Edrich would not be allowed to bat. It was the height of folly. Bill could be stubborn and infuriating in taking an opposite view. He told his despairing team-mates that he was unshaken in his resolve. They watched helplessly as he changed and started to buckle on his pads.

David Montague, the Middlesex physiotherapist, made one last plea: 'You can't go out to bat with a fractured cheekbone,' he said. Edrich, with a wild grimace, replied: 'David, if I could fly bombers over Germany in the war, I can go out and bat against Frank Tyson.'

Tyson remembered the sight of Edrich, shoulders

held high, coming out to the crease at the fall of the second wicket. 'He looked like a war casualty. His jaw was in a sling tied at the top of his head, his face was more black and blue than pink, and his eyes were almost closed by the massive facial bruising.' Edrich's re-emergence presented Tyson with a dilemma. 'First-class cricket is no place for sentiment and I wanted to give him another bouncer. I looked across towards Denis Brookes, my skipper, at mid-off. He nodded and Bill got a bouncer first ball, which did not please the Middlesex supporters. But, believe it or not, Bill tried to hook it. You simply could not intimidate him. He went on to get 20 before being caught in the slips.' *Wisden* laconically commented: 'After being hit in the face while batting, Edrich spent the night in hospital, but he resumed batting on the last day and showed customary steadfastness.'

The beleaguered Edrich had made his point; it was a mark of pride that he should grasp the nettle in adversity. An injury of such proportions entitled him to extended sick leave from cricket. He continued playing as if nothing had happened. Less than a week later he was in opposition again to Tyson at Northampton. The assault on his dignity was not forgotten. Bill hit an avenging century to settle the score in his favour. Brian Edrich recalled his own disbelief and concern when his brother visited Canterbury in early August. 'I didn't recognise Bill when he played against us. The side of his face, where Tyson had cracked his cheek-bone, had collapsed. But it didn't stop him playing.'

The eagerness and vitality of Edrich's batting gained the respect of all his rivals, none more so than Ray Lindwall and Keith Miller, in four post-war series against Australia. Alfred Gover, another fast bowler of high repute, has dwelt upon the frustrations of bowling to players showing a penchant for the hook shot. 'Anyone who can hook fast bowlers is a good batsman. It puts him in the ascendancy and you on the defensive.'

Lindwall remembered one Test occasion at Lord's in 1948 when he squandered a chance of laying a snare for Edrich. He disobeyed, to his chagrin, the instruction of his captain, Don Bradman. 'Bradman wanted me to put a fellow in front at square-leg. Bill hit a sitter to where I should have placed the bloke.' In his next over a rueful Lindwall asked for the field to be rearranged as had been suggested. Bradman said: 'It's too late now – he won't play that shot again.'

Trevor Bailey has reflected on the bravery of Edrich against Lindwall and Miller and their ally, the left-hander, Bill Johnston. He maintained that watching Bill hook Lindwall was one of the most exhilarating sights he had witnessed on the cricket field. Bailey also believed that Edrich, as a Lilliputian among the Gullivers, would not have been dismayed by the steepling bounce of the modern West Indian giants. 'His technique was good enough to have coped with them.' Edrich himself did not consider that his contests with Lindwall and Miller would have paled by comparison with latter-day duels with Ambrose or Garner. 'Keith and Ray certainly didn't bowl as many bouncers but the surprise element, when they came, made them just as dangerous.' Remorseless fast bowling did, he considered, transform a beautiful game into a bore. 'We played our cricket for the sheer enjoyment of it. We didn't set out to maim one another.'

Denis Compton has expressed his regret at the decline in back-foot play, which was a key characteristic and counter of all really good players against quick bowling in his time. 'Against exceptional pace Bill and I were on the back foot before the ball was bowled.' Keith Miller once passed on the complaint: 'The one thing I didn't like about you blokes was that I couldn't see the stumps.' Denis added: 'Keith always liked to see all three.'

Edrich, like Herbert Sutcliffe in an earlier generation, almost seemed to welcome his bruises as the regalia of gallantry. On one occasion, batting with him, Bailey watched as Lindwall toppled him with a bouncer. 'Bill was always a gutsy player. I made the mistake of going down the wicket to ask if he was all right.' He was firmly rebuked for his solicitude. 'Of course I'm all right,' was Edrich's abrupt response. 'Bill jumped to his feet and carried on batting.'

Edrich, in his retirement, was not unsympathetic towards those of his juniors reduced to nervous wrecks. He had experienced the palpitations of fear in more severe circumstances. He conceded that the terrors of war gave his generation a yardstick by which to judge the comparative hazards of facing dangerous fast bowling. In addition, his mental reserves would have withstood any psychological pressures. He would have quickly stifled the intimidatory tactics of the bruisers of modern cricket. Any verbal exchanges would have been sharp and to the point. An even more likely reaction would have been an amused disdain. The encounter would have been resolved by a barrage of blazing hooks. John Dewes, who played under Edrich's captaincy in the 1950s, has underlined the combative strain of a born fighter. 'Bill was magnificent in defence. He was always rock solid behind the ball and glaring at the bowler. You wouldn't want to meet him on a dark night, if he didn't like your looks.'

Jim Swanton, interestingly, judged Edrich superior to his great mentor, Wally Hammond, against fast bowling. It was a view endorsed by Les Ames, who considered that this frailty was revealed in the waning command of Hammond against hostile pace in later years. In a post-war appreciation of Edrich, Swanton wrote: 'Bill is a fine swinger of the bat. The remarkable leverage which he engenders from those broad shoulders of his makes his on-drive one of the most powerful strokes in cricket. Perhaps, now that Hammond's batsmanship is but a memory, only the off and straight drives of Keith Miller are quite so fierce.'

Jack Robertson, a close friend and associate from their early days at Lord's, remembered how Edrich 'wielded his bat like a broadsword, cutting, pulling and driving, with a nice late cut and leg glance'. One of Bill's favourite shots was the pulled drive, inimitably his own, and conceived as a vivid and violent riposte. Batting from the Nursery End, he would strike the ball high to Q Stand beside the pavilion. The strength and certainty of the stroke, said one sorely tried off-spinner, was a constant irritant. 'It was actually quite dangerous to sit in that stand,' added Robertson. 'Bill really did pepper that area.'

The expert testimonies of Denis Compton and others have refuted suggestions of fallibility against leg-spin and the ball leaving the bat. It is an allegation which seems less than exact when considering Edrich's weight of runs and the opposition in the immediate post-war years. England could then call upon a formidable contingent of leg-spinners, who included Hollies, Wright, Brown, Jenkins and Peter Smith.

The charge against Edrich may have been largely fostered by his experiences against Bill O'Reilly in his first Test series in 1938. O'Reilly amusingly recalled his supremacy in a message of goodwill on Edrich's seventieth birthday. 'Passing through Sydney and carrying his lamp, Aladdin promised me a return to the days of my active cricket life if I were to touch his light and wish for it,' wrote O'Reilly. 'I asked him for time to think seriously about it and then agreed on the express condition that my mate, Bill Edrich, was given the same privilege.' O'Reilly explained that his reasons – six winning appeals – were so demanding that he would be happy to weave his own spell once again. Edrich, for his part, never failed to acknowledge those moments of torment. 'Hey, Tiger, here is your rabbit,' was his greeting in the following years. O'Reilly concluded: 'It was Bill who said it. I would never have dared.'

Compton regards Edrich as a superb player of off-spin bowling. 'Bill would drive the ball, with no element of indiscretion, wide of mid-on and over the top. He would guide it to elude the field.' Trevor Bailey has referred to this lofted shot as a cross between the on-drive and a 'cow shot', which brought Edrich a vast number of sixes on the largest of grounds.

Alf Gover, with memories of Edrich's tussles against Lock and Laker, has also referred to his application on the uncovered and rain-affected wickets at The Oval. Brilliant footwork enabled him to counter the lifting ball. As late as 1956, Edrich hit an innings of 82 against Surrey's vaunted spin twins. 'It was an innings of technical skill and concentration on a turning wicket,' commented *Wisden*. Gover, along with other rivals, regarded Edrich's record on bad wickets as second to none. 'Bill could play either turn and used his feet quickly to play the ball down.' Stuart Surridge, the Surrey captain in their great years in the 1950s, was another admirer of a resolute opponent. 'He's a so-and-so nuisance to us,' was a compliment to treasure.

Alan Moss, one of the younger Middlesex brigade in Edrich's time, shares with another contemporary, Doug Insole, the view that their senior would have adapted easily to the one-day game. They present Edrich as an obvious fast scorer in reasonably propitious conditions. 'Bill could score quickly without apparent effort,' said Moss. 'Off-spinners were bread and butter to him. You were always in with a chance against him. But you were never going to bury him in his crease.' George Mann, the Middlesex captain in the late 1940s, also recalls the aggression of Edrich. 'He was a solid oak of a batsman, a fine player off the back foot, not only defensively, but in hitting any ball short of length, even if it was turning. He was ever ready, if need be, to take a couple of paces down the wicket to cover the spin.'

The effervescence of Edrich's batsmanship was illustrated in one of his finest hours against Yorkshire at Leeds in 1947. Essentially, his general approach was to stress enjoyment in cricket. Winning was of less importance than communicating your love of the game to the crowd. If it wasn't fun for you, the spectators would also be gloomy, and the game would be a waste of time on both counts. This was an example of his transparently honest nature touched with an engaging naïveté in his years as Middlesex captain. He governed a happy dressing-room before the age of sponsors and the urgent need of success to serve commercial interests. A grimmer side did surface when the battle was joined with Surrey or Yorkshire. The cavalier man of Lord's was transformed into a grittily purposeful cricketer. Denis Compton said his partner possessed many attributes in common with the doggedness of the North-country cricketer.

The evidence was provided in Bill Bowes' benefit match at Headingley. On the first day Middlesex lost four wickets for 17 runs inside thirty minutes. Edrich rescued his side with a defiant 70, occupying two and a half hours, on a spinners' wicket. In the morning, as J. M. Kilburn related, 'Yorkshire were inspired to a level of magnificence that was once a day-to-day characteristic. Fortunately, for Middlesex, there was comparable inspiration in Edrich. The hundreds he has made on Test match wickets were great feats of endurance and persistent technique, but this was an occasion calling on all the arts of batsmanship, swift feet, an alert mind and a brave heart.'

Middlesex, on a topsy-turvy day, scored only 124 but still gained a first innings lead of 39 runs. Yardley, with 41, attempted to stem the tide in unenviable conditions for batting. Edrich was fresh enough to open the bowling in each of the Yorkshire innings. He capitalised on his runs by quickly sweeping through the defences of Hutton and Watson in the first innings. He made another early breakthrough when he dismissed Watson in the second innings. Yorkshire seemed to have reasserted their authority and obtained a match-winning position in another reversal on the following morning. Middlesex were in disarray at 88 for six. Robertson, Brown, Denis Compton and Robins, the latter two in the space of three balls, all fell to the spin of Wardle by the end of the first half-hour.

'Within the next hour Middlesex had regained their dominance by as fine a display of batting as one of the best of our contemporary batsmen can ever have shown,' reported Kilburn. Before the onslaught Wardle and his partner, Ellis Robinson, appeared in the possession and encouragement of a wicket of spinners' dreams. 'Edrich took complete charge of the situation, not only hitting boundaries more or less at his own pleasure, but so contriving his singles that he had almost all the bowling to himself,' continued Kilburn.

Edrich's superb innings was a reflection of a batsman dictating his destiny – and that of his team – in mounting a stunning orgy of power play. Yorkshire, at length, acknowledged his conquest and could not bowl a length to him. They had held back, rightly in view of the expected rout by spin, in claiming the new ball. It could no longer be rejected; but it only had the effect of increasing the momentum of Edrich's bombardment. In Smailes' first over, Edrich hit 22 runs – four fours and one spiralling straight six which hurtled over a distance of around 110 yards into the members' rugby stand enclosure. Each of his hits flew off the bat like a rocket. As the ball was tossed back at the end of the over, Brian Sellers, the Yorkshire captain, stared uncomprehendingly at the bowler. 'Hey, Frank,' he called out, 'what have you done with that nice new ball I gave you five minutes ago?'

'There were no more worlds for Edrich to conquer and the completion of his century just before lunch was a rightful assumption of the laurel wreath,' concluded Kilburn. Edrich's bounty of 70 and 102 were the only scores above 50 in the match. He had once again defied the odds and prospered while others, less adventurous, had faltered and failed. Yorkshire, briefly cheered if only consoled by a late flurry of runs by Wardle and Robinson, were beaten by 87 runs.

Neville Cardus presented a typically vivid description of Edrich as the furious bowler of high temper. 'He bowled as boys and men bowl on the village green. He slung or hurled the ball at the wicket as fast as he could make it go, at the risk of breaking his back. The energy of his action carried him sprawling halfway down the pitch, as though drawn in the draught of his own velocity. I expected to see dust and newspapers eddying in the air whenever he bowled fast – like the tremendous atmospheric disturbance which happens on a railway station platform as an express train thunders through.'

While unstinting in his praise of Edrich as a courageous and resourceful batsman, Alec Bedser considered that his former partner's bowling was of negligible quality. 'Bill did put everything into each delivery and tried to bowl as fast as he could,' said Bedser. 'But he was not fast in a true sense and not really a bowler of class. He could be termed a slinger.' Bedser calculated that he had as many as seventeen new-ball partners during the threadbare years before the arrival of Bailey, Statham, Tyson and Trueman. It is, however, instructive to recall that Edrich held his England place in South Africa before the war largely because Hammond approved of his all-round potential. Edrich opened the batting and bowling in the first Test at Johannesburg and shared the opening attack with Ken Farnes in three matches in that series. Even as late as 1946, when Edrich was a late choice for the tour of Australia, the selectors were undoubtedly swayed in their decision by his haul of four wickets for 68 runs against India at The Oval. Godfrey Evans, who made his debut for England in that match, maintained that Edrich was the fastest bowler in the country at the time. Edrich could hasten the best batsmen into error. His tally of 479 wickets (41 in Tests) included the prized ones of Bradman, Morris and Hassett. Alan Melville, the South African captain, was his victim on four occasions in 1947.

Jack Robertson remembered Edrich 'exploding at the wicket with a flurry of arms and a slinging action. His follow-through was such that I expected him to reach the other end before the ball. Bill would give his all for half-a-dozen overs.'

Brian Edrich also believed that his brother was genuinely fast in the years preceding the war and up to 1947 when a shoulder injury in late summer caused Bill to curtail his bowling. (In succeeding years Edrich reverted to off-spinners, suffering, as one wag said, a strange delusion that he could bowl them.) 'He was a slinger with a quick right arm,' said Brian Edrich. 'The

101

ball would skid through faster than you expected and keep a little low. Bill did not waste his energy on a long run. He would pound up to the wicket from around 12 yards. The impetus of the delivery was gained from his body action. He also developed the off-cutter which came back off the seam at you.' Godfrey Evans remembered Edrich in bowling action – 'the left leg raised high in the air and the right arm stretched back to its fullest extent at the point of delivery'.

George Mann has paid tribute to the energy and stamina of a loyal team-mate. 'We depended on Bill and he allowed us to depend on him, despite the fact that he was a principal batsman. He was so keen; he would make runs and then bowl his heart out for a few overs.' Mann recalled that, after the war, Middlesex were sorely handicapped by limited fast bowling. Laurie Gray, the main bowling spearhead, was beginning to be troubled by arthritis. A succession of recruits were called up to support him, and it was not uncommon for the wicket-keeper, Leslie Compton, to take the new ball, with Sid Brown going behind the stumps. Edrich, having watched this experiment, offered his services. 'Let me have a rip at them first, skipper,' he said. Mann said Bill would fulfil a quota of six or seven overs and often make a crucial breakthrough. What impressed the Middlesex captain was Edrich's 'willingness to have a go. He was capable of getting the best batsmen out.'

There was, in addition, the bonus of Edrich's alertness as a slip fieldsman in his prime years. He was as prehensile as a pickpocket in this position. His record of 529 catches, taken with unusually small hands, was the product of superb anticipation and lightning reflexes. 'Some of his catches, executed with a dive like a teal's coming downwind, were phenomenal,' said one observer. The intelligence of Edrich's fielding was shown in a match between Middlesex and Yorkshire at

Lord's. He had watched Barber awkwardly and carelessly playing Smith off his body. His response was to sidle up, unnoticed, until he was only five yards from the bat at short-leg. Smith bowled again, the batsman pushed the ball away, but Edrich flung himself straight forward, and took the ball with the fingertips of his outstretched hands.

Ray Lindwall, perhaps, captured the essence of Edrich as the batsman/bowler, who characteristically was prepared to trade bouncers even with him. 'Bill was quick when I played against him in 1946 and 1948.' In 1948, at Manchester, Edrich had the temerity to bowl an over of bumpers at Lindwall. One of them struck the Australian a fierce blow on the arm. His quietly rhetorical reply promised a royal battle when England batted again. 'Don't you think I've got another bowl in this match?' he asked. Edrich had said that Lindwall and his partner Keith Miller attacked him, as a batsman, with impunity. Miller, as a keen racegoer, affected a roguish puzzlement at the expression. He wondered if Bill was referring to the horse he had wrongly backed in the 3.30 at Pontefract. Edrich considered, despite the raillery, that he was entitled to measure his expresses against those of his Australian rivals. Bradman would not allow Lindwall to retaliate against Edrich in England's second innings. Lindwall was understandably exasperated by the instruction, which deprived them of an enjoyable contest. 'Bill had plenty of guts. He wouldn't have minded at all getting six out of six from me.'

Sir Pelham Warner, in his Foreword to W. N. Roe's book on *Public Schools' Cricket 1901–1950*, named Edrich as a member of one of his selected teams. They included six England captains – Wyatt, Allen, Hammond, Jardine, Chapman, J. W. H. T. Douglas – and other Test players, Duleepsinhji, Fender, G. T. S.

Stevens, John Clay, Reg Simpson, J. C. White and Farnes. Warner's accolade is endorsed by another of his candidates, Trevor Bailey. Bailey has rated Edrich as a great player who would have been an automatic choice for a world eleven at his peak: 'Bill for five years – it could have been longer but for the war – was the complete master, with a magnificent defence. Few in my experience have watched the ball so closely. The harder you hit him, either with bat or ball, the greater became his determination.' As a comparison, Bailey ranked Edrich alongside Ken Barrington and Tom Graveney and below the exceptionally gifted play- ers such as Denis Compton, Leonard Hutton and Gary Sobers. His assessment excluded the immortals – Bradman, Hammond and Hobbs.

The intervention of the war precludes a definitive verdict on Edrich's talents; but Bailey believed that England, during the brief pre-war interlude, produced the best four professional batsmen of all time in Edrich, Compton, Hutton and Hardstaff. 'Bill was very quick on his feet; one of the best on-drivers – for a little man he hit the ball very hard – and a fine hooker and cutter. As he grew older, the flamboyancy departed and he lost the "eye" shots; he then anchored and built his innings on correct, responsible defence.'

Edrich's recuperative powers, so well demonstrated as a RAF bomber pilot, were a tribute to an amaz- ing constitution. As Robin Marlar put it, he could teach a rising generation something in this regard. Edrich did not consider early nights a necessary prerequisite for cricket. 'Find out your own capabil- ities and limitations and within these enjoy yourself to the full,' was his advice to young cricketers. Peter Parfitt, as one of the recruits under his command, said there was no insistence on a curfew. 'If you wanted to stay up, he would stay up with you.

But woe betide you if you faltered on the field next day.'

Alfred Gover recalled a conversation with Edrich during a wartime game at Lord's. 'I had been on an army night exercise and did not get back until four in the morning. I was a little tired.' He confided to Bill that he was feeling 'knackered'. Edrich replied: 'I was night-flying. I was not only knackered, I was also a bit scared as well.'

Brian Edrich tellingly recalled an instance of how his brother was able to combine the roles of reveller and cricketer. A reunion with a former RAF Bomber Command friend, Alec McKenzie, then an hotelier in Canterbury, preceded a century against Kent. Brian, along with his county colleague, Arthur Phebey, was having a quiet drink in the bar. 'Bill arrived with Jack Young and a mighty party ensued.' Brian and Phebey, then young Kent players, discreetly retired to bed around midnight. In the morning Brian learned that the carousel had lasted until three o'clock. Their host looked distinctly haggard. Brian's immediate reaction was that Bill would also be afflicted by a raging hangover. On arrival at the St Lawrence Ground – around 10.30 – he was astonished to find Bill in the nets. Laurie Gray and Alan Moss, the Middlesex fast bowlers, were moving in vigorously to bowl at him. 'Half an hour later Bill came in, bathed in sweat,' said Brian. 'He knew he had had a heavy night and had to work off the ale. I reckon he deserved his hundred that day.'

Alan Moss related a similar story concerning Keith Miller. During the match between Middlesex and the touring Australians at Lord's in 1953, Edrich and Miller had dallied until the early hours out on the town. On the following morning Miller had almost literally to be helped in to his pads. Bill was gently guided out to his customary position at first slip. He called out to

Moss: 'Pitch it up; he hasn't been to bed.' Miller tossed back his hair in a familiar gesture; and glared through blood-shot eyes at the Middlesex bowler. 'You think I'm pissed, Mossie; I could play you with the bat handle.' Keith stumbled into position and smartly glided the first ball to the mid-wicket boundary. He might have played this delivery from memory; but his brains rapidly sharpened as he went on to score a brisk 71. Edrich, watching the reeling bowlers, rocked with laughter at slip. As a postscript, Moss observed: 'There is no-one today with the character or ability to enjoy a party, as Bill and Keith did, and then go out next day and play cricket just as heartily.'

The brazen fortitude of Bill Edrich had more than a passing acquaintance with Jacques Tati's Monsieur Hulot. Like the lugubrious Hulot, he seemed to attract physical mishaps, if not in the dumb show of this visually inventive humorist of the cinema screen.

Cricket raconteurs, including Jack Fingleton and Doug Insole, remembered the merrymaking of Edrich, notably before and during the Centenary Test at Melbourne in 1977. Fingleton, the former Australian Test cricketer and noted writer, recalled the flight out to Australia and said, as quoted in David Foot's *Beyond Bat and Ball*: 'I won't forget that Qantas trip. Dear old Bill, in his haste to make fun with good cheer, over-imbibed and fell over the recumbent John Arlott who dotted him one'.

Insole, who was then chairman of the Test and County Cricket Board, was in charge of a distinguished contingent of cricketers visiting Australia, including Arlott. The champagne flowed freely during the flight out. Arlott was deep in reverie, listening to music on his earphones. Edrich was in mischievous mood, after liberally sampling the hospitality. He had twice staggered down the aircraft aisle and attempted to engage Arlott in conversation. In his second bid he raised the volume on the cassette. Arlott, startled by the unexpected crescendo, involuntarily lashed out and hit Edrich straight in the eye. 'Bill, within the space of twelve hours, sported the most tremendous shiner,' said Insole. 'It really was beautiful – all the colours of the rainbow – and by the time we landed in Australia it was an absolute belter.'

The jollifications continued unabated at a Melbourne hotel on the eve of the Centenary Test. Bill, according to his brother, Brian, had never been so alarmed on a cricket field, as he became during a heated debate after the official dinner. Under discussion were the merits of different fast bowlers through the ages. Bill, as the senior member of the company, which included his former England colleague, Fred Trueman, was asked to nominate his favoured rivals. Frank Tyson and Ray Lindwall headed his list, and Bob Crisp, the South African, came third. But he unaccountably neglected to include Fred among the contenders. Bill no doubt simply intended to tease the Yorkshireman. Trueman was, though, rightly aggrieved and glowered with anger at his omission. It required many soothing words to reduce the tension from others in the room and avert the threat of fisticuffs.

Edrich's zest was not in the least diluted by his frolics on the Australian fiesta. 'We were rolling into Heathrow on our return journey,' said Doug Insole. He was alerted by a tap on the shoulder. It was Bill presenting his compliments. 'I just thought I'd like to tell you. This has been the best ten days of my life,' he said.

CHAPTER 7

Body Blows at Brisbane

'Edrich played an innings of quite tormented obstinacy. We could see him almost torn from the crease, but by the ligaments of his own tenacity he was held there.' – *Neville Cardus*

The frenzy of the elements at Wooloongabba produced an indigestible pudding wicket which could only have been mixed by a malevolent chef. Each time the ball pitched it built up a ledge of mud which confounded the laws of batsmanship. Bill Edrich displayed the fearlessness of an extraordinary gladiator in defying the curse of a terrible wicket. The innings at Brisbane confirmed his credentials as a Test cricketer on his first tour of Australia in 1946–47.

Edrich, imperilled by wavering selectors, was close to missing the tour. He was not included in the first list of twelve names published in July; and his selection, along with the other choices of Laurie Fishlock and James Langridge, was not confirmed until three weeks before the MCC tourists set sail on the RMS *Stirling Castle* at the end of August. The validity of Edrich's selection was to be amply justified in the months ahead. While Hutton and Compton strove to discover their true form, he stood firm as the mainstay of England batting.

A grave injustice to a great cricketer would have

been perpetrated if he had been omitted from the party, for this first tour was the watershed in his fortunes. It was his chance to disperse the lingering accusations of lack of temperament. A cabal of critics still harassed him. It is astonishing to note that few voices were raised in his defence. 'Of course,' said one dissenter, 'there is an awful danger that they might put Edrich in again.' The prejudice ran deep, dismissive of his form in the Victory Tests against the Australian Services in the previous season, when he had headed the England batting averages.

In 1946, Edrich redeemed a bad start with a flurry of runs – 937 in six weeks from mid-July onwards. He made one score of over 200 and hit five centuries in all. One innings surpassed all his other achievements this summer: against Gloucestershire at Lord's he was unbeaten on 127 out of 166 runs scored from the bat. In two hours and twenty minutes, 158 runs were scored while he was at the crease. Only one partner, Price, reached double figures. The rest of the side totalled 16. Edrich did not bat in his only Test against India at The Oval, but there was the salvation of valuable wickets. 'In a sense this was the real turning-point, for his bowling success sealed his selection for Australia,' commented *The Cricketer*.

The violence of the storms, which twice water-logged the Wooloongabba ground within twenty-four hours in December 1946, was unparalleled in Brisbane's history. They were regarded as positively immoral after Australia had scored freely and monumentally to reach 645 – their highest total at home – before the deluge. The course of the match was put irretrievably beyond England's grasp by the denial of Bradman's wicket. The great Australian, struggling to regain his pre-war powers, survived a much debated and controversial decision while his innings was still in its infancy. He

109

had scored only 28 when a catch, taken shoulder-high by Ikin in the slips off an attempted yorker by Voce, was disallowed as a bump ball. Bill O'Reilly dryly said that to get such a ball to reach this height at a speed sufficient to spin Ikin side-on, as he effected the catch, needed an uncanny propulsion seldom seen in cricket.

Norman Yardley, fielding at gully at the time of the vital incident, commented: 'Bradman attempted one of his favourite strokes, a drive just wide of cover-point. The ball flew from the top edge of his bat and straight towards second slip where Jack Ikin caught it beautifully.' Bradman himself said the point at issue was whether the ball had finished its downward course before making contact with the bat. In his opinion, the ball had touched the bottom of his bat just before hitting the ground and therefore was not a catch. It was, whatever the rights or wrongs, and the views were divided on the decision, a psychological reverse of severe dimensions for England. Bradman went on to score 187 before being bowled by Edrich. He shared a third-wicket record stand of 276 with Hassett. The plunder was reinforced by the Test debutants, Keith Miller and Colin McCool, who capitalised on the advantage with further century partnerships.

The ensuing treachery of the wicket duplicated the conditions in which England had overwhelmed the hapless Australians ten years earlier. Neville Cardus said a description of its terrors would have taxed the language of the Old Testament and Joseph Conrad. 'The atmosphere was greedy for the Englishmen's ruin; the fieldsmen stood on tiptoe, and in the feverish vision of the batsmen they would surely have appeared each to have many hungry arms to stretch, seize and throw up into the air without pity.'

The irony of the predicament was that Australia

might have been the distraught victims but for a catalogue of fielding errors. Hassett was dropped three times. McCool, who went on to hit 95, was missed behind the wicket off Bedser, with his score on one. Jim Swanton considered that if England had held even half their chances the Australian score would not have been unsurpassable. He dwelt upon the significance of Bradman's reprieve before the storms rendered the pitch utterly unplayable. 'Had he gone for 28, making Australia 74 for three, it could have been they in their second innings who were caught on a rain-ruined wicket. As it was England were snared, one by one, the only extraordinary thing being the time needed for their dispatch.'

Godfrey Evans, England's twelfth man at Brisbane, agreed with this verdict. Paul Gibb, the first-choice wicket-keeper and soon to be replaced by Evans, failed to recapture his pre-war form. Gibb was a major culprit, dropping three catches behind the stumps. 'Australia scored over 600 instead of 350,' said Evans. 'Had they been dismissed earlier, we would have batted on a good wicket and caught them on a bad one.' Evans believed that England's total of 141 on a vile pitch would have far exceeded Australia's resources. 'If they had batted on that wicket, they wouldn't have got 30.'

Ray Robinson, the Australian writer, also commiserated with England in an article in The Cricketer. 'As if the disparity in bowling, age and range of batting did not weigh the scales enough, the luck of the toss and two thunderstorms denied the Englishmen a chance in the first Test. Even more exasperating was the luck of the umpiring. Usually, debatable decisions work out fairly evenly over a Test rubber, but the weight of evidence suggests that the umpires were mistaken in giving Bradman not out in the first Test, Edrich lbw in the third Test, and Washbrook caught behind the wicket in the fourth Test.'

Robinson considered that the dismissals came at such crucial points in England's bid to gain an advantage that they could almost be called the turning-points of all three games. The umpiring also came under the searching microscope of English correspondent, E. M. (Lyn) Wellings. He maintained that it was a curious fact that the worst umpiring against England in Australia occurred during a series in which they had no chance of winning. Norman Preston, in *Wisden*, delivered the view that the reason why England did not fare as badly as their predecessors, who lost all five timeless matches in the 1920–21 series, was because the games were limited to six days each of five hours' duration.

A divide in experience at first indicated an open series in 1946–47. England had selected seven players – Hammond, Hutton, Edrich, Compton, Hardstaff, Voce and Wright – who had played against Australia before the war. Australia, by contrast, had only three survivors, Bradman, Hassett and Barnes. The hastily arranged tour did not, however, allow the English selectors time to take stock of the situation. The intervention of the war had blunted the abilities of the old guard and disturbed the advancement of those approaching their prime time. The key factor was the veteran status of the MCC tourists. Only four of the party were under thirty and others, including Hammond, had left their best years behind them.

In the event, it was a triumph for Australia's emerging Test recruits, buoyant and strong in their youth. As a demonstration of their all-round strengths, three of their leading bowlers, Miller, Lindwall and McCool, scored centuries. England did find consolation in the blossoming talents of their newcomers, Godfrey Evans, Alec Bedser and Cyril Washbrook, who had made his debut for England against New Zealand at The Oval in 1937. After the initial reverses at Brisbane and Sydney, they achieved commendable draws at Melbourne and Adelaide. Denis Compton, in a welcome purple patch, led the recovery with two centuries at Adelaide. In the final Test at Sydney, where Australia won by five wickets, Hutton was stricken by tonsillitis after scoring a century and did not bat in the second innings.

The pattern of the series was shaped by the calamities of the first Test. The thunderstorm on the Monday night at Brisbane first signalled the looming spectre of a bowler's pitch. It was followed, with unjust perversity, by another of greater ferocity on the following afternoon. The winds reached a velocity of 79 mph; in half an hour '250 points of rain fell', according to the *Sydney Morning Herald*; transport services were disrupted and power lines were torn down; city buildings and roads were flooded; and a barrage of hailstones left a trail of wreckage. Surfers at a nearby seaside resort, wounded by the jagged pieces of ice, had to be treated for head injuries.

The *Sydney Morning Herald* reported on the amazing scenes as the hurricane rushed through the exposed stands at the Wooloongabba ground. 'Many cricket enthusiasts had left the ground at the first warning of the storm, but thousands were huddled in the stands and under improvised shelters. A terrific thunderstorm was accompanied by vivid lightning; hailstones the size of cricket balls hammered on the iron roofs, portions of which were ripped off and hurled skywards.' Bradman also recalled the intensity of a stupendous downpour: 'In half an hour one could have sailed a boat across the oval. Water was halfway up the boundary fence. The stumps, which had been left in the middle, floated away. One sightscreen had been blown over the fence by the cyclonic wind, and the hailstones on the roof

113

sounded like machine-gun fire. We were marooned in our dressing room.'

England, before the intervention of the afternoon storm, had fought heroically to reach 117 for five wickets. In the morning, old internationals, who had witnessed the phenomenon of play starting at noon after the overnight rain, voiced their amazement. Before long they had more cause for wonder at the resolution of the England batsmen. On this turf of malice, as Cardus related, 'the full range of the anatomy was brought into play; strokes were at the last moment checked in carrying power; wrists were dropped or thrown up at the final perilous flash of a second when the ball was in the danger zone'.

Miller's first ball of the morning swept off Washbrook's cap and grazed his forehead. In the same over Edrich was thrice struck on the body. He looked, as Neville Cardus put it, 'like a boy straddled on a very slippery slide'. Edrich was impervious to the blows which assaulted him as he resisted the Australian attack for one and three-quarter hours. In *Wisden* Norman Preston wrote: 'Edrich scored only 16, but his was one of the most skilful batting displays I have ever seen.' Another writer, Cliff Cary, marvelled at Edrich's 'nonchalant contempt for danger. He seemed content to be battered black and blue rather than lose his wicket.' Godfrey Evans said: 'Bill was always a great fighter when you were in trouble.'

Denis Compton, Edrich's partner for forty minutes during the battle for survival, calculated that Bill's score, paltry on paper, delivered much less than it was worth. He remembered an 'impossible wicket and leaping half-volleys'. Keith Miller, said Compton, 'bowled at only half-speed, yet his deliveries, on pitching, rose straight into the air'. Compton added that in England the conditions would have been admirably suited to the spinner. 'The Australians, by contrast, used medium-pacers and kept the ball straight and up to the batsman.'

Edrich described the contest as resembling a round with boxing heavyweight champion, Joe Louis. He said that a completely new technique had to be improvised on the spot. 'It consisted in not playing the ball; but the decision could only be taken after the ball had pitched and one could be sure it would not hit the wicket. It was a tense business. I became so engrossed in it that I forgot the spectators and almost everything else.'

Keith Miller, remembering the bravery of a 'marvellous little man', also considered the wicket at Brisbane as the worst in his experience. 'It was so bad that one ball would hit the batsman's ankle and the next endanger his head. I thought I was going to kill someone and eased off.' Bradman, remorseless in his pursuit of the batsman, told him: 'Nugget, bowl fast. It makes it harder.' Miller did obey the command: 'I thought if this is Test cricket, I don't like it. But I did bowl faster and Bill just stood there and took it. He was unflinching. He scored 16 runs and it was one of the greatest innings I ever saw. It was worth 200 on any other wicket.'

Wally Hammond was a declining force in his last Test series. His domestic affairs at the time were at a worrying crisis and the news of his divorce was made public as the tour began. He scored only 168 runs in eight innings before he was stricken with fibrositis and replaced by Yardley as captain in the final Test at Sydney. He did, however, provide one last glimpse of his majesty at Brisbane. It was a classic exhibition of bad-wicket play. His near-miraculous 32 in England's first innings vied with his artistic poise on another evil pitch at Melbourne in 1936. Bill O'Reilly, who watched both innings, concluded that Hammond had no peer in twenty years of international cricket as an all-weather player. 'From the first ball bowled to him he proved to be the absolute master of the situation,' reported O'Reilly. 'Hammond is second to none in playing the "dead bat" at the lifting ball. He played it so well that one might have been excused for thinking that his right arm was either broken, or made of jelly, so little pressure did he place upon the bat.'

The cruel arrival of the second awesome storm mocked England's defiance. Ernie Toshack, Australia's left-arm medium-pace bowler, had been spoken of as the man who would demolish a Test innings, if he was given the opportunity on a bad wicket. In the event he struggled to live up to expectations. He did not recognise his task until after Bradman and Hassett had tutored him on the field before play on the final morning of the match. The procedure was simple: bowl to half-volley length and don't worry about spinning the ball. Toshack belatedly responded by taking nine of the last fifteen England wickets. Keith Miller, regarded by the less than prophetic O'Reilly as a supernumary bowler on this occasion, was Australia's match-winning agent. Miller's seven wickets in the first innings was the crucial thrust to deprive England of any hope of recovery.

The tempest at Brisbane did, for a time, offer the beguiling promise of an escape. Jim Swanton, for one, had anticipated a drawn game. 'What was extraordinary was the strength of the tropical Queensland sun which sucked away the moisture, so that against all prediction, and thanks also to the sandy soil perfect for drainage, play was possible sharp to time,' he said. Swanton had described the scene of desolation in a broadcast on the last morning. At eight o'clock part of the playing area still lay under a foot of water. He quoted the Brisbane curator as thinking that there could be no more cricket that day. 'English listeners, who had gone to bed with this comforting information, had to be told when they woke next morning that fifteen wickets had fallen and the game was over,' recalled Swanton.

Australia were again the victors by an innings in the second Test at Sydney. Bradman and Barnes each scored 234, the latter, it was said, sacrificing his wicket at the same innings total, so as not to usurp the authority of his captain. Australia scored 659 for eight wickets to exceed their Brisbane aggregate. Their victory by an innings and 33 runs demonstrated the gulf between the teams. Only once before had England been defeated twice by an innings in successive matches: A. E. Stoddart's team on the 1897–98 tour.

Bill Edrich, as always revelling in an uphill fight, was not to be denied his own personal triumph. Bill O'Reilly described him as the complete Test cricketer and said that Edrich's all-round performance distanced him from the slapdash methods of many of his colleagues. Edrich's batting was complemented by a spirited bowling spell. He took three wickets – those of Morris, Johnson and Hassett – for 79 runs in 26 overs. Of his century, following 71 in England's first innings, O'Reilly said: 'His cricket was a shining example of the grit and determination expected from a stout-hearted England Test batsman'.

England were overthrown by the spin of Johnson and McCool at Sydney. Their troubles began in the second over when Fred Freer, the Victorian fast-medium bowler, who was deputising for the indisposed Lindwall, bowled Washbrook. The reports, which paid tribute to Edrich's pluck in his rallying innings, could not have expressed awareness of the events preceding it. Denis Compton shared a room with his friend at Sydney. On the evening before the Test Denis had

117

been surprised but not unduly concerned by Bill's absence. In the morning he was perturbed to find the accompanying bed undisturbed. He took the precaution of ruffling the bedclothes. A knock on the door interrupted his thoughts. He breathed a sigh of relief. 'Here's Bill at last', was his reaction; but his visitor was the England captain. 'Where's Bill?' asked Hammond. Denis had to think quickly to protect his friend in those more disciplined times. He assumed his most serious manner. 'Oh, didn't you know, Wally, Bill takes a long early morning run to prepare himself for the cricket. He'll be back in a few minutes.' Hammond appeared to accept the explanation and replied: 'Well, tell him not to be late; the coach leaves for the ground at ten o'clock.'

The dinner-jacketed Edrich sneaked in undetected shortly after the conversation. His eyes were bloodshot; he clearly had had a very good night out. Denis sternly admonished him. 'Bill, for goodness sake, get under the shower,' he said. Edrich explained that he had met a former bomber pilot comrade after practice on the previous day. They had flown together in the war. Bill said: 'I'm sorry, I bumped into a great friend of mine – a very brave man – and he invited me to his home. We have spent the night talking about old times. I'm afraid the bottle got the better of us.'

Compton, only slightly appeased by this recital, was less composed when they arrived at the ground to find that England had won the toss. It was a good wicket for batting; but this was an occasion when a spell in the field would have been beneficial for his friend. 'Bill did look rough and, to make matters worse, we quickly lost a wicket. He was the next man in. I wondered whether he would find his way out to the middle. For about fifteen minutes he was awful, but eventually he got sight of the ball and he then played one of the best innings

118

I've ever seen. He was a remarkable chap. I couldn't have done it.'

Godfrey Evans also recalled his amazement but he was baffled by Bill's dismissal, lbw to McCool's quicker delivery. When Edrich returned to the pavilion, Evans offered his congratulations. 'Well played, Bill,' he said. 'What a magnificent innings. Tell me, what did you get out for, you were playing so well?' Edrich replied: 'Godders, I think I'd sobered up by then.'

Another great batsman was goaded into furious action at Sydney. Bill Bowes recalled a conversation with his former Yorkshire colleague, Len Hutton, before England's second innings. 'You know what they're saying, Len? They reckon you're freetened of fast bowling.' Hutton did not respond to the allegation; but his characteristically swift and luminous smile signified his acknowledgement. Bowes was well aware that Hutton would not allow this notion to linger in the minds of the Australians. Neville Cardus said one of the tragedies of the match was the way an enchanting innings by Hutton came to an end. 'It is not reckless to assume that a century of grandeur was nipped in the bud, a rare page blotted in the book of cricket's history.'

The exuberance of Hutton's strokeplay bore the indignation of an affronted man. 'He survived an appeal for lbw off the first ball; and then, in a most easeful sequence, he rippled the sunlit field by stylish drives, quick and wonderfully late,' wrote Cardus. In less than half an hour Hutton struck six boundaries. England reached 49 in a glorious counter-thrust. 'In the last over before lunch,' added Cardus, 'the cruellest bolt of mischief brought Hutton down to prosaic earth.' He attempted another forcing backstroke off Miller and, after hitting the ball, lost the grip of his bat with one hand and the uncontrolled swing of it broke his wicket.' Hutton's 37 runs took him only 24 minutes. It was a classic cameo of an innings and, reported the *Sydney Morning Herald*, even the most ardent partisan would have welcomed another hour of Hutton's majestic strokeplay.

Bill O'Reilly also paid tribute to a 'showpiece effort'. 'He began by hitting the short stuff so hard that even if Australia had had fifteen fieldsmen the fours would still have come. Those who were fortunate enough to witness his remarkable display must have grieved with me that such a superlative innings was nipped in its golden prime.'

With reason to feel that luck was an accomplice, Australia's slow bowlers, McCool, Johnson and Tribe, went avidly into action on a wearing pitch in the afternoon. Washbrook was caught by McCool at forward short-leg off Johnson's sharply rising off-spinner. Edrich reached his second 50 of the match, always combining opportunity with instinct and sturdy strength. 'He stimulated confidence that showed, as far as he was concerned, this was no occasion for an English collapse,' commented the *Sydney Morning Herald*. 'Edrich played a staunch innings and, after a nebulous prelude, Compton's lissom batsmanship massaged the lined face of the England innings,' reported Cardus. Edrich and Compton, during a period of increasing command, were associated in England's first century partnership – 102 for the third wicket – of the series. They offered for a time the prospect of a match-saving partnership. 'Once again, disaster fell on England at the pinch,' said Cardus. 'Compton flashed at an offside ball from Freer fatally and was quite ghoulishly caught by Bradman only twenty minutes from the long day's end.'

Hammond's dismissal, caught off an indulgent big hit, sealed England's defeat on the last day. His last scoring shot was a straight four off McCool. 'It had a kind of grand pathos about it – like a dying bull struggling to its feet to defy the matador before the kill,' wrote Tom Goodman in the *Sydney Morning Herald*. Edrich went on to complete his first century against Australia. The innings, occupying over five hours, called upon his immense powers of concentration. He had a stern tussle against the unorthodox spin of Tribe on a turning pitch. Other English batsmen would experience bafflement when the Australian plied his trade for Northamptonshire on uncovered county wickets. Edrich's determination to succeed was, however, proof against any discomfort. 'He battled on with his team disintegrating at the opposite end,' reported O'Reilly. 'He proved beyond any doubt that he of all the English batsmen was best equipped for the struggle.'

O'Reilly perceived other troubled times for England: 'The present Australian attack looks like developing into the best array of wicket-takers this country has possessed for many years. It must have been a novel experience for Don Bradman to have had the handling of such a well-balanced attack.'

Ray Lindwall expressed his firm conviction that he did not unfairly deprive Edrich of another century in the drawn third Test at Melbourne. He was unrepentant about his demanding appeal. 'We all thought Bill was out. The ball shot low, and if it did hit his bat, I didn't hear or see it. Otherwise, I wouldn't have appealed, at least not in earnest, or expecting a decision in my favour.' Edrich had reached 89 when he was adjudged lbw to Lindwall. Reports indicated that he struck the ball so sharply on to his pad that it could be heard in the pavilion. The undetected snick occurred when Edrich and Washbrook were renewing their overnight century partnership. Edrich had spent considerable time the previous evening cleaning his bat. When he went to the wicket the following morning, there was not a mark on it. After his dismissal, he angrily paraded the dent on the inside edge of the bat where, he claimed, the ball had struck before the fatal decision.

Compton said he had never seen his friend so upset at a cricket match. Bill's temper was not improved by the apparent loss of a cash bonus. A wealthy English industrialist and cricket patron, visiting Australia, had offered the incentive of £100 to England players scoring centuries in the series. The businessman supporter, holding a watching brief at Melbourne, shared Edrich's displeasure. Bill did receive his money. 'I could hear the smack of your bat on the ball,' said the patron. 'I'll sign this cheque for you, William, and make sure you do get a hundred next time.'

The presentation was a reward for Edrich's tenacity in an unavailing cause. His form in Australia was to prove a prelude to other feats of valour in the post-war years. In three innings, one on the Brisbane gluepot and two others in the throes of another heavy England defeat at Sydney, he had silenced his critics. An enormous burden had been lifted from his shoulders. 'I was no longer worried,' he recorded, 'by the anxiety to prove, before it was too late, that I deserved my place in the side.'

Edrich headed the England Test aggregates with 462 runs in Australia. He had typically summoned his best efforts in the hours of need. The heroism of his batting earned him the soubriquet of 'lionheart'. 'Now that the tour is over it seems almost unbelievable that he was nearly left at home,' commented *Wisden*.

CHAPTER 8

Dear Bill

'Ginger, ginger, you all know captain Ginger.
Jolly old sot, O-T 'ot.
Ninety-nine in the shade, what, what!
He loves the ladies, but none of them would he injure.
All the ladies are fond of gin,
Gin, gin, gin, gin, Ginger!'

Those boon companions who shared the boisterous ballads and enchanted evenings of Bill Edrich hold wistful memories of an incorrigible rogue. He was the unabashed romantic who stole so many hearts in his whirlwind romp through life. He was a restless Peter Pan figure, appealingly vulnerable to his worshipping women carers; and a cavalier who strode outrageously through his merry 'never-never' land.

Edrich's volcanic temperament did upset those who sought to check his eruptions. John Arlott wrote: 'He could be furiously argumentative. He was convivial, but could be intemperate. If some of his actions were ill-judged, he also could be wise and thoughtful.'

The zest of a remarkably resilient man communicated a 'terrific love of life', in the words of his sister, Ena Taylor. As a Bracondale schoolboy in Norfolk, Bill had shown thespian inclinations. One local reviewer, passing judgement on his swaggering portrayal of Bob Acres in Sheridan's *The Rivals*, had unerringly sensed

123

the dramatic style, which was to punctuate Edrich's roles off-stage. The critic remarked: 'He tended to rush his lines and not make allowances for the necessary pauses.' Bill rarely did acknowledge the need for reflection, even in his mature years. 'He did not think about the consequences of his actions; he could never have been careful,' observed Ena. 'He was intelligent and clever, but did not want to get tied up in the realities of everyday existence.'

Frank Tyson, an admiring England comrade, has reflected upon the innate honesty of Edrich, who shot his verbal darts straight from the shoulder. 'What you saw is what you got. Bill always believed that life and cricket were meant as a personal challenge to be interfaced with team effort and, above all, to be enjoyed. He met life and the game head on and tackled it as he was, warts and all.' Tyson maintained that the zeitgeist of 'carpe diem' was not uncommon in the late 1940s and early 1950s. Edrich, in common with other survivors of the war, was surprised to be still alive. The elation was manifested, in many cases, by a total disregard for future security. A certain fatalism had entered their souls.

Keith Miller, who served in the Royal Australian Air Force, was similarly heedless of the swings of fortune. Tyson remembered the refreshing philosophy of Miller in one conversation. It was a reminder that the weightiest of anxieties is excess mental luggage. 'What were you worrying about last year, or last month?' rhetorically asked Keith. 'Then why did you worry?' Tyson concluded: 'Bill was like that, I thought.'

The changed perspectives did lead to cynicism – or as others unaffected might describe it as a contrariness of outlook – among the returning servicemen. It was in character that Edrich then, and later, saw no reason to ease down into sobriety. The country boy from Norfolk came whooping into the post-war world as the courtly, decorated Squadron Leader, metaphorically twirling his moustaches, and setting his cap at the ladies. It was a state of intense consciousness and, in the view of one friend, Trevor Bailey, Edrich did not leave his realm of fantasy. 'Bill lived in a dreamland. He never grew up,' said Bailey. 'He was always falling in love.' The ardent disposition never faltered. Bill was sixty-seven when he married his fifth wife, Mary Somerville, a Chesham hairdresser, in September 1983.

Ena believed that the gallantry of her brother would have served him well had he lived in the days of the Crusades. Rescuing 'damsels in distress' was part of his challenging campaign. 'He was quite hopeless – you had to laugh – he couldn't resist a woman.' In his defence, it must be said that at least two of Bill's conquests, miserable in failed marriages, rebounded blissfully into short but happy times. The compulsive philanderer was following the example of his forebears. 'Earthy stock, I believe, the Edriches, working and playing hard, with an eye for a pretty woman,' wrote a Norfolk historian. 'Add to that,' said Ena, 'some drops of Cumbrian blood from similar stock, with a little more romanticism, and you have the mixture that was Bill.' Edrich himself dwelt upon the benefits of his mother's antecedents, the Cumbrian farmers and his maternal grandmother, who was related to John Peel. Two of his cousins were Cumberland and England front-row rugby forwards, hell-raising and terrifying men. 'It was a pedigree for virility and stamina,' he said.

The complexities of Edrich's character juxtaposed honourable and wanton elements. He was caring and kind and never deliberately hurtful. Ena has related how Bill was a very involved member of her family: 'I have seen him on numerous occasions, interacting with the elderly relatives, and always with courtesy.'

Jack Robertson, while in the throes of a serious illness, remembered Edrich's deep concern and how his old friend and cricket colleague regularly rang his wife to check on his progress.

Edrich was, in a sense, a man rent in two by his fame. Before the war Norfolk was a remote and enclosed community, snug and warm in its own rituals and customs. Bill was an ambitious boy, but he must have been overwhelmed by the transition to big city life in London. Alfred Gover, with memories of the Norfolk burr, was taken aback by the change in tone at a wartime meeting with Edrich at Lord's. 'Why are you talking like that?' he asked. Bill had by this time assimilated an accent befitting a RAF officer. He was instantly classifiable as a gentleman in manner.

Did, perhaps, Edrich's legendary peccadilloes mask the shy country boy which was his true self? It could be argued that he adopted the machismo style to suppress an inferiority complex. The wayward tendencies were undoubtedly a symptom of recurring bouts of loneliness. They did hide a sensitive spirit. The inconsistency of his dealings with women – unlike those with men – disguised the fact that he possessed a great depth of feeling. His faults, as with Shakespeare's Othello, were that he loved not wisely but too well. 'He could never open himself up to be with one woman for any length of time because it became too mundane,' commented Ena.

Bill's younger son, Justin, has said that his father inspired affection among so many people, men as well as women, but was unable to cope with the practical aspects of life. 'I think it is sad that he spent so much of his life battling with various demons and never reached the stage where he was truly contented. Dad got his pleasure from short-term highs rather than overall fulfilment or peace.'

The closeness of Bill's relationship with his mother was another impediment to marital stability. 'Bill was looking for a girl like his mother as a model for a wife,' said one of the departing ladies. It was a quest as forlorn as chasing a rainbow. Edith Edrich was a stern protector throughout all the trials of her erring son. After Bill had been censured by a cousin for breaking one pact, she loyally remarked: 'Yes, dear, I know. But Bill is my boy and he hasn't killed anyone yet.'

The heartbreaks of the estrangements might justifiably have produced bitterness; and yet one of their intriguing features is the legacy of lingering affection. One consequence of the marriages was the harmonious intermingling of children – half-brothers and step-sisters – at the celebrated Edrich family matches in the picturesque Norfolk village of Ingham. The tender forgiveness of Bill's ladies in retirement is a testimony to an infuriating but disarming man. The first of his marriages, at the age of twenty, was to Betty, a London girl, whom he met during his apprentice days at Lord's. She was succeeded by Marion, a WAAF officer (considered a 'surprise choice' in family circles) in an association which lasted until after the war. The rules of engagement did exceed the bounds of propriety when Bill literally carried off his next bride, Jessy, a former Yorkshire repertory actress, during a visit to her home at Castle Donington in 1948. Bill, playing for Middlesex in a county match at Trent Bridge, was invited to spend the weekend with Jessy and Dick, her husband. The two men had met on a staff training course at Camberley during the war. 'Bill kept on saying how unhappy he was,' recalled Jessy. 'And I was miserable too at that time. We just ran away. It was complicated because my two daughters were then quite tiny.'

Jessy Edrich, vivacious and sociable, was the ideal

consort for Bill during the hedonistic days and parties of thanksgiving following the war. 'Bill presented me with a lovely son, Jasper, and we had four very happy years together. They were wild and hilarious times.' Jessy remembered how Bill enjoyed the role of the 'gentleman player'. 'He was not a social climber, or a snob, but he liked to move in that circle. The problem was that he disliked protocol and did not always see eye to eye with the cricket hierarchy. Bill was silly and impulsive and sometimes less than tactful. He was honest to himself, didn't crawl or pretend to people who might have bettered his cause.' A recent newspaper article called attention to the handmaidens of Edrich's halcyon years. Jessy was asked by her grand-daughter if she belonged to this admiring throng. She replied: 'Certainly not – it was before my time.'

The idyll of Jessy and Bill was broken by a letter from an Australian girl, who had snared Bill's affections on a cricket tour. The marriage was not immediately severed, even though it was closed as a love match. It led to a supposition in the family that it might endure. It was, however, a false premise; and Jessy, whose name still springs readily and nostalgically to the lips of cricket contemporaries, sadly slipped out of Bill's life.

'The only thing that matters is the holiness of the heart's affections,' is a line of Keats, a poet greatly admired by Edrich. He would have approved the sentiment which counters the image of him as a libertine. Denis Compton, along with many others, regards Edrich as a strictly honourable man. He was certainly conscientious in his more serious liaisons in properly tying the knot. The merest exchange of glances with a pretty girl across a crowded room was a signal for romantic action. Compton recalled a cocktail party which led to one swift declaration of love. 'We were fielding in the slips on the following day. Bill said: "I saw someone last night whom I'm going to marry." ' Denis thought this rash and imprudent, even by Bill's standards of courtship. 'Don't be silly, Bill,' he said. 'You've only just met her.' Bill was adamant and set on his course. 'He was true to his word; he did marry her.'

The comforting Valerie, the fourth of Bill's wives, was regarded by the family as a stabilising influence. It was a typically decisive encounter. Bill never did waste time. Valerie was a consultant with the Australian Mutual Provident Company in the late 1950s. The romance blossomed following a business meeting at which Bill promised to put her in touch with potentially lucrative clients in the tomato-growing industry. In the event, the unrealised offer concealed another agenda; the succeeding dinner engagement produced a proposal of a different kind. 'Bill was an absolute charmer. I had a large mansion flat in Frogmore. A lodger occupied one of the big front rooms. He was given notice and Bill moved in. We were married three months later in March 1960.'

Jack Belton, a fellow RAF cadet at Cranwell and a future business associate, recalled the episode. It had been preceded by the association with the Australian girl (the source of the break-up with Jessy) who worked for the Qantas airline. At Bill's insistence, she had actually travelled to England to meet him. Her journey was in vain: 'By this time Valerie had come on the scene and Bill had completely forgotten about this Australian conquest,' recalled Belton.

One of the conditions of their marriage, as Valerie related, was that Bill should give up drinking. He remained abstemious throughout the first year and the drought was not broken until the birth of their son, Justin, in January 1961. This was a serene interlude at the seventeenth-century farmhouse at Wyverstone in the Suffolk countryside. 'Bill basically hated London; it was anathema to him. Give him a garden to dig in and dogs to go shooting with, and he was happy,' declared Valerie.

This view was supported by Jack Belton with whom Edrich stayed at his Hoddesdon home between the marriages to Jessy and Valerie. 'Bill was a shy man, not an outgoing type, and really ill-at-ease among the bright lights.' Belton also refutes allegations of alcoholism. 'Bill did drink but he couldn't really take it. He was just a boozer, who enjoyed a few pints, a game of shove'a'penny or darts, and a chat with the locals at our village pub.' Bill's intake, while excessive at times, was a continuing palliative to drown the lost voices of friends killed in action. Denis Compton firmly believed that it was a legacy of the war. 'He would obviously need a few beers to restore himself between operations. And this becomes a customary habit if you do it for a long time in such circumstances.' Eric Edrich, less addicted than others in a drinking family, remembered that his brother was always on his best behaviour on the visits to his home near Huntingdon. 'Bill was as good as gold; he never got tight once.'

The return to his country roots in Suffolk in 1963 was at first welcomed by Edrich. He was restored in health and apparently reconciled to the role of the squire. It was the perfect sanctuary in which to attend to his business pursuits in poultry and insurance and enjoy highly competitive cricket duels with his young son, Justin, in the garden net. There was a host of regular visitors for weekend parties. He enjoyed the blessings of his two step-daughters, Jane and Judy (Valerie's children); and bantering comradeship with his eldest son, Jasper, on holidays. Justin recalled how immensely proud his father was of his sporting achievements, in cricket (the younger Edrich was later to play in the Minor Counties championship with Suffolk) and football. There were fierce table tennis contests in the attic at Wyverstone. 'He was just better than me; he would never let me win. I would be around eight or nine at the time, diving around all over the place; and tears of anger and frustration would well up as Dad beat me 21–18 in the final game.'

Valerie Edrich has described Bill as a 'Victorian-type' husband, incredibly possessive, and with the additional handicap of being utterly helpless in household tasks. She does, though, remain steadfast, with becoming kindness, in assessing his character. 'Bill was a good man; our relationship was marred by his possessiveness. If he had been less demanding, I'm sure we could have worked it out.' She has no regrets. 'Given the chance again, I would still marry him.'

There was, inevitably, the other woman, to stifle the contentment at Wyverstone. Bill spotted Margot, a friend of Valerie, who lived in a neighbouring village. There were attempts to shore up the marriage until Justin was eighteen. Margot was an enchantress who dazzled males and Bill was quickly her captive. He desperately wanted to marry her. He was for once repulsed – largely on the advice of Valerie – and Margot, a highly independent lady, became his long-standing companion but not his wife.

As a postscript to the break with his mother, Justin Edrich presented his own verdict. 'Dad seemed to be fairly happy leading a peaceful rural existence as a sort of lord of the manor; but ultimately it wasn't enough. He had to start his travels again and return to London when he met Margot. His roots – and his real comfort – were in a tranquil country setting; but he had been elevated into the world of international sportsmen, and the lure of this circle proved too strong.'

The eccentric pattern of Edrich's life did hurtle him at times into despair. Ena Taylor described her brother as the quintessential 'tragic-romantic'. 'There was a great loneliness in him,' she said. In times of crisis he was drawn back into the family fold, seeking reassurance from his parents and brothers. Jack Borrett, the former Ingham captain and president, provided evidence of the filial tug. Bill was conscious of the alarm which would be caused by the final rift with Valerie in 1973. He enlisted the moral support of Borrett when he came down to Norfolk to report the news to his mother and father. His friend said he would accompany him, but only as far as the door. He waited outside while the discussion took place. 'How did you get on?' he asked, when Bill rejoined him. 'Ma was very upset,' said Bill. Borrett next asked for Bill senior's reaction. After the talk with his mother, Bill had turned to his father to seek his opinion. Old Bill was buried in the racing pages of his newspaper. There was more than a hint of resignation in his reply. He did not directly refer to the topic but simply said: 'Who do you reckon's going to win the National, Bill?'

The carousing antics of Edrich at the Scarborough Festival have passed into legend. Godfrey Evans recalled the rapture of this cricketing holiday time for players and their wives. Bill was in bold and extravagant mood amid the whirl of parties, banquets and balls. The cavortings resembled a crazy royal court. Jessy Edrich remembered the riotous assemblies. 'You were a queen for a fortnight at Scarborough. However did we manage to appear at dinner in our finery!'

Edrich's crowd-pleasing centuries did not betray the fact that he scarcely slept and often arrived dinner-jacketed for breakfast. Frank Tyson remembered one occasion when Bill, enthusiastically tackling a kipper breakfast in his room, lost his false teeth. He had to go down to the hotel kitchen and retrieve them from the detritus. The pattern of the festival was admirably in tune with cricketers on holiday. Godfrey Evans said: 'We didn't start the cricket until twelve o'clock. Lovely hours they were. We would call in at the Royal at eleven to quench our thirst. They served some nice draught bitter. It was just a gentle stroll from the bar to the ground.' Edrich revelled in this carefree atmosphere. 'All I've got to do is wake up, sniff the air, and I'm away,' he said.

The glamour of the splendid terraced ground in North Marine Road laid its spell on players and supporters alike. Huge crowds watched the three traditional matches – Yorkshire v. MCC, Gentlemen and Players, and H. D. G. Leveson-Gower's XI against the touring team. The tents of the festival president, the town mayor and the Scarborough members bedecked with gay flags, billowed in the sea breezes. 'The sun shone and there was the usual large and appreciative crowd spilling over the mound near the main gate,' wrote Gerald Pawle in an article in *The Cricketer*. 'The Town Band played the 'Eton Boating Song' and selections from *Rose Marie* with the brio and that reckless disregard for their conductor which had made them famous.'

The lunch and tea gongs in the adjacent boarding houses in Trafalgar Square boomed rousingly to call in the spectators for their victuals. On the field there was the ritual of refreshments being brought out by a uniformed butler and a retinue of waitresses. 'Each night,' wrote Pawle, 'the amateurs, dinner jackets de rigueur, dined in the Cricketers' Room at the Grand, the opulent Victorian hostelry on the cliffside. After dinner they repaired to whatever haunt was in favour at the time.' It was sometimes the St Nicholas Hotel where Bill Edrich shuffled happily in his favourite slow fox-trot, as he led the dancers on to the gleaming glass floor. At other times the rendezvous was the ballroom of the Royal where anyone not arriving in evening dress was promptly ejected. Lindsay Hassett, the Australian captain, on one occasion, was hastily arrayed in a jacket and tie before he was allowed entrance. Another great festival venue was an hotel in the main street which did not close its doors until dawn. 'The deafening music of a Hammond organ was played by a prominent local doctor,' related Pawle. 'It made conversation a little difficult, but in those garish surroundings there was much learned discussion in the small hours on the arts of batting and bowling, and the iniquities of umpires.'

Bill Edrich made his mark in a sporting as well as a social sense at Scarborough. It was always said of him that he made a point of playing at least one innings of distinction at the festival to book his invitation for the following year. He hit 135 out of 193 for MCC against Yorkshire in 1950. Three years later the match between the Gentlemen and Players was dominated by Leonard Hutton. Hutton, captaining the Players, scored 241 in an innings of imperious power. He still finished on the losing side. It was a match of three declarations. The Gentlemen were set a victory target of 251 in two and a half hours and won by five wickets. Edrich masterminded a breathtaking assault on the Players' bowling. He raced to 133 and when he departed, ten minutes from the end, only eight runs were required. He scored another century, vainly, in 1955, when the Players were the victors by two wickets in a thrilling finish.

In the last of his festival appearances, in 1956, he belied his advancing years with another pugnacious display. 'Edrich set the mood of the Gentlemen's innings and, indeed, the whole game with an exhilarating exhibition of controlled hitting,' reported *Wisden*. Edrich's buoyant 133, hugely entertaining in a lost cause, was in keeping with his adventurous spirit beside the sea in Yorkshire.

The effervescence of Edrich's batting at Scarborough merited an advertisement extolling the effects of good wine. The glow of alcohol could last well into the afternoon when, as happened on one occasion, fatigue overtook him, causing a sudden, toppling lurch backwards on the field. Edrich, in his version of the incident, said that he was fielding at mid-wicket when Jack Hill, the Australian, broke his bat. He settled down on the grass for a moment's rest while the bat was replaced. 'The grass felt so cool and healing,' he recalled. 'Suddenly I jerked into a sitting position. Hill was crouched over his bat, the bowler was about to begin his run-up, and the fieldsmen were poised.' Bill had to shake himself awake. He had fallen asleep. Edrich, after the previous evening's festivities, usually took the precaution of hiding behind the wicket-keeper, or retreating to fly slip. Tom Pearce, the festival organiser after the retirement of Leveson-Gower, recalled one instance of Edrich's exceptional powers of recovery. On one festival morning, having enjoyed a short nap before play, he was padded up by his team-mates and almost literally escorted out to the wicket by his opening partner, Reg Simpson. 'Bill was in a terrible state, just about conscious really,' said Pearce. 'But he got himself better quickly and scored a century.'

Roy Tattersall presented another variation on this theme. 'Bill was truly "kalayed" before the start of one game against the Australians. It was a lovely day and there was the usual big crowd. Bill went out, played very well, and scored 40. The Australians weren't feeding him any runs. After his dismissal, he took his pads off, and was instantly fast asleep on the dressing-room floor. The spectators, watching Bill batting, did not realise anything was wrong.' Ron Burnet, the former Yorkshire captain, remembered a bleary-eyed Bill playing earnestly down the line oblivious of the fact that the ball was bouncing perilously around his ears. The mists cleared and he played properly to score a hundred.

All of Edrich's contemporaries at the festival and other social events have recalled the spellbinding entertainer, the exaggerated hauteur of his speech, the hooked nose curling in disdain in a tantrum, and the silly smile which played around his lips as a prelude to taking the stage on team party occasions. One of his setpieces, conducted with a total disregard for convention, was mired in confusion like those of the professional joker, Tommy Cooper. It was a conjuring trick involving an egg. This was always far more entertaining when it failed than when it was successful, a view not shared by one cricket correspondent whose white tuxedo never looked quite so immaculate again. It was an act in which Bill placed a raw egg in an egg cup, on top of a tray, on top of a glass of water. The plan was to strike the tray with the side of the hand thus causing it to spin away, and for the egg to drop from its perch into the water. Bill's judgement was not infallible and, as Frank Tyson remarked, the besmirched walls of some Australian kitchens bore witness to his inaccuracy.

Bill had an extensive repertoire of songs which were delivered in a husky baritone voice that only just carried. Romantic ballads as well as other bawdy numbers acquired in wartime featured in his cabaret performance. The saucy tongue-twisting tale of Susie 'sitting in her shoeshine shop' was a special favourite.

It was a particular triumph when it was rendered as a duet in company with either Lindsay Hassett or Leonard Hutton. This was an hilariously rewarding comic turn. It provoked streaming tears of laughter and was encored long into the night. 'If Bill was having fun, so was everyone else,' remembered Alfred Gover.

By contrast, Edrich could tumble into embarrassment away from his intimate circle of friends. Jack Belton remembered a visit to the London Palladium to see the Crazy Gang. Bill had earlier in the day scored a century against New Zealand. Jimmy Nervo, one of the comic gang, came to the front of the stage to announce the feat and the fact that Edrich was in the audience. 'Bill went all the colours of the rainbow and disappeared under his seat,' said Belton.

Edrich was always entertaining in drink and never aggressive or bad-tempered is the view expressed by Denis Compton. 'It did not seem to affect him on the field; he never let Middlesex or England down at cricket.' Denis recalled one especially intoxicating divertissement when he and Bill were invited to Dublin to open a new cricket ground. They received a typically hospitable Irish reception. At dinner, in the evening, they were introduced to the sweet blandishments of Irish coffee. 'They say it is potent, but it tastes just like cream,' said Denis to his friend. Denis had managed to restrict his own intake before the speeches. He was steady enough to deliver a few well-chosen words. Bill, however, was swaying like a sheaf of corn in a windswept field. 'He really was plastered and I wondered what he was going to do.' Their hosts politely indicated that Bill should remain seated. 'Here is Denis's twin,' announced the master of ceremonies. Bill looked round uneasily and stuttered sluggishly: 'Gentlemen . . .' He didn't say another word before launching into song. It was the opening verse of 'When Irish Eyes are Smiling'.

The faces of the guests were instantly wreathed in smiles of delight. The chorus grew in vigour as they all joined in. Cheers rang out around the room. 'I've never known anyone get such an ovation as Bill did. They loved him.'

Geoffrey Howard, the MCC manager on Edrich's last tour of Australia in 1954–55, recalled another party at which Bill, rather late in the evening, did insist on making a speech. The content was indecipherable – people could see his lips moving, but no sound whatever was coming out. 'I can still see the young Colin Cowdrey, on his first trip to Australia, standing open-mouthed in sheer astonishment,' said Howard.

Edrich's reputation as a partygoer gained him followers all over the world, not least on *The Cricketer* holidays to the Greek islands. Sharing the fun on these riotous occasions were cricket celebrities, Brian Johnston, Jim Swanton, Christopher Martin-Jenkins and Bob Wyatt. Bill became a popular figure in Nidri on Lefkas, as he was in Corfu in other years. He was called 'Vassilis', the Greek for Bill. Ben Brocklehurst, *The Cricketer* chairman, recalled the evenings spent in a Nidri taverna. Bill and his burly partner, Panos, the local police chief, won a special round of applause when they performed a little Greek dance. 'Panos was embarrassed afterwards because he was dancing in uniform, much to the delight of the watching islanders.'

On another occasion, in the Nidri hostelry, Bill spotted a fisherman gliding past in a very small boat with a powerful paraffin light in the bows. The fisherman carried a forked spear to impale the squid and any other fish attracted by the light. Bill hailed the man, an old friend, who picked him up. It proved to be the ultimate restorative, a speedy way to clear the senses. 'Bill was forced to stand with his legs apart in a "tipperly" boat in pitch dark until the fisherman finally relented and released him ashore an hour or two later,' said Brocklehurst. Christopher Martin-Jenkins related another episode in which Bill failed to master the art of sail-boarding, mainly because of his arthritic hip. 'He tried for hours to learn the knack,' said Martin-Jenkins. 'Bill was undeterred by the repeated duckings, as the board flipped over. He bobbed up time and time again to clamber aboard.'

Brian Johnston recalled a good mind beneath the carefree spirit. Bill was always the champion in pursuits beyond cricket. One year, in Nidri, against stiff opposition, Bill won the annual Scrabble tournament. As in all his activities, he addressed this contest in a most serious manner. His extraordinary competitiveness was also revealed in backgammon encounters and he was among the first to complete the *Telegraph* crossword. 'He showed great knowledge and intelligence at Scrabble,' said Martin-Jenkins. 'He also displayed a fiercely argumentative streak if ever one of his words was challenged.'

The fervour of Edrich's lifestyle was given a new impetus among his young cricket pupils when he returned to Norfolk in the late 1950s. He was then at an age when most people would be reining in their energies. Instead he cavorted as if he had rediscovered adolescence. In his forties, he was firmly of the opinion that he was a heart-throb, and that all the ladies loved him. Tracey Moore, one of his disciples, has referred to Bill's unquenchable enthusiasm. 'He was an amazing man; he never tired, and was always full of beans.'

Edrich's inspirational qualities and strict regime on the cricket field was less responsibly matched in the bizarre social round. The cricket disciplinarian, off duty, invariably required the protection of his young charges. At this time Bill drove a Rover car, which he called 'Roy'; and his escapades had the élan of the comic hero. They certainly did not stall in recklessness. The Norfolk team had celebrated freely after one match at Ingham. There was consternation in their ranks when Bill took the wheel on their departure, insisting upon acting as chauffeur. The first obstacle was the sightscreen which was knocked over; he then drove out of the village and immediately plunged into a hedge. 'Come on, Bill,' went up the cry. 'Let someone else take over.' Bill could be headstrong after drink. After righting the vehicle, he said: 'We're all right now; we're on the road.' Their erratic progress was halted yet again as they skidded into the wall of a pub. Within 250 yards, after leaving the ground, he had had three accidents. Bill, at last, realised his incapacity as a driver. 'Perhaps you're right,' he conceded, as he swung away from the wheel of the car.

Edrich's dignity was even more severely affronted during another game at Bishop's Stortford. The Norfolk manager, Harry Wright, an early riser, customarily went out early in the morning to buy a newspaper. As he left the hotel, he chanced upon the returning Bill, who was struggling to keep his feet, like an athlete at the end of a marathon race. There was little recovery time before the match, just a brief and rudely interrupted sleep. Bill was quite confounded when the maid reported to his colleagues that 'she couldn't wake up that old gentleman in room No. 30'.

All his Norfolk cricket friends remember Edrich as the vocalist and choirleader. 'If we had a singer in the side, he wasn't allowed to go to bed. Bill didn't always know all the words,' said one team-mate. The Ballad of Molly Malone, delivered with eloquent, hand-waving gestures, was a regular number. Overwhelmed by the emotion of the song, Bill once punched himself in the

a) A flourish against Leicestershire at Lord's, 10 June 1953.

b) Lindwall leads a chorus of appeals against Edrich.

a) Prehensile as a pickpocket, Edrich catches Davidson for 22 at slip off Laker against Australia at The Oval, 1953.

b) England's team at The Oval, 1953.

c) In the moment of victory Compton and Edrich have to run the gauntlet of excited England supporters.

Concentration and attack : a) Edrich's defiant 82 against Surrey and the spin of Laker and Lock,August 1956; b) Edrich employing his favourite pulled drive against Gloucestershire at Lord's, May 1957.

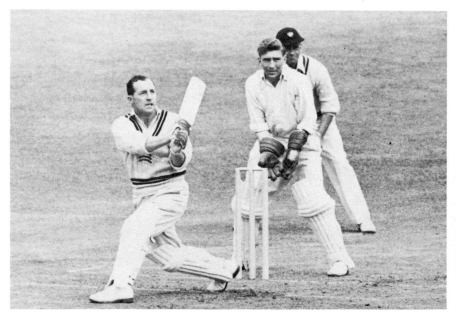

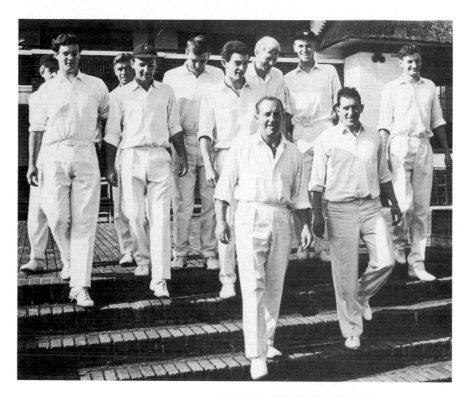

a) The returning champion leads the Norfolk team out on to the field.

b) Down on the farm : Edrich cradling newly hatched chicks.

a) Party glee.

b) Keith Miller and Bill Edrich reminisce.

a) Bill and Valerie Edrich.

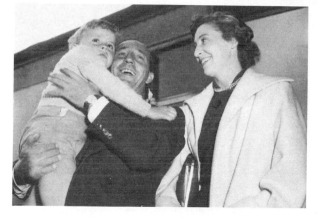

b) Bill and Jessy with
   their son Jasper.

c) Bill welcomes his
   cousin, John Edrich,
   at Lord's in 1974
   when India scored
   their lowest Test total.

a) The multi-faceted wreath for Bill Edrich's memorial service at St Clement Danes, the Central Church of the RAF.

b) Denis Compton opens the Compton and Edrich stands at Lord's in 1991, watched by Colonel John Stephenson, Secretary of MCC, and Justin Edrich.

mouth. He retired to examine the damage. He returned to the assembly in indignant mood. 'You didn't tell me my mouth was bleeding,' he complained.

Tracey Moore, the recipient of the tirade, recalled a journey to an all-night diner for breakfast halted by the call of nature. They stopped by the roadside to relieve themselves over a hedge. Moore, a six-footer, leaned nonchalantly on one of the overhanging branches. Bill sought the same support, put his hand out, and promptly fell into a ten-foot ditch. He looked up wonderingly from his bed of brambles. 'What happened?' he said. Moore explained the reason for the sudden descent. 'Well, I'm taller than you, of course.'

Edrich did have an engaging sense of the ridiculous; he thoroughly enjoyed a joke, even when it was against himself, as when a teasing junior filled his pipe with cotton wool and he went through a box of matches trying to light it. He was only slightly peeved when one hotel porter denied him a whisky nightcap. He had attempted to pull rank in making the request long after closing hours. He was perplexed but amused when the man said he did not know him but he was acquainted with his brother. 'Fancy him knowing Brian,' was his bemused response. There were those youngsters who tried to straddle the conflicting demands of enticing social dates and the imperatives of cricket fitness. One of them, torn between having a late night, or going to bed early, earnestly sought Bill's advice. The old campaigner replied: 'I've been struggling with that problem all my life. There's no answer to it.' It was a telling rejoinder from a man who could feast on two fronts. The Norfolk players, now in middle years, became boys again, as they trod the path back to their youth. 'They were the happiest years of our lives,' was the unanimous verdict. 'Bill was tremendous fun and everyone respected him. You could not dislike him.'

Edrich exuded an identical appeal for other young men in his late Middlesex phase. Peter Parfitt, a fellow native of Norfolk, said: 'In the early 1940s Bill went through a stage when he was regarded as an out-landish inebriate. But as he got older people idolised him because he was consistent and never varied.' Bill was never given the cold shoulder, except perhaps as the motoring madhatter. Jack Belton always insisted on driving; at other times the law imposed a ban to put this out of the question. Alan Moss related one audacious motoring anecdote which brought a con-tingent of Middlesex players within a hairsbreadth of disaster.

The incident occurred following a match against Kent at Maidstone. Bill's passengers in his Mercedes were John Warr, Sid Brown and Moss. 'We were coming like the clappers down this hill,' said Moss. 'Suddenly, Bill started pumping away on the pedals with his feet.' Warr said: 'What's wrong, master, brakes gone?' Bill replied: 'Yes, they (expletive deleted) well have.' He frantically attempted to get the car into gear and slow it down. The prospect of a frightening colli-sion loomed. 'We hurtled down towards the main road and over a roundabout,' recalled Moss. 'Bill somehow manoeuvred us into the traffic and we didn't hit a thing. When we looked back, we couldn't see a gap in either direction. It was a remarkable escape.'

Among the less perilous but just as unnerving activ-ities in the Middlesex quarters were the notoriously competitive games of cards when rain stopped play. The autocratic Gubby Allen once eavesdropped on a game of brag. He was horrified to discover a mountain of money – cheques and cash amounting to around £90 – in the centre of the dressing-room table. Edrich and Denis Compton were the senior players in the young company. Allen peremptorily called Bill away and sternly rebuked him for looting the boys' pocket money. Bill politely listened to the verbal broadside. He then declared both his and Denis's innocence. 'Don't be silly, skipper, it is all our money in the middle.'

Alan Moss has paid tribute to the generosity of two great sportsmen. 'Bill and Denis were big spenders. They were never mean and would give you the world, if they had it. Ten minutes later they would have forgotten the gesture. If there was a consequent crisis in their affairs, they would cross that bridge when they came to it.' Edrich, in his later years as a successful financial consultant, was equally generous in his counsel. Brian Johnston and Michael Denison, the actor, and fellow Middlesex cricketers were among a host of people who hugely benefited from his transactions and were grateful to him for his advice. Bill, despite the urgings of his manager, who knew about his high income need, did not make the same provisions for his own future.

Geoffrey Howard, as a tour manager, was also aware of Edrich's financial profligacy. One of his duties was to call upon the players to pay any hotel extras (not chargeable to the MCC) which they had incurred. These were discussed at individual interviews each month. One England player, a tight-fisted character, disputed every item in his bill amounting to eighteen shillings. Edrich was next in line. He could not help overhearing the prolonged talk. 'I wouldn't like your job, Geoffrey. I feel sorry for you.' Howard replied: 'Stop being sorry for me and start feeling sorry for yourself. You owe me £38!' Bill hardly raised an eyebrow. 'If you say so, Geoffrey,' he said. He appended his name to the account with a flourish and a smile, as if he was signing a mess bill. Howard added: 'Bill had probably spent most of the money on long-distance telephone calls to his girlfriends.'

Illuminating the life of Bill Edrich was an innate

grace and courtesy. Donald Carr, as a thirteen-year-old schoolboy, first opposed him in a friendly match against a RAF XI at Mickleover, near Derby. In 1940 Bill was stationed at the nearby training unit at Burniston. Carr recalled how his elder brother, David, in this scratch game, bowled their famous opponent for four runs. 'Bill was then the fastest bowler in England; but he only bowled donkey drops at us boys; and, to our immense delight, we beat the RAF team.'

There was a remarkable sequel to this cheering episode. Carr, at three days' notice, replaced George Pope in the England team to play the Australian Services in the 'Victory' Test at Lord's in 1945. It was his first-class debut and an unexpected baptism. 'I poled up at Lord's with my cricket bag on the Saturday morning,' said Carr. The officer cadet, attired in his battledress, looked shyly around the dressing-room. There was a cursory glance from the England captain, Wally Hammond. His assumption that Carr, then unknown to him, was carrying the bag of another player was understandable. In the opposite corner of the room there was a signal of recognition. The bearer of the inquiring look was Bill Edrich. 'I think we've met before,' he said. 'Come here, lad, and strip next to me.'

Carr was a surprised young man, unable to believe that Edrich, after his hazardous years, could possibly have remembered their fleeting encounter at the beginning of the war. 'He was a lovely person and I will never forget him for such a wonderful gesture.'

CHAPTER 9

Twinning the Records

'It was the last great pyrotechnic display before the game was taken over by egalitarian times. The combined run spree of Edrich and Compton has not been approached to this day.
– *Basil Easterbrook*

The home fires burned high and low in the magical summer of 1947. A mood of escapism prevailed among the war-wearied populace in days meant for happiness. A fever of absenteeism caught hold as the cricket crowds, scorning unpalatable austerity, flocked to watch the exploits of two great cricketers. The soothing balm of record runs was at odds with the desperate economic crisis. Amid the sporting excitement fears were expressed that county cricket – and the tour by the Australians in the following season – might have to be abandoned in the interests of national survival.

The threat was averted and the charms of cricket were renewed in this troubled peace time. As the touring South Africans and their accompanying wives gratefully acknowledged, they were given a comfortable ride in terms of hospitality off the field. They came to a beleaguered country disfigured by bomb damage and reduced to minimal food rations. All around them austerity tightened its grip; but it scarcely touched the tourists, who were sensible of their privileged position as feted and conspicuously popular guests. From meagre larders their hosts miraculously extracted such delicacies as plaice and chicken, and sausages and kippers for breakfast.

'What a summer it was that burned down that year,' related the South African cricket writer, Louis Duffus. 'It seemed to bleach even the dark future of a crisis-ridden kingdom, and sent seventeen cricketers bowling along, with accumulating batting averages, past fields of golden crops and the serene sights of a cloudless season.'

The sun did, in fact, sizzle this year, but late. The temperature dropped to freezing-point at Worcester, and it rained all one day in Dublin. At Old Trafford, in July, the north-west winds gusted mightily from the Stretford End to topple the sightscreen and scatter the bails. They said it was like watching cricket in mid-winter. 'Drink your tea, love, while it's wa-arm,' urged one thoughtful Lancastrian vendor.

There is, of course, nothing like a good blow to clear the air; the gladdening warmth, as the chills dispersed, cast a glow on the lavish entertainment. The joys of the union of Edrich and Compton, the champions in the fight against dullness, brought pleasure to thousands of post-war supporters. They were the perfect matching pair; twins in comradeship if not by birthright. It was an alliance which has few equals, at the county and Test levels, in the history of the game. As R. C. Robertson-Glasgow described them, 'They are the mirror of hope and freedom and gaiety; heroic in the manner of school stories; the inspiration, and quarry, of the young, because in a game that threatens to grow old in the saddest sense, they do not outgrow the habit, the very mistakes of youth. They seem to be playing not only in front of us and for us, but almost literally with us.'

3,539.

BATTLING BILL
In War and Peace!

Roy ULLYETT.

A glorious evening of reminiscence was spent at the Hilton Hotel, London, in October 1984. An illustrious assembly of diners gathered to pay homage to Edrich and Compton. The guests were there to rejoice in a spirit which everyone believed them both to personify. It was a celebration of a proud association which had started fifty years earlier. They watched the clips of newsreel film, which had been put together as a celluloid tribute, flickering on the screen like a silent film of the Chaplin era. The perky cavaliers walked out to bat again, the Movietone News cockerel crowed its overture, and the commentator's impeccably long-vowel sounds reached back into the past. Roy Hattersley, the ardent Yorkshireman, with memories of his infatuation with Len Hutton, was able to cast aside the old rivalry and pay his tribute to the two paragons of the sophisticated south. Hattersley described them as the apotheosis of effortless superiority. 'Both were batsmen of professional technique rather than flawless elegance,' he said.

John Arlott, in his own recollections of their mastery, recalled 1947 as a 'legendary time of gallant cricket, played in the glory of sunlight'. The massacre of the South African bowling was of towering proportions. Altogether, during a remarkable summer, the tourists conceded to the Middlesex pair over 2,000 runs, 1,187 to Compton and 870 to Edrich. Of these, Edrich scored 709 and Compton 745 in seven consecutive innings for Middlesex and England against the visitors. Each of their dizzily careering figures, harvested in magnificent style, exceeded the record of 3,518 runs established by Tom Hayward in 1906. Compton's 3,816 runs included 18 centuries, which surpassed Jack Hobbs' tally of 16 in 1925; and they included six hundreds – and a 97 for the MCC – against the South Africans. Edrich, at one stage the leader in the record chase, totalled 3,539 runs. He vied with his partner in a season of incredible virtuosity. 'We helped each other,' said Bill, 'and between us we didn't give the bowlers much hope.'

'It was our destiny to be touring England when these two men reached the peak of their form – and to bowl at them for hours and hours on end. We were just unlucky to bump into them,' said Lindsay Tuckett, the South Africans' opening bowler and one of the victims of the bombardment. 'The big thing about Edrich and Compton was that they worked so well together. Bill had usually been at the wicket for around half-an-hour when Denis came in. He would nurse his partner through his first 20 runs. They were clever. As soon as you started worrying them, they began to steal short singles – tip and run, we called it – and this was really upsetting. Blocking them meant that we left other gaps in the field.'

Tuckett considered that Edrich was the likeliest of the two batsmen to succumb to the bowling because of his unbridled aggression. 'He had a penchant for the on-side; his on-drives and pulls were invested with a resonant power. He thumped the ball hard, getting well over and on top of it.' Edrich was never afraid to loft the ball, which gave at least a vestige of a chance to the perspiring bowlers. By contrast, Compton, in Tuckett's view, was very thorough in his approach to batting. 'He was unbelievably quick on his feet, nimble as a ballet dancer, and he seemed to position himself sooner than other batsmen. He played some unorthodox and cheeky shots, which would have ensured a severe reprimand from any coach.' Tuckett remembered his exasperation as Compton waltzed yards down the wicket. 'Sometimes he would stay there, sometimes he would go back. It was most disturbing in its effect upon your rhythm and concentration.'

Compton was at his most brazen in his scampers

down the wicket in the second Test at Manchester. 'He was like a ruddy yo-yo, forward and back down the track,' said Tuckett. 'I'd done a lot of bowling, fifty overs in the innings; and I was tired and irritable.' As Compton again ventured down the pitch, Tuckett propelled the ball at his head. Denis evaded the challenge. With one hand on the ground to keep his balance, he flourished his bat with the other to prevent the ball from going through to the wicket-keeper. 'It was the fantastic reaction of a great player,' said Tuckett.

Athol Rowan, the South African off-spinner, in one discussion with his fellow spinner, left-armer Norman 'Tufty' Mann, devised a plan: 'We thought we had a better chance of getting them out if we tossed the ball over their heads.' Mann was the first to try out the manoeuvre. Compton, in his shuffle down the wicket, was suddenly confronted by the ball flying about his head. 'Denis just played a tennis serve and it went straight to the boundary,' related Rowan.

Mann, who died at the age of thirty-one only five years later, was grudgingly accurate as a bowler. He headed the South African bowling averages in 1947 and on the following tour in 1951. He began his first Test appearance with eight successive maiden overs to Edrich and Compton. Altogether he conceded only 104 runs in eighty overs on a 'feather-bed' Nottingham wicket. On the second day of the fourth Test at Leeds he took four wickets for 59 runs in 42 overs. His immaculate length was reflected in the fact that he bowled 350 maidens in his 954 overs on the tour. His spinning partner, Athol Rowan, was the only South African bowler to take a hundred wickets; but in the Tests he was expensive with 12 wickets at an average of nearly 56.

Louis Duffus dwelt upon the development by Edrich

of a formidable defence, allied with intense concentration, since his pre-war tour of South Africa. 'His movements are quick and on the off-side he faithfully follows the line of the ball with his bat. He excels in on-side play, exploiting a range of strokes from a drive wide of the bowler to neat deflections to fine leg.' Duffus thought that Compton was the more versatile of the two players. 'He is a polished, brilliant batsman who commands all the conventional strokes and, like Bradman, from whose example he may possibly have benefited, daringly exploits some which contravene the canons of correct cricket. Perhaps more than anything his prolific scoring is founded upon the high art of placing the ball.'

John Dewes, a younger colleague who played for Middlesex from 1948 to 1956, believed that the excellence of the partnership of Edrich and Compton lay in the fact that, in many ways, they were at the opposite ends in batting methods. 'Bill was at his best against fast bowling and he was prepared to be unorthodox against slow bowling. Denis was so much the all-rounder. He would do it with twinkletoes and the poor bowler wouldn't know where to bowl next.' Dewes considered that Edrich, to some extent, was refreshed in appetite by the presence of Compton. 'He might not have achieved the record he had without Denis at the other end. But as a pair they made opposing attacks look so stupid.'

Roy Tattersall, the Lancashire and England off-spinner, was another admiring witness. 'Denis did have a greater variety of shots, some played off his backside. Both of them could break a bowler's heart; but they were always giving you a chance.' Tattersall confessed that 'Bill wasn't on my mantelpiece too many times'. But he intriguingly and delightedly recalled that he had claimed the wicket of another feared batsman,

Len Hutton, between ten and a dozen times. It was an accomplishment to savour. In a Roses context, especially on one side of the Pennines, it had a particular significance.

Edrich always acknowledged the unique qualities of his batting companion. In their momentous summer Compton basked in an adulation to outrival that accorded to a famous film star. 'Denis was a genius,' said Bill. 'He used to play shots that nobody dreamed about; they came out of his imagination.' Geoffrey Howard also recalled the audacious improvisations of Compton. 'He is one of only two players – Ken Grieves was the other – I've seen who actually hit a yorker on his leg stump through the covers for four.'

Sir Donald Bradman said that although their names were indelibly linked – like salt and pepper – it was always Compton and Edrich, and not the other way round. 'And so perhaps Edrich will never be accorded the distinction that his skills merited,' he added tellingly. Jack Plimsoll, a South African quick left-arm bowler, agreed with this: 'Bill would have been on a pinnacle if Denis hadn't been around,' he said. Alfred Gover, on the other hand, believed that the divide tended to be exaggerated, at least in terms of their respective run-rates. 'Denis was more attractive to watch, but he didn't really overshadow Bill in run-scoring.' Another writer in *The Cricketer* said of the pair that in style and technique no twins were less identical: 'Compton was a cavalier who could ad-lib his strokes: Edrich, equally well-equipped in stroke production, was more down-to-earth. He was an efficient plumber who knew his taps.'

Geoffrey Howard described Compton as a 'nominator', who would promise and deliver a century on a certain day. On other occasions he would tell the next batsman: 'I shan't be long. Make sure you're ready.' Howard said Edrich was less content. 'Bill would want to make a hundred every time he went in to bat.'

The rhapsodic notes of the batting were smudged in the orchestration of the running between the wickets. Their frequent misunderstandings, according to Hubert Doggart, gave rise to the joyous enunciation of the 'three-call trick'. The first call was the basis for negotiation, the second a considered statement of policy. The third in the sequence was: 'Damn, I've done it again,' as one or other of the batsmen made their way back to the pavilion. John Warr said: 'Denis was the only player to call his partner and wish him luck at the same time.'

Jack Robertson, in more serious vein, could never understand why Compton, as a top-class player, was such a bad judge of a run. 'If you were batting with Denis, you had to take over and, when necessary, refuse a call quickly and firmly. Bill and I were always prompt in this way, and we generally survived.' Robertson said the rules changed when Denis was paired with the lower order batsmen. 'They would not, perhaps, want to say "No" to the great man. In their eagerness to assist him, they might be run out by inches on the third run.' Robertson added: 'None of the run-outs were intentional. Denis was not a selfish man.'

George Mann, as the Middlesex captain in 1948 and 1949, believed that the hazards accumulated over the course of time. Bill became, perhaps justifiably, rather nervous about what was going to happen and runs were lost on occasions. Their major partnerships did present ample opportunities for confusion. 'It was always a little worrying for those of us in the pavilion to watch the hesitations and discussions when both of them were out of the crease,' recalled Mann.

153

Compton himself conceded that he was not the greatest judge of a run. He could not offer an explanation of this deficiency. In his own defence, he maintained that he ran himself out more often than his partners. Edrich, Peter May and Godfrey Evans were adamant that he presented few anxieties as a runner. He once asked each of his England colleagues to confirm their unanimity on this vexed question. They all replied: 'As long as we ran straightaway when you called, it was all right. If there was just a second's hesitation, we had problems.'

In the drawn first Test at Nottingham in 1947, South Africa came tantalisingly close to victory. 'Our team had the aspirations of a lifetime within reach and could not grasp them,' wrote Louis Duffus. South Africa totalled 533 and England were surprisingly dismissed for 208 on a perfect batting wicket. 'What a situation for a visiting side in the first match of a Test series!' exclaimed Duffus. England, following on, lost four wickets for 170. They were rescued in the nick of time by Compton and his captain, Norman Yardley. It did not escape notice, to judge from the smiles of the buoyant Springboks, that Evans, the next man in, was the last of the recognised batsmen. The smiles should have broadened before the stand developed. England still needed 41 runs to make South Africa bat again when Yardley was crucially missed by Bruce Mitchell at first slip off Tuckett. It was the turning-point of the game. The recovery was sealed by a record fifth-wicket partnership in England of 237 runs. Compton scored 163 and Yardley's tenaciously garnered 99 deserved the accolade of a century. A wickedly brilliant 74 by Evans was followed by the last back-breaking straw of 51 runs piled on outrageously and protractedly by England's tenth-wicket pair of Eric Hollies and Jack Martin. 'I shall never forget the forty-five minutes of that last partnership and its emotions that sank from imminent jubilation to exasperating despair,' recalled Duffus.

Sir Leonard Hutton praised the artistry and enthused about the classical dimensions of the strokeplay of Alan Melville. The South African captain scored two centuries – 189 and 104 not out – in the Nottingham Test to add to his 103 in the last meeting between the two countries at Durban in 1939. He was to hit another century in the second Test at Lord's to equal Jack Fingleton's record of four centuries in successive Test innings. Melville and Dudley Nourse, in the first innings at Trent Bridge, scored 319 together for the third wicket in four hours to establish a South African Test record for any wicket. 'Afterwards Melville sat in the shower-room, happily but physically exhausted,' wrote Louis Duffus. 'I'm glad I managed to do well,' said Alan Melville. 'A lot of people thought I was too old.'

The slimly-built Melville was in his thirty-eighth year in 1947. The strain of the tour caused him to lose 20 lb. in weight. Jim Swanton also recalled that the food rations in England were not enough to sustain the tourists. 'They were all absolutely shattered by the end of the summer,' he said. Lindsay Tuckett said that they were praying for rain in the final weeks of the season. He was burdened by a persistent groin injury, sustained during a long bowling spell at Nottingham; and in his unaccustomed round of daily cricket there was no time for rest. There was also for the wearied South Africans a sense of hopelessness as the rampaging Edrich and Compton reinforced their toil.

On their arrival in England in April the tourists had been the guests of the British Sportsman's Club at the Savoy Hotel in London. Bill Edrich had welcomed them on behalf of the MCC. A Tom Webster cartoon on display depicted a smiling lion dressed as an umpire. It was cheeringly inscribed with the words: 'Greetings to South Africa. The British umpire welcomes you. May your stumps be small and your bats tremendous and the ball be always joyful for you.'

The friendly greeting set the tone for a series, regarded by Norman Yardley as the happiest of his career. Duffus related that large crowds stood in queues for admission – and sometimes throughout the games. At Lord's, in the second Test, the atmosphere of enthusiasm was reflected in the besieging crowds. The gates were closed half an hour before the start, with an official figure of 30,600 inside the ground and an estimated 10,000 vainly waiting for admission beyond its walls. The multitude, spilling on to the edges of the boundaries, watched a sedate opening partnership by Hutton and Washbrook. In ninety minutes before lunch, England scored only 58 runs, which included only one boundary by Washbrook. Hutton, with elaborate care, spent nearly two hours in scoring 18, and was then bowled by Rowan.

South Africa bowled the statutory 55 overs, then in force to allow the quicker taking of the new ball. It brought them the wicket of Washbrook, jugglingly caught by Tuckett at slip off Dawson. It was an achievement of mixed blessing, since it brought together Edrich and Compton. 'There was no more peace for South Africa,' related J. M. Kilburn. 'If the first wicket stand had done anything, it was to survive an awkward period, and Edrich and Compton accepted an inheritance of ease in full appreciation. The only essential difference between the two batsmen lay in the choice, or direction, of their strokes. Edrich collected most of his boundaries through on-drives, Compton stormed the covers with off-drives and square-cuts. As a variation, they ran innumerable short singles. Their joint mastery was complete.'

The Springboks were left to repent a missed stumping chance by Lindsay off Mann when Edrich had scored 47. The costliness of this lapse, as in Yardley's escape at Nottingham, was emphasised by Louis Duffus: 'Missed chances in a Test match grow magnified in retrospect,' he declared. 'But there is no doubt that in the first two games against England the South Africans could not clinch vital opportunities, which in one case might have won them the game, and in the other saved them from defeat.'

The weather at Lord's waxed with increasing brilliance, according to Duffus, to match Edrich and Compton in their imperious command. 'As the two picked up the pace of the pitch, the flow of runs broadened and deepened,' related John Arlott. The London *Times* reported: 'Suddenly a storm of runs burst upon the South Africans. Just as it is difficult to recollect the first flash of lightning, so it is to remember the particular stroke which set this assault in motion. It may have been one superb forcing shot by Edrich off the back foot which sent the ball scuttling to the boundary; or perhaps it was an off-drive by Compton to the Mound.' By tea the total had advanced to 187; Edrich and Compton had scored 111 at better than a run a minute. By the close of play, the Middlesex pair added 216 runs. Edrich reached his first Test century in England and Compton his second 100 in successive innings.

The *Rand Daily Mail* in Johannesburg reported on the accuracy of South Africa's spinners, Mann and Rowan, and the unflagging and often inspired fielding. The two bowlers shared 118 overs, half those bowled in the innings, in conceding 273 runs. 'The South Africans still bowled a length and set a tight field,' commented Kilburn. 'But the willingness to accept risk can turn a good length ball into a half-volley, and when a batsman is hitting the ball as he chooses, there are not enough fieldsmen.'

Edrich and Compton were in full cry on the following morning. They advanced the score, not with hilarity (the South Africans did not permit a full-blooded assault), but with certainty. There was a sudden spate of runs when Melville at last introduced his leg-spinner, Ian Smith, into the attack. Smith had twice taken Edrich's wicket at Nottingham. He responded ferociously to the menace. Smith, in his first over, pitched the ball so irregularly that Edrich struck four deliveries to the leg-side boundary. After lunch, both Edrich and Compton sacrificed their wickets in the quest for quick runs. England, at one stage 466 for 2, lost six wickets for 88 runs. Tuckett, helped by two dazzling catches by Rowan at short-leg, reaped a well-earned reward by taking five wickets for 20 runs in his final spell of seven overs.

Edrich was bowled by Mann. He had scored 189 and his partnership of 370 runs with Compton was the highest for the third wicket in matches between the two countries. It is still an English record. 'It was,' said *The Times* correspondent, 'a splendid innings by a splendid cricketer, who is always well and truly in the game. Once, in attacking Rowan, he had been lucky to feel the ball glance off the edge of his bat, but for the rest his innings was as near as could be immaculate. Compton, in his double-century, as ever placed the ball to beat the well-set field. He was once beaten by a leg-break from Mann, but these rare mistakes serve only to emphasise the perfection of their craftsmanship.' Louis Duffus, discussing the merits of South Africa's aggressors, described Compton as the personification of confidence. 'It almost seems that he gives inspiration to Edrich, who seldom plays better than when he is at the other end.'

Duffus, contemplating England's massive 554, was unfazed by the total and South Africa's deficit of 227 on the first innings. The England bowling was by no means hostile and his compatriots had, after all, also topped 500 in the first Test. He believed that a draw was a reasonable expectation. His optimism was confounded in the ensuing events. 'It was our batting that snapped, not in one fell collapse but in unexpected moments just when it seemed most stable. This was the primary cause of South Africa's defeat by ten wickets, sudden frailties of batsmanship coupled with opportunely brilliant feats by England in the field.

'Before we had felt the first premonition of defeat,' Duffus went on, 'the last morning was upon us and Edrich had sensationally laid low Nourse's middle stump with the first ball of the day. For South Africa it was the most fateful ball of the game. A flame had suddenly leapt across a seemingly fireproof roadway and the sounds of destruction were all at once crackling overhead.'

From that moment on all that remained to be settled was the margin of England's victory. It was one of those occasions when the leg-spinner Doug Wright could do no wrong. His length was good and he exploited sharp spin and lift to take ten wickets in the match. Edrich's contribution was three wickets – the prized ones of Melville, Viljoen and Nourse – for 31 runs in 13 overs; and he sealed a superb all-round display by ending the resistance of Mitchell (80) with an acrobatic catch off Wright. A deflection struck the wicket-keeper's pad and the ball flew wide of first slip. Edrich flung himself sideways at full stretch and then, with a terrific lurch, he grasped the ball safely in his right hand.

The presentation of Edrich as the batsman all-rounder, while sound in general terms, did him less than full justice. His South African rivals thought he was undervalued as a bowler. Jack Plimsoll remembered the heave of his opponent's powerful shoulders, which caused the ball to speed dangerously off the wicket. Lindsay Tuckett said Bill had the knack of getting wickets at opportune moments. 'He upset our applecart at Lord's, taking two quick wickets to set us back, and this brought about our defeat.' Bruce Mitchell, the implacable batting veteran of three tours of England, recalled the need for care against Edrich. 'He had a natural away-swinger and the ball came through nice and fast.'

Jackie McGlew, a later South African tourist in 1951 (as well as 1955 and 1960), offered a corresponding view of the bowling qualities of a 'cheerful and true friend'. He endorsed the widely held opinion that Edrich was the fastest bowler in England in 1947. 'He used to come charging in at you like a 100-yards sprinter and then jet-propel the ball at you at tremendous pace. Bill's energy and ability to crack open an opposition side was always feared.' McGlew also praised Edrich as a quicksilver fieldsman. 'He was tremendously agile. As a slip fieldsman, he had hands that could grasp anything within reach.'

Charles Fortune, the doyen of South African broadcasters, described Edrich as a resolute but genial player. He considered that the Englishman's battles against South Africa spanned the productive years of his career. Fortune remembered Bill's gallantry and 'the smile just lurking around the corner of his face'. Edrich could afford to relax into a full-throated chuckle of glee after his magnificent all-round cricket in the third Test against South Africa at Old Trafford. He scored 191 in another exhilarating partnership with Compton;

and, amid fears of the demands being placed on his stamina, bowled 57 overs for a haul of eight wickets. Wally Hammond, his old mentor, was among those who warned of the dangers of overbowling a premier batsman. 'Edrich is a glutton for work,' conceded Hammond. 'When he starts waving his arms about in the slips, it is a sign that he is anxious to be bowling again.'

'The splendid crowd at Old Trafford found themselves suddenly transported after tea to unusual ecstasies,' related Neville Cardus. This was a felicitous overture to the batting assault of Edrich and Compton. England, replying to South Africa's first innings total of 339, considered by John Arlott as a match-winning score, had lost two wickets for 96 runs. 'Hutton,' wrote Cardus, 'incredibly unrelated at present to his own superbly organised technique, fell to a catch at the wicket at 43. A moment later Washbrook could not get his bat out of the way of a vicious ball from Tuckett outside the off-stump. It came up with fangs at an acute angle.'

Discretion was the keynote of the opening stanza performed by Edrich and Compton. The pitch was fiery in keeping with the behaviour of the wickets at Old Trafford in this season. Of the 26 innings played before the Test, only four had reached 300. After the heavy rain, it was demonstrably in harness with pace and the admirable length of Tuckett and Plimsoll. Edrich, forced into taut defence, was restricted to five runs in half an hour. 'For a while it was the sort of wicket which calls for keen eyesight and compels a batsman to think himself clever to use the middle of the bat,' related Cardus. 'Edrich played back and forward with time to spare; there was a propulsion even in those strokes which possessed none but wicket-saving intent.'

161

The dangerous advance of the South African bowlers was at first curbed and then countered in a flush of remarkable strokeplay. 'Edrich,' said John Arlott, 'took his life in his hands to hit Plimsoll off before he could wreck the England innings.'

The momentum of the partnership was hastened when Melville took the new ball. It almost seemed to enhance the clarity of the batsmen's vision under the lowering clouds. The shine on the ball rapidly disappeared. Three overs yielded 38 runs and 60 came in half an hour, of which Edrich scored 42. Plimsoll was hit for 40 in five overs.

The brutal fusillade began with an on-drive by Edrich off Plimsoll for four. He then sallied down the pitch, and with his favourite pull-drive, struck the same bowler far over long-on for six. The next ball was guided sweetly across the green for another four. Compton in the following over, bowled by Tuckett, edged a boundary through the slips, then cut and drove two more fours which defied interception. Plimsoll, in his next over, was twice hit for six by Edrich, one of them a glorious full-blooded pull which sent the ball hurtling among the spectators.

'Against all probability,' commented Arlott, 'Edrich and Compton were once more on top, batting as if obvious difficulties did not exist. More than once the ball stood waist-high – even chest-high – from a length, only for one or the other batsman to cut it, hook it, or steer it wide of the field with an assurance which confirmed all that had been ever said of their greatness in this summer.' Arlott tellingly added that Jim Laker, in taking nineteen wickets against Australia on the same ground nine years later, achieved his feat with less help from the pitch.

A vintage partnership ended when Compton, having reached his third successive Test century, was caught by Tuckett at short-leg off Dawson. The stand had staggeringly realised 228 runs in ten minutes over three hours. The savagery of the enterprise, and the skills which made it possible, were acknowledged by Jim Kilburn. 'Throughout the day,' he wrote in the *Yorkshire Post*, 'the ball was a menace to the fingers and ribs and a constant stimulative to the slip fieldsmen. It was a wicket to give bowlers hope and yet permitting batsmen to make strokes. It was, in fact, a wicket fit for cricket, and magnificently did Edrich and Compton play on it. They not only collected runs but created them.'

Edrich, on a rain-curtailed third day and on a rapidly deteriorating wicket, completed an epic innings in a blaze of strokes. His 191 (out of 375) occupied five hours and twenty minutes, and included three sixes and 22 fours. 'He was missed once but a hundred times worthy of fortune,' enthused one observer.

England lost their last four wickets for 48 runs. South Africa required 139 to avoid an innings defeat. They suffered an early setback when Dyer was bowled by Gladwin. Mitchell was caught by Hutton at slip, off a ball from Compton which kicked chest-high. Melville, after passing his 50 serenely, was clean bowled by Edrich, who tore out his middle stump and sent it whirling through the air back to Evans. Nourse, with a belligerent century, as gallant as any in the series, added 121 with Viljoen for the fourth wicket. They frustrated England for an hour and a half before Edrich exuberantly yorked Nourse to stifle mounting concern. South Africa, with a draw apparently certain, lost their last seven wickets for 50 runs in an hour.

England needed 129 to win in two and a half hours. It was by no means a leisurely stroll on a wicket drying out under the sun. Washbrook was aware of the impending perils. He scored 40 out of

63 for the first wicket in under an hour. The spinning zeal of Mann accounted for Hutton and Compton. Cardus thought that, with victory on the doorstep, 'it was gently ironical to see Edrich and Compton coerced into unwonted anxiety and parsimony'. Arlott more considerately remembered Edrich displaying the 'alacrity of a cat' as he took command of the situation. The marathon man at Old Trafford was still there at the end to steer his team to victory by seven wickets. He had been on the field for all but half an hour of the match.

John Arlott said the match might go down in history as the most disastrously wasted opportunity for bowlers in any Test. 'It was a savage commentary on the others that the most successful bowler of the match was Bill Edrich with eight wickets: no one else took more than four.'

Neville Cardus, watching Edrich at Manchester, had impishly observed: 'It is clear that the time has come when something needs to be done, legally if possible, about him. It might be fair and proper to put him on a run ration, a book of coupons to be handed to the umpire at the promptings of vigilant scorers. A proviso might be made that no other ration book bearing the name, or names, of Edrich, be negotiable.'

Edrich's average at this stage was 101. By the start of August he had scored 2,358 runs to Compton's 2,071, averaging 107 against his partner's 76. He seemed certain to be the first to reach 3,000 runs. He had also taken 67 wickets at an average of 22.58 runs each. A shoulder injury, sustained against Kent at Canterbury at the end of the month, ended his bowling for the season. It prevented him from emulating Jim Parks senior's record of 3,003 runs and 101 wickets established by the Sussex all-rounder in 1937. The gulf in runs between Edrich and Compton was narrowed in the final stages of the season. Denis did overtake his partner to pass Hayward's record in the match between a South of England team and Sir Pelham Warner's XI at Hastings in September. Seven days later it was Bill's turn to reach that milestone. Compton was, inevitably, his encouraging partner in another violent conquest at The Oval. Denis hit 246, then his highest score in England, and Bill 180, as Middlesex, the champion county, beat the Rest of England by nine wickets.

South Africa were spared further martyrdom when Edrich withdrew from the England team in the final Test at The Oval. Jack Robertson was his deputy in a match made memorable by the concentrated vigil of Bruce Mitchell, whose unbeaten 189, following a century in the first innings, carried the Springboks to within 28 runs of victory. At Leeds, in the preceding Test, Hutton restored his England credentials, if they had ever been in doubt, with a masterly century before a delighted home crowd. Edrich and Compton were relative bystanders, compiling only 73 runs between them, as England won by ten wickets. Ken Cranston, the Lancashire all-rounder, in the finest feat of his short Test career, took four wickets in an over without conceding a run to end South Africa's second innings.

Middlesex, runners-up in five successive seasons, at last hoisted the championship pennant at Lord's in 1947. It was their first title since 1921 and it was recorded under the dynamic leadership of Walter Robins in his last season as captain. In all matches, four Middlesex batsmen – Edrich, Compton, Robertson and Brown – scored 12,193 runs. The tally included 8,213 in the championship, in which the quartet obtained 33 of the county's 37 individual hundreds. Robertson and Brown shared nine century opening stands, including 310 and 222 in successive innings. The triple hundred against Nottinghamshire was scored in three and a half hours. It beat the Middlesex first-wicket record of 306 achieved by Warner and James Douglas, also against Notts, in 1904.

Denis Compton, looking back at a wonderful year, has stressed that the key to Middlesex's success was the opportunism of their cricket. 'We had an inspiring captain in Robins. He would insist upon 400 runs by tea, or soon afterwards. Anyone who was out of form was firmly told to get out and let someone else come in. This gave us about an hour's bowling against the opposition. We invariably got two or three wickets in this time.'

Denis deplores the recent introduction of the four-day championship programme. 'It will encourage the moderate player with not too many shots. In our three-day cricket we had some terrific finishes. The attitude was one of a sense of urgency.'

Jack Robertson also recalled the captaincy demands of Robins, who would not brook slow play, either by his own team, or the opposition. Robins could be ruthless in imposing an increased tempo, even when Robertson and his partner, Sid Brown, had posted a century before lunch. 'I want it three times as fast from now on,' would be his instruction during the interval. Robertson said: 'After lunch Sid and I would go mad and probably get out. Of course, one or other of us did enjoy big partnerships with Bill and Denis. But it was very nice to have them come down after us.'

Geoffrey Howard, as a neutral observer, put forward the argument that Middlesex would not have scored the runs they did, or as rapidly, if Robins had not been captain. 'It was a beautiful summer and the wickets were good. Robbie would say: "I shall be declaring at five o'clock whatever runs we have on the board." He needed time and Middlesex batted right down the order on many occasions.' Howard believed Edrich and Compton would not have made as many runs for Yorkshire, where the balance of the team was different. 'The circumstances at Lord's did help Bill and Denis in their marvellous achievements.'

The drive for quick runs was dictated by the limitations of the Middlesex attack. Edrich and Laurie Gray shouldered an immense burden as new-ball bowlers. Jack Young, the left-arm spin bowler, who also opened the bowling on occasions, was paired with the veteran, Jim Sims. The two spinners shared nearly 1,800 overs in taking 222 wickets. Aiding them was Denis Compton who experimented, often profitably, with his newly discovered unorthodox left-arm spin. So the accent was on securing a cushion of runs to allow maximum time to dismiss opponents twice. The spinners had the incentive to be extravagant and buy their wickets, if it proved to be necessary. In 1947 Middlesex passed 400 eleven times, and failed to total 100 only once. They declared in twenty innings, against three opposing totals of 400, six of less than 100, and two declarations, both by Kent.

Alec Bedser has refuted allegations by at least one player of a later generation that there must have been easy pickings for Edrich and Compton in their record year. 'There were still some good bowlers around although they were a little older. They were by no means duffers, perhaps not exceptional; but they obeyed the principles of length and direction. They didn't bowl long-hops all day. It was a very hot summer and you do get tired, especially when you are bowling against batsmen like Bill and Denis.' Bob Appleyard, another England colleague, added: 'When big scores are being amassed, bowlers do become weary and dispirited. However strong your will, once you get tired you lose your effectiveness. As a bowler on good pitches, you know you are going to have a job to dismiss great players because everything is in their favour.' Doug Insole made another interesting point on the modest bowling forces: 'Runs were easy to come by for such fine players because they had obviously played against better all-round attacks.'

The portrayal of 1947 as an idyll for batsmen has substance in that there were 364 individual innings of 100 or more, an improvement by more than a hundred on the first (wet) post-war season. It does, though, neglect another conclusion on the economy of the leading bowlers in that summer. Tom Goddard, Jack Young and Dick Howorth, all spinners, each bowled in excess of 1,000 overs and boasted averages of little more than 17 runs per wicket. Goddard, the wily Gloucestershire off-spinner, played a major role in his county's keen struggle for the championship with Middlesex. He obtained 238 wickets at an average of 17.30 runs apiece. Altogether twenty-one bowlers took over 100 wickets. Within their ranks were such stalwarts as Doug Wright, Eric Hollies, Jack Walsh, Harold Butler, George Pope, Alfred Gover, Reg Perks and Arthur Jepson.

One of the most striking examples of Middlesex's enterprising approach occurred in an astonishing finish to the match against Leicestershire at Leicester. Edrich was captain for the first time since turning amateur in the spring. The preliminaries had yielded a cascade of runs, including a rousing double-century by Edrich. Leicestershire's first innings total of 309 was eclipsed in tumultuous style by Middlesex: Robertson and Edrich put on 159 for the second wicket, then Edrich and Compton added 277 in 130 minutes. In twenty minutes over two hours, between lunch and tea, the total rocketed upwards by 310 runs. Leicestershire, requiring 328 to avert an innings defeat, staged a notable counter-attack. Les Berry hit 154 and, vigorously partnered by Tompkin, appeared to have slammed the door on a Middlesex victory. At lunch on the third day, Leicestershire led by 17 runs, with six wickets left. Only eighty minutes remained for play.

'We didn't seem to have a chance of completing the match,' recalled Jack Robertson. The dispatch of the remaining wickets for 48 runs in 35 minutes offered a slim hope. Denis Compton remembered the thrilling finale. 'Bill said: "We're not in bad form. Why not come in with me?"' Robertson, relegated to first-wicket down, put on his pads and sat, waiting expectantly, by the sightscreen. He was not needed. Bill and Denis, chasing a target of 66 runs in 25 minutes, won the match with four minutes to spare. 'There was no panic and no swiping,' said Robertson. 'It was just good controlled cricket.'

A total of 1,405 runs scored in the match, including 663 on the second day, provided sumptuous fare for the spectators at Leicester. Denis Compton fruitfully purveyed his unorthodox slows, recommended and taught by Jack Walsh, the Australian who played for Leicestershire. Denis could be erratic in this bowling mode, but it was not always a wasteful occupation, as shown by his career figures of 622 wickets. He took three of the last six Leicestershire wickets to fall in their unexpected collapse.

Bill Edrich always acknowledged the excellence of Robertson and Brown in easing the path of Denis and himself in Middlesex's championship year. There was, however, no denying the immensity of the contributions of the two gladiators. The aggressive and match-winning pursuit of runs rarely faltered. At Northampton Edrich followed his 222 in 1946 by hitting another double hundred, 267 – the highest score of his career.

One Northampton correspondent, then a schoolboy on holiday, recalled that Edrich narrowly missed demolishing the old pavilion clock with one mighty strike. Edrich batted for five and a quarter hours, sharing a third-wicket stand of 211 with Compton, and another of 155 with George Mann. 'He then opened the bowling and clean bowled Dennis Brookes before the close of play. For half-a-dozen overs he was as fast as anyone on the county circuit. Everyone was amazed by his stamina.'

Another pulsating display in torrid heat against Surrey at The Oval produced a sympathetic response from *The Times* correspondent. 'Dante could not have thought of a harder penance for bowlers on a perfect wicket,' he reported. The only regret for Middlesex partisans was that Brown missed his century by two runs after an opening stand of 211 with Robertson. Middlesex totalled 537 for two wickets on the first day. Edrich (157) and Compton (137) added 287 in two and three-quarter hours without being separated. 'Not even the Surrey wicket-keeper, Arthur McIntyre, unbuckling his pads and going on to bowl, could shiver them,' amusingly commented one observer.

Alfred Gover, one of the hard-pressed Surrey bowlers, was free of blame. A severe cold checked his endeavours. 'I had picked up this cold in the previous match and wasn't really fit to play.' He was called into action and bowled off a short run. Edrich expressed his amazement. 'Why are you bowling off this poovy run, Alf?' he asked. 'I could play you with a broom handle off this stuff.' Gover explained the need to conserve his energies. Bill and Denis quietly conferred and then just played down the line. They both said: 'Alf has got the flu.' Gover recalled: 'Bill had a tremendous grin on his face. He just kept gently pushing the ball away. It was a lovely gesture.' It was an instance of the charity of two fine sportsmen not prepared to take advantage of a handicapped opponent. Gover said it was entirely in keeping with Bill's character. 'He was a very kind chap.'

The reverence in South Africa for the two masters of cricket is exemplified by the tribute of a later player. This witness is Johnny Waite, the Springbok wicket-keeper-batsman, who toured England in 1951, 1955 and 1960. Waite was taken by his father to watch his boyhood hero, Bill Edrich, score 219 at Durban in 1939. As he now says, he little realised that he would be opposed to Edrich when he reached manhood. One of his treasured memories, undulled by time, is the match against Middlesex in 1955.

'I know the "terrible twins" would have dearly loved one final triumph over the Springboks,' says Waite. For once Edrich and Compton were subdued, scoring only 69 runs between them. Waite points with pride to two entries in the records: D. C. S. Compton, st Waite b Tayfield, 8; and W. J. Edrich, c Waite b Heine, 25. 'No wicket-keeper could hope for two more illustrious victims, nor two such marvellous opponents, against whom it was always a privilege to play.'

CHAPTER 10

Banished by England

'Freddie Brown made a very costly error in refusing to let the selectors give him Edrich.' – *Sir Pelham Warner*

The jurors, called in to explain the omission of Bill Edrich from the MCC team in Australia in 1950–51, have indicted the selectors on the grounds of mismanagement. Edrich was at the centre of a *cause célèbre*, which now seems of trifling significance when compared with other recent indiscretions. His transgression – and lapses in conduct rebounded heavily against offenders in those days – was to enjoy himself too freely during the first Test match in the preceding summer against the West Indies at Old Trafford.

The irony of this misdeed was that he was celebrating not his own achievement, but Godfrey Evans' maiden Test century. Evans, partnered by Trevor Bailey, had pulled England out of the doldrums in adding 161 runs for the sixth wicket. Bailey recalled the events of a critical weekend for Edrich at the team's Cheshire headquarters at Alderley Edge: 'I was a little surprised to see Bill in his dinner-jacket at breakfast on the Sunday morning. But that was excusable, with a rest day ahead. The problem was that he had to be put to bed on the *Sunday* night. The porter undertook this task and Bill was so paralytic that he woke everyone up.'

Edrich, in his own version of the episode, said: 'After a personal failure in the first innings, I got involved in a party. I returned to my hotel room in the small hours, and apparently went to bed rather noisily. It wouldn't have mattered had not the chairman of the selectors, Bob Wyatt, been occupying the next room.' After the match Edrich was upbraided by Wyatt, told that his conduct was disgraceful, and that he would have to report the matter to Lord's.

'I was arraigned before a high-powered committee at Lord's,' continued Edrich. 'We've had this report from Bob Wyatt,' said Pelham Warner, who presided at the meeting. 'Would you like to withdraw your name from the list of possibles for the tour of Australia?' he asked. Edrich refused point-blank to surrender his place on a much-coveted assignment. Flashing across his mind during this tense interview was his disastrous series against Australia in 1938 and the succession of dismal failures in South Africa in the following winter. He had proved to himself at least the futility of going to bed early. In the middle of the 'timeless' Test at Durban he had accepted an invitation to a party. His 219 scored over the next two days was, he considered then and on other occasions, ample justification for his frivolities.

Edrich was a conformist on the cricket field. He reserved his formidable invective for sporting prima-donnas. Indiscipline, in any form, was repugnant to him; those players who strayed from straight dealings were guilty of a disservice to the game. He was, though, wary of people who primly objected to his lifestyle. For others, like his two England captains, Norman Yardley and Leonard Hutton, who gained his trust, he demonstrated his standards of sincerity. Geoffrey Howard, as a future MCC tour manager, was another who found Edrich an affable companion. 'There was nothing coarse about him, even in drink. If he stepped

173

out of line, and he knew he had done something wrong, he was very apologetic.' The overwhelming sadness, for Edrich's family and friends, was that his topsy-turvy private life laid waste his virtues. His divorces brought about an estrangement with the cricket hierarchy and ultimately barred him from the high office of the England captaincy.

Edrich could be an obstinate man; he was less than tactful at those times when a situation demanded a temperate response. His anger surfaced when he felt that he was being judged in an unreasonable manner. There was, almost certainly, a stormy exchange with Bob Wyatt at Manchester. According to Edrich, the deciding factor was that Freddie ' Brown, the third-choice captain for the Australian tour, did not want him in the team. Edrich said that he had sought an explanation from Brown in a meeting at Scarborough. Brown told him: 'If the selection had been left to me, I would have taken you.'

Godfrey Evans, as his party companion at Manchester, believed that greater wisdom should have prevailed. 'It was nothing serious. Bill was, perhaps, a little foolish. The penalty of a suspension for a couple of Tests would have been sufficient punishment.' Jim Swanton believed that bridges should have been mended, and the quarrel 'patched up'.

The vexatious muddle has perplexed many people. Edrich was excluded from Test cricket at an important stage in his career. A giant was felled and it did seem that the selectors were happier with dwarfs. Peter May, a future England colleague, has expressed his puzzlement at the 'enormous gaps in Edrich's Test career for a player of his ability'. Edrich himself ruefully reflected on his absences, extending over series against Australia, South Africa and India, after the escapade at Manchester. 'It amounted to a three-year suspension.

I'd done an indiscreet thing, but it didn't warrant the heavy punishment meted out.' He did not play for England again until his recall against Australia in 1953. The olive branch of reconciliation was then belatedly presented to him by Freddie Brown, then chairman of the selectors, and Bob Wyatt, another member of the panel for that series.

In 1950, at Manchester, Edrich provided evidence of his recuperative powers and his devotedness to England's cause. The protracted revelries did not prevent him from scoring 71 in a rescuing partnership with Norman Yardley. He was at the wicket, battling tenaciously, for over three hours in England's second innings. He demonstrated his expertise on a wicket which assisted spin from the first day of the match. Jim Swanton thought it was almost the worst Test wicket he had ever seen. The West Indian manager, Jack Kidney, said: 'It has been unsafe from the first ball and the batsmen have been more concerned with avoiding physical damage than in making the strokes the crowds want to see.' Swanton added: 'Eric Hollies bowled a leg-break which flew over the slips and went for four byes without touching anything. It was quite staggering.'

Wisden also reported on the state of the Old Trafford pitch: 'In their earnest desire to adjust the balance between batsmen and bowlers, the Lancashire ground committee issued an edict to the groundsman before the season that less use should be made of water and the heavy roller in the preparation of the pitch. Throughout the summer the wicket at Old Trafford was in favour of spin bowlers, and the Test proved no exception. A week of hot weather before the game hastened the crumbling effect.'

Alf Valentine, the twenty-year-old West Indian slow left-arm bowler, took eight wickets on his Test debut

175

at Old Trafford. It heralded his supremacy, along with another astonishing young man, his mesmeric and 'unreadable' spinning ally, Sonny Ramadhin. The English batsmen, said Swanton, were faced with a class of bowling unknown in their experience. 'Ram' and 'Val' were just as spellbinding in their time, as was Shane Warne for Australia in 1993. Two other spinners, Bob Berry and Eric Hollies, shared seventeen wickets for England. Edrich, Evans, Bailey and Hutton were England's batting heroes. Jeffrey Stollmeyer was equally resistant for the West Indies; he scored 78, out of a total of 183, in his team's second innings. England were the victors by 202 runs, their only success of the series.

Crawford White, the *News Chronicle* correspondent, said the West Indies did not mind their honourable defeat at Old Trafford. 'They are well used to it,' he wryly remarked. But retribution was swift and sudden when Ramadhin and Valentine – those 'two little pals of mine', in the words of the calypso – spun the West Indies to a famous victory at Lord's. The story might just possibly have taken a different course had not a catch been spilled off Edrich's bowling in the West Indies second innings. Clyde Walcott was the favoured batsman, with his score on nine. He took full advantage of his reprieve with a tremendous forcing innings. Walcott was unbeaten on 168 and he and Gerry Gomez established a then record Test stand of 211 for any West Indian wicket in England. Hubert Doggart was the fielding culprit at slip, as the ball leapt from Walcott's bat at Lord's. 'Bill bowled very fast,' recalled Doggart, 'and I was able only to knock diagonally up, but alas back, a shot which Clyde hit with his normal double-arced swing of the bat. The ball fell to the ground behind both Alec Bedser and me.'

It is beyond doubt that Edrich's summary exclusion

in 1950 would have been averted if either Norman Yardley or George Mann, the first and the second choice to captain England in Australia, had been available. They were unable to tour because of business commitments. Freddie Brown was chosen to lead the team. He enhanced his credentials with a barnstorming innings for the Gentlemen against the Players at Lord's. Brown's 122 recalled Hugh Bartlett's fierce onslaught in the corresponding fixture against the Players in 1938. He scored all but nine runs of the 131 accumulated during his 110 minutes at the wicket. He reached his century in bravura style with a six into the pavilion.

The decision to omit Edrich from the MCC party aroused the indignation of many cricket followers who considered him to be the ideal tourist. Alex Bannister, writing in the *Daily Mail* before the team was finalised, said: 'If Edrich is passed over, English cricket will want to know why, for there are some players, with steamship tickets in their pockets, who are not within a mile of his class and lack his experience and specialist fielding ability.'

George Mann recalled the friendship and supportiveness of Edrich – and Denis Compton too – during his two-year term at the county helm. It is instructive to record his unswerving admiration for Bill and his dismay that the newly turned amateur was barred by a new business venture from accompanying him when he led the MCC team to South Africa in 1948–49. 'Bill, along with my father, who was then the Middlesex president, came to Waterloo to see us off. I was sorry he couldn't be with us, and I feel sure that Bill was disappointed not to be on the tour.' Mann stressed that Edrich would have been one of the first selections for South Africa. A similar imperative would have applied if he had been able to captain England in Australia two years later. 'I wouldn't have gone without him,' he said.

Mann, typically, offered a general statement on mis-guided tour management, rather than a direct response to the rashness of Edrich's omission. He believed that it was a reflection of confidence, or the lack of it, in deal-ing with problems. 'If a player is picked for England, it does not mean that he is naturally an easy, or even a nice person. What it does mean is that he is a bloody good cricketer. As a manager, or captain, you have to cope with misdemeanours and try to help players to avoid them.'

Mann enjoyed high esteem as one of England's best captains in his brief and regrettably curtailed reign, being regarded as a disciplinarian and a firm but sym-pathetic leader of men. He maintained: ' I do think we are inclined to believe that people should not err in their behaviour. As a touring captain, you take out a team of cricketers who are a cross-section of the community. You cannot expect them all to come out of the same mould.'

Under the microscope in 1950 was the question of an England captain to succeed Norman Yardley. Freddie Brown had taken over the leadership in the final Test against the West Indies at The Oval. As early as May there were strong advocates in the media proposing Edrich as a future captain. He was, however, placed fifth in one newspaper's captaincy poll among its read-ers. Wilf Wooller, the Glamorgan captain, combative and enterprising, headed the list with twice as many votes as his rivals. He was followed by Washbrook, Hutton and Brown. The England captaincy was an honour dearly coveted by Edrich; members of his family have confided how bitterly disappointed he was not to fulfil this aspiration.

Crawford White, writing in the *News Chronicle* in 1948, considered that Edrich – 'unpopular in certain quarters' – was the only amateur fitted for the post. 'But this is only his second season as an unpaid player and MCC traditions are hard to break.' He enlisted the support of the Australians in his testimony. 'They just cannot understand why Edrich's claims are not recognised. Quite openly, rightly and unashamedly they tell you they are all amateurs, and the best player gets the captaincy.'

There seems every reason to suppose that Edrich had turned amateur in 1947 with the target of the England captaincy in mind. Trevor Bailey believed that Edrich, having followed the example of Wally Hammond's assumption of amateur status in 1938, had substantial hopes of claiming the prize. Hammond, it is thought, may himself have raised these expectations. 'As a result of the war,' said Bailey, 'Bill had moved into the officer class from which the average amateur emerged at that time. He felt he was right for the job, and went that way.'

In Bailey's view, Edrich took a calculated gamble in dismissing a bumper benefit, which would have been his due as a professional and acclaimed war hero. Bill would have been the recipient of a benefit amounting to £14,000, the equivalent of £200,000 today. Alfred Gover, another close friend, was bewildered by Edrich's decision. 'Cricket supporters, with your DFC fresh in their minds, wouldn't be able to get their hands into their pockets quick enough to reward you,' he said. Bailey also thought that Edrich might have been wiser to remain a professional. 'On the other hand, the award of the England captaincy would have counterbalanced the loss of the benefit proceeds.'

The quarrel behind the scenes in 1950 was masked by an injury. A strained back had forced Edrich to rest for several weeks, during which time he might have scored enough runs to make his omission unthinkable.

179

His tally of 1,760 runs was commendable for a curtailed season. A knee operation also kept Denis Compton out of action for two months. The subsequent events compounded the error of the non-selection of Edrich for the Australian tour. Denis, it now seems ludicrously for a player of his stature, scored only 53 runs, at an average of 7.57, in the series. He was disappointed by his failures, especially as he made runs against all the Australian Test bowlers in the state matches. In all first-class matches on the tour Compton scored 1,095 runs, and was second to Hutton in the MCC averages.

There is general agreement that England fielded a weak combination in Australia; others more forcibly described it as one of the most disastrously selected teams to leave these shores. The newcomers, Gilbert Parkhouse, David Sheppard, John Dewes and Brian Close between them totalled only 152 runs in the Tests, including 41 by Sheppard in the fourth Test at Adelaide. Hutton alone was peerless in his command. He batted magnificently to score 62 not out on the second of the three sticky wickets to tax England at Brisbane after the war. At Adelaide, he hit an unbeaten 156 (out of 272) in a vain attempt to avert another defeat. Hutton headed the batting averages in the series with 533 runs (average: 88.83). He exceeded by nearly 200 runs the aggregate of the next highest batsman, Reg Simpson.

Australia, who won an important toss, were narrow victors by 70 runs at Brisbane. At Melbourne, where Compton was absent with his recurring knee injury, England paid the price of excessive caution. In a low-scoring match, they were set a target of 179 and lost by 28 runs. Injuries deprived England of the services of Wright and Bailey in the conclusive Test at Sydney. Australia's new spinning recruit, Jack Iverson, took six wickets, and England lost by an innings. Iverson, England's *bête noire* in Australia, was a giant of a man, a six-footer and weighing over sixteen stone. He took 21 wickets in the series at an average of 15.23. The delicacies of Iverson's spin contrasted with his physique. *Wisden* reported: 'He doubled back his middle finger under the ball, imparting sharp spin, mostly off-breaks, and maintained a precise length. His flight and pace were not such to allow batsmen to leap out to him easily (the tactic was afterwards employed to nullify his advantages). His direction, at the leg stump, and carefully planned field settings permitted few liberties.'

The close gulf between the sides in the opening two Tests in Australia bolsters the strongly expressed view that Edrich was the missing link to help bind an immature force. Trevor Bailey believed that the presence of Edrich, then a better player than on his last tour of Australia in 1954–55, could have provided a winning slant. Denis Compton was another who regretted the omission. 'Bill should have been with us out there. We needed someone with backbone. He could have inspired the rest of us, and given us that vital extra strength, which we needed so badly.' Compton insisted that Edrich was the ideal tourist because of his great love of the game and fondness for those with whom he played. 'He was loyal to the game, and loyal to cricketers. Seldom, if ever, did you hear Bill say anything detrimental about another player.'

John Dewes added: 'Bill was always the man for the crisis and that is why he would have been so good. He would have made all the difference to our fortunes. Unfortunately, Denis never got going. Had he averaged at least 20, the situation would have been altered. The rest of us didn't have the confidence to use our feet against Iverson. Apart from Len, none of us measured up to the task.'

Philip Snow, then president of the Fiji Cricket Association, provided a telling postscript to the Australian tour. Snow organised a welcoming ceremony for the MCC party during the stopover in Fiji. Meeting the team face to face after the resounding Australian triumph, he was struck by the frailties of a unit which contained so many untried players. It cried out for two all-rounders of proven experience. The fielding alone of the young players had been ridiculed in the Australian media.

On his return to England shortly afterwards, Snow and his brother, C. P. (later Lord) Snow, the novelist and physicist, entertained their old friend, Sir Pelham Warner, at a dinner at the Savile Club in London. There was much discussion about the reverses in Australia. Snow expressed his great admiration for the leadership and personal performances of Freddie Brown. Warner said promptly: 'Yes, but he made one very costly error in refusing to let the selectors give him Edrich, who would inevitably have made his mark and would probably have tilted the series in England's favour. Brown should certainly have taken the risk.'

The belief now exists that Brown had second thoughts, unhappily not implemented, in seconding the decision not to include Edrich in the MCC party. Edrich's injury, while clearly not the primary cause of his non-selection for three Tests against the West Indies in 1950, did afford the selectors the opportunity to disregard him for the Australian tour. Brown, despite his later misgivings, viewed Edrich with extreme disfavour, regarding him as a problem cricketer. 'I've enough on my plate without taking Edrich,' he was reported to have said.

In his conversation with the Snow brothers Warner recalled: 'I was faced with a very similar challenge and took it. I insisted on the selectors letting me take Len Braund (the Somerset all-rounder) on my tour of

Australia in 1903–4. I guaranteed getting him sober and on to the field. He not only enjoyed the tour in every possible way, but the vitality of his all-round performances proved essential for my team.' Freddie Brown, claimed Warner, should have adopted the same course with Edrich. 'I'm sure,' he said, 'that the tour results would then have been quite different.' Listening to his ardent championship, both Philip and Charles Snow were left in no doubt as to Warner's loyalties. 'It was plain to us that his admiration for Edrich's courage as a cricketer and wartime exploits was unbounded.'

Bill Edrich had been secure enough in his self-esteem and in the approbation of the England selectors on the arrival of the Australians in 1948. There was no hint of any clouds of displeasure when he resumed his merry adventures with Denis Compton against Somerset at Lord's in May. The Middlesex 'twins' accelerated once again with their punishing bats to amass 424 runs in an unbroken stand lasting four hours. 'It was,' said Denis, 'a leaf out of our 1947 book,' and it beat all third-wicket records except for the New Zealand partnership of 445 between W. N. Carson and P. E. Whitelaw for Auckland against Otago at Dunedin in January 1937. At Lord's Compton hit 252 and Edrich 168, the pair making 209 of their runs in seventy minutes after tea against an attack which included two England bowlers, Arthur Wellard and Maurice Tremlett. Middlesex declared at 478 for two wickets fifty minutes before the end of the first day. 'Bill encouraged me with his flow of strokes, and I encouraged him. It was a mutual infection,' said Compton.

Jack Robertson recalled the whirlwind progress of the two batsmen at the height of their mastery. 'The wicket was pitched on the top Grandstand side at

Lord's. It was rather unpleasant sitting in the small "A" stand (the predecessor of the Warner enclosure). There was a little off-spinner, Coope, playing for Somerset. Poor chap. Oh dear, they murdered him.' Coope, an occasional bowler, was hit for 61 runs in six overs. His seniors, Wellard and Buse, did not fare much better. There were centuries against their names and dented morale.

The individual achievements of Denis Compton salvaged England's pride against Don Bradman's all-conquering Australians in 1948. They included the valour of his 145 not out in the drawn Test at Old Trafford. He was struck a staggering blow on the head as he attempted a big hit off à 'no-ball' bouncer from the hostile Lindwall. He was ordered to rest after stitches were inserted in the wound; Edrich then held the fort with exemplary technique for more than three hours against some of the fastest and most dangerous bowling of the series. It allowed Compton an interlude of quiet before he restarted his innings at the fall of the fifth wicket. An eighth-wicket partnership of 121 in two and a half hours with Alec Bedser carried England to 363 in what might have proved to be a match-winning total. Bedser then took four wickets as Australia were bowled out for 221. England increased their lead to 306 before the intervention of rain prevented play on the Monday and did not permit a resumption until after lunch on the Tuesday.

This was a time when England had an opportunity to edge back into contention after their reverses at Nottingham and Lord's. Victory at Old Trafford would have given them a lifeline and, had this happened, the pattern of the series ought to have undergone a change on the spinners' wicket at Leeds. It is a valid evaluation, even allowing for the superior strengths of the tourists. The monumental strokeplay of the Australian batsmen, seven of whom passed 1,000 runs on the tour, was given significant support by Lindwall and Johnston, who each captured 27 wickets in the series to equal the fast bowling record of Ted McDonald in 1921.

The passage of events in the fourth Test at Headingley, in which England held the keys to victory until the fateful last day, must be regarded as a lamentable tale. Before the bushfire of shameful runs, the Australian march had been halted. A vast Yorkshire crowd, the attendance figures of 158,000 amounting to a record for a match in England, nudged shoulders expectantly as victory beckoned. 'Just how many people would have seen play at Headingley, if all could have got into the ground, it is impossible to imagine,' reported a correspondent. 'Thousands remained outside close to the turnstiles, and messages were sent back to the centre of the city to turn away latecomers.'

A first-innings century of breathtaking ferocity by the nineteen-year-old Neil Harvey gave a foretaste of his future mastery. It checked an ascendant England, who had slipped from the prosperity of 423 for two wickets to 496 all out. The total was still formidable but less than seemed likely after three century partnerships, including one between Edrich and Washbrook, and another between Edrich and the sprightly nightwatchman, Alec Bedser. Edrich had been an onlooker, never a position he relished, for most of the first day. But he arrived at the wicket determined to consolidate the advantage so handsomely won by Hutton and Washbrook. His century vindicated his retention by the selectors and sealed his batting revival after having only once previously passed 50 in the series.

One observer, watching the mounting frustration of the Australians during the Edrich-Bedser partnership, reported: 'The batsmen stayed in comfort and dignity, offering no suggestion that this was an alliance between

Nos. 3 and 10.' At lunch on the second day, the total was 360. In the afternoon the pair moved on serenely until Edrich, hooking Morris for four, hoisted his 100 and 400 for England. This was the climax of the stand, but not quite its end, for not until the score had reached 423 did Bedser slightly mistime his drive to offer Johnson a hard return catch. He had scored 79. Jack Fingleton wrote: 'Bedser came in to keep watch overnight, but so brilliantly and confidently was he batting at one time that he seemed certain to become a centurion. I have never seen a man so embarrassed as Bedser was when he returned to the pavilion. He was positively blushing at being acclaimed as a batting hero.'

England had the prize of victory in their grasp on the last day. Edrich and Compton were again the revellers in a quickfire century stand. They added 103 at just over a run a minute to build on the second opening century partnership of Hutton and Washbrook in the match. What followed was a sad indictment of England's bowling resources. Australia feasted hugely on a diet of long-hops and full-tosses on a pitch tailor-made for spin. Their target was 404 runs in five and three-quarter hours, and they won in a canter by seven wickets. For a large and glum Yorkshire crowd, proud in their memories of Rhodes and Verity, it was an act of abject surrender. Australia triumphed with what was then the highest winning total in Test history. Don Bradman, unruffled as if he had just completed an extended net practice, was undefeated on 173 in his farewell innings at Leeds. Bradman and Morris hit 301 runs in just over three hours. Sixty-six fours were struck by the rampant Australians.

England were gripped by a fielding palsy which had the spectators rubbing their eyes in disbelief. Bradman was missed three times and Morris escaped twice as catches were spilled and stumpings not accepted. Australia, if truth were told, were not seriously looking for victory after the early morning declaration. England's lapses meant that they could hardly help winning the match. The astonishing upset enabled Australia to maintain their supremacy at Leeds which was to last until 1956.

Jim Laker, mature and assured in his spinning skills eight years later, was a major disappointment in the Headingley fiasco. His match figures were three wickets for 206 runs in 62 overs. Norman Yardley, the England captain, had to place his hopes in the eccentric left-arm spin of Denis Compton and, briefly, in a pre-lunch gamble, in the leg-breaks of Len Hutton, who bowled only rarely for Yorkshire in the post-war years.

Godfrey Evans, England's wicket-keeper in a nightmare match, looked back ruefully on a woeful episode. While admitting that he had a terrible game and was as guilty as anyone in England's decline, Evans remembered that the Leeds pitch was unpredictable in its behaviour. 'Three balls in an over would come straight through and then, when you were least expecting it, the ball would turn and lift. It was completely out of character with what had happened before.' Evans believed that the capricious wicket handicapped England's bowlers. 'The ball did not turn regularly and, in consequence, it was difficult to power the spin, or control the direction of the ball. My problem was that I did not know which of the deliveries was going to act strangely.'

The crucial wicket was that of Bradman and, as the discomforted Compton remembered, if it had been taken England would have won the match. He had made the early breakthrough in accepting a return catch to dismiss Hassett. Evans then missed a stumping off Morris. 'For some extraordinary reason Norman took Bill Edrich out of the slips and put him in the covers,' said Denis. 'Jack Crapp, normally a safe slip, replaced him. I suppose dear old Jack couldn't read my googly, which Bill did, of course. Bradman was missed twice, dollies off me, at slip, before he had scored 10. I did feel sorry for Jack, but if Bill had been there the chances would surely have been taken.' Denis recalled a later conversation with Keith Miller. 'Keith said the Australian team had already packed to leave the ground early because they thought the match would be over by four o'clock.'

A conflicting postscript to the game was presented by another Australian, Ray Lindwall. He made light of the conditions and said that his side' had not envisaged defeat. 'The wicket at Leeds was spinning but not dangerously. Our fellas were on top for the whole day after the first session.' Lindwall played a key batting role in a match which yielded five centuries. 'I only got 77 but my innings was important because we pushed the score along.' Despite heavy punishment from Harvey, Miller and Loxton, England still held the upper hand. Australia were 141 runs behind when their eighth first-innings wicket fell. Lindwall, aided by Johnston and Toshack, put on 103 to restrict England's lead to 38 runs. 'But for my knock,' said Lindwall, 'we would have had a heavy deficit. We would have had no chance if I'd got out. It made all the difference.'

It was exactly right that the triumvirate of Edrich, Compton and Hutton – the standard bearers in the previous post-war series against Australia – should take centre stage in the Coronation Year of 1953. No fiction writer could have constructed a more rewarding scenario. The wheel had come full circle and the three exciting batting discoveries of the pre-war generation were reunited in wrestling the Ashes from Australia in a tumultuous finale at The Oval. It was the turn of the tide. England achieved their first Ashes victory, by eight wickets, since the bodyline series in Australia twenty years earlier. It was unsullied by the rancour attending Douglas Jardine's triumph. In a tiny room at her London flat, Jessy Edrich was the hostess at a boisterous celebration following the match. Members of both teams displayed their camaraderie in the high spirits of an impromptu game of rugby. Jessy was thrust into a scrimmage of joyous cricketers. Her husband Bill, as Ray Lindwall remembered, wrestled furiously in a tackling bout with his Australian opponent. Honours were shared. Both men, with their knees skinned, ended up in a heap at the bottom of the stairs outside.

Leonard Hutton, whose deeds are now commemorated by a magnificent sculpture at the main entrance to the ground, was the England captain at The Oval. Edrich, cold-shouldered by the selectors in 1950, had been recalled with the avowed intent of taming Lindwall in the third Test at Old Trafford. In all matches in 1953 Edrich scored 2,557 runs, more than anyone else, and he averaged 47. It was like old times to see the Middlesex twins once again in harness against Australia. At Leeds, on a rain-affected wicket, Australia gained a lead of 99 runs. In the second innings, Hutton and Graveney were dismissed cheaply. 'Then came Compton,' reported *Wisden*, 'and he and Edrich withstood hostile bowling from Lindwall, Miller and Archer. They were subjected to a series of bumpers but stayed together to add 77 runs in two and a quarter hours.' Keith Miller later conceded: 'It's a waste of time bowling bumpers at Bill.' Jim Swanton praised Edrich's 'intense concentration' during this duel, and his joy in the fight carried out as usual with the utmost contempt for personal risk.

Hutton was a relieved captain in the tense finish to the game. Australia, in the end, needed only 30

189

runs for victory. They had been set a target of 177 in three minutes under two hours. Despite the loss of Hassett, who played on to Lock, and Morris stumped off Laker, it was quickly apparent that they had taken up the chase. In a golden half-hour Harvey and Hole scored 57 runs. Bedser was hit for 12 in an over and 13 runs came off Lock. The whirling scoreboard promised a win for Australia, with time to spare. Harvey had scored 34 before Bedser trapped him lbw. Bailey, finally introduced by Hutton, halted the gallop. His concentrated attack on the leg stump was sufficient to lower the tempo. 'Until the end the young Australians made strokes and took all they could from them, but the opportunity had slipped,' reported Swanton. 'Bailey's six overs had cost only nine runs, and it was his excellent support of the unflagging Bedser that had tipped the scales. Bedser toiled for two hours unrelieved and, in the process, took his 100th wicket against Australia.'

The reprieve at Leeds enabled England to hand a sporting crown to their young sovereign. Lock and Laker cast a spinning blight on Australia at The Oval. By the end of the third day England needed 94 runs to win their first rubber against Australia in this country since 1926. It was achieved despite the loss of Hutton, who was run out twenty minutes before the end of this session. Swanton said the dismissal induced a feeling of complete and quiet stupefaction. Australia, on the last day, made strenuous efforts to deny England their coveted victory. 'Lindwall, from the Pavilion End, kept up a ceaseless, fast and accurate attack,' reported Swanton. 'Edrich and Compton had to watch with all their eyes and wits.' Edrich was unbeaten on 55 and it took two hours and forty minutes to make the winning runs.

'Edrich,' commented *Wisden*, 'magnificently hooked two successive bouncers from the Australian bowler.'

This was the moment when the excited throng knew that the Ashes had been won. Hassett, with an impish grin, at last conceded defeat and handed the ball to Morris. Compton, spinning on his heels, swept the ball to the boundary. He just headed his partner in the scamper back to the pavilion as the milling crowds descended upon the field to greet a famous victory.

Peter May, one of the emerging and best and most commanding of the new guard of batting stylists, assisted in the final rites at The Oval. His boyhood idols had been Hutton, Compton and Edrich. He recalled the security of batting with them at the other end. 'Their presence was reassuring. It gave you confidence, as a young player, because they always looked so solid and didn't look like getting out.' The most important lesson he learned and profited from was the placing and timing of the ball. 'I always used to think it is no use hitting fine shots at the fieldsmen. Basically what batsmen are trying to do is miss them. To score runs you have to do just that. The best players, like Len, Denis and Bill, hit the gaps.'

The vitality and strength of Bill Edrich, which so impressed Peter May, were to prove of inestimable value to the England captain, Leonard Hutton, on a physically draining tour of Australia in 1954–55. As boys more than twenty years earlier, they had first taken measure of each other as Norfolk and Yorkshire rivals in a Minor Counties match at Lakenham. Hutton and Edrich were complementary in their outlook on cricket. Above all, Len had great confidence in Bill as an adviser and appointed the Middlesex man as one of his selectors on the tour. For both of them, it was a farewell to Test cricket; they were inseparable even in their averages, sharing 400 runs and taking one wicket between them.

Bob Appleyard has dwelt upon the demands of a

191

tense low-scoring series in which the speed of Frank Tyson, coupled with the unflagging accuracy of Brian Statham, ultimately capsized the Australians. Adding to Hutton's burden was the fact that he lacked a consistent and solid opening ally. He had four different partners: Reg Simpson, at Brisbane; Trevor Bailey at Sydney; Edrich at Melbourne and Adelaide; and Tom Graveney in the final Test at Sydney.

Hutton, in fact, had to be persuaded to play in the vital third Test at Melbourne, where England gained a 2–1 lead in the series. He was in a low state and had scored only 75 runs in four innings in the preceding Tests. Appleyard said that Hutton was struggling to maintain his fitness at this stage. Geoffrey Howard remembered that he was so overwrought that he asked for a doctor to be called on the night before the Test at Melbourne. Edrich and Godfrey Evans joined Howard when the examination was carried out on the morning of the match. The doctor announced a clean bill of health and urged Hutton to take a shower, have breakfast, and go to the ground. It was, as later transpired, a psychosomatic illness. 'Len was devastated; he wanted to be told that he was unfit,' said Howard.

The reason for Hutton's indisposition was that he had decided to leave Alec Bedser out of the team. As a considerate man, he was deeply worried about the impending omission of his senior professional and one of England's most loyal and successful campaigners. Melbourne was also one of Bedser's favourite bowling venues. He had taken 22 wickets in three Tests there. 'Len didn't want to hurt Alec; but he refused to delegate the task to Edrich, who was prepared to convey the sad news,' recalled Howard. To make matters worse, Hutton did not advise Bedser of his decision; the Surrey bowler, having already changed for the match, was confounded to discover that his name was not included on the team sheet pinned up on the dressing-room notice board. 'Len had actually taken Alec out to inspect the wicket,' said Howard. 'With all the other problems pressing on his mind, he still couldn't face communicating his decision to Bedser.'

Godfrey Evans recalled that it was largely at Edrich's instigation that Hutton was prevailed upon to play in the match. 'We had levelled the series after being beaten by an innings and plenty at Brisbane. Psychologically Len had to be out there with us at Melbourne.' Evans and Edrich shepherded the England captain into a cab and travelled with him to the ground. 'We don't care a bugger what you do, Leonard, but you must go out on to that field,' was their exhortation.

Hutton's despair was exacerbated by his own downfall when England batted. In ninety minutes before lunch England lost four wickets for 41 runs. Keith Miller took three wickets for five runs in a spell of nine overs, which included eight maidens. His prized victims were Hutton, Edrich and Compton, while Lindwall, at the other end, dismissed May. Colin Cowdrey, with a chanceless century of astonishing maturity, rescued England. His 102, out of a total of 191, dragged Hutton out of his lethargy. Howard recalled: 'Len was miserable after getting out so quickly. He did not take his pads off and just sat in the dressing-room, staring glumly at the wall. His mood changed when he realised, from our excitement on the balcony, that Colin was playing so well. Before long he had joined us to share our enthusiasm.'

The controversial allegations of a watered pitch, vigorously disputed by the Melbourne Club, aided England in their second innings. Jim Swanton related that, over the intervening weekend, a hot north wind blew, and the heat grew increasingly intolerable. 'After Melbourne had experienced the hottest night in its history England, going out to field on the Monday morning, were amazed to find evidence of moisture in the pitch. They had left it desiccated and friable; now the sprigs on their boots, which had slid over the baked, shiny surface, cut lines in the turf.' The artificial refreshment, added Swanton, suited England well, for it gave them the truest surface of the match for their second innings. Frank Tyson, who was to cut a swathe with his fast shooters through the Australian batting, said: 'Had the curator not acted, there can be little doubt that there would have been hardly any wicket left by the Monday.' Australia, with eight wickets left, needed 165 to win before the dramatic last stages of the match. 'Tyson blazed through them like a bushfire,' reported *Wisden*. In seventy-nine minutes the match was over, the eight remaining wickets falling for 36 runs. Tyson took six wickets for 16 runs in 6.3 overs; and Statham, as his immaculate foil, captured the other two wickets for 19 runs. 'I wonder now who would have withstood Tyson as he bowled on this pitch on this January morning,' enthused Swanton. 'In little more than an hour 50,000 people were applauding him in and then wending their way home, chattering adjectivally, I expect, in profane disbelief.'

Bill Edrich enjoyed his last tour of Australia and revelled in the triumphant atmosphere. 'Bill was one of the senior players in Australia and Len relied on his experience,' said Bob Appleyard. 'It was a test of character in those low-scoring matches, with wickets falling around your ears. He was pushed in as opening batsman in two matches to stay there, which was totally against his attacking instincts. But he was always a great battler. My lasting impression of Bill is that he was a first-class team man. He would always do what you asked him to do.'

Geoffrey Howard has recorded that Edrich, far from being difficult to handle, posed no problems on this last tour. 'We did have to "rescue" him on one or two occasions but he always co-operated in the nicest possible way.' Frank Tyson remembered that Edrich arrived at Bunbury in Western Australia for the opening game against a country eleven, just before he had to go out to bat. 'We had all travelled down some hundred miles by car on the night before. But, as. Bill put it, he and his driver, "ran into a bar en-route".'

On another occasion, at the end of the deciding Test at Adelaide, Edrich went off to celebrate the victory with his former RAF bomber crew friend, Ernie Hope. He was away for two days. Howard recalled: 'We had to leave for Sydney about five in the morning. We were all waiting in the coach. I went to Bill's room. He was stark naked and fast asleep in bed. I finally roused him and gave him his air ticket. I told him to come along on the next plane.'

Edrich was highly indignant to be so rudely swept out of his slumbers. He raised himself sleepily on the pillows. 'This is very irregular,' he said. 'I want my friend, Compton.' Howard retraced his path down the stairs and explained the situation to Denis. Five frantic minutes later, Edrich, escorted by Compton, sheepishly took his seat on the coach. He was not properly awake, but he was fully dressed. 'It was all done by Denis,' said Howard. 'Bill couldn't have made it on his own.'

Before the euphoria of England's Ashes triumph, Edrich and Godfrey Evans – and the rest of the MCC party – demonstrated their faith in a successful outcome to the series. The odds against an England victory were 8–1, reflecting the expectancy of Australia, after they had overwhelmed their opponents at Brisbane. 'All the boys clubbed together to put £100 into the kitty for the bet,' said Evans. When victory was finally sealed, Godfrey and Bill were deputed to go along to Tattersalls to collect the winnings, amounting to £800.

They entered the seedy premises in a state of some apprehension. In the darkened office they encountered a group of steely-eyed and roughly attired bookmakers. It is perhaps not overstating the matter to say that in these quarters they seemed likely to be assaulted. All of the men showed an obvious reluctance to part with the money. Bill said: 'We've got to be careful here, Godders.' Godfrey whispered words of encouragement. The prospect of a battle, extending to fisticuffs, loomed. The cricketers were undeterred. Bill replied: 'Let's get the money and move out quickly.' Their resolve won over the bookmakers. The wager was acknowledged, the winnings released, but it was a close call. Bill and Godfrey thankfully sought the safety of the street.

Edrich never did waver in a crisis, nor did he ever give way to pain. A competitive soccer interlude in Australia provided one example. At the age of thirty-eight, he resumed his role as a soccer winger in a match between the MCC and the press on Christmas Day. It was played on the beach at Glenelg, just outside the team's headquarters at the Pier Hotel. Frank Tyson recalled: 'Bill received the ball and made his way towards the opposition goal, slowly sinking lower and lower as he yielded to the earlier festive spirits and the taxing demands of the sand under foot.

'Eventually he sprawled full-length in the shingle, skinning the whole of one side of his face. It was an awful mess. But he got to his feet immediately, shook and wiped the blood away and carried on playing.' Tyson added: 'I don't know what the spectators thought when they saw "Scarface" going jauntily out to bat on the following day at the Adelaide Oval.'

Edrich belied his advancing years in another outrageous escapade. It was a daring and exuberant display of his own joy, as the England players celebrated the winning of the Ashes at the Pier Hotel. He revived memories of his childhood, incorrigibly climbing trees at home in the Norfolk farmlands. His stunning late-night party trick was to swarm twenty feet to the pinnacle of a glistening marble pillar in the foyer of the hotel. He stayed there, like a puckish Nelson, grinning hugely and refused to come down. He was, in a manner of speaking, on top of the world. His team-mates, in a nervous huddle below, could not help but laugh and rejoice with him.

CHAPTER 11

Homecoming of a Veteran

'Seldom can the enjoyment of the players have been better communicated to spectators; seldom can a side have had a better team spirit. – *David Armstrong, former Secretary, Norfolk CCC.*

The goal of a chivalrous man was to entertain and never to allow the taint of foul play to smudge the honour of his conquests. Bill Edrich, as a captain, flourished in Norfolk, where he ruled with evangelical fervour and infused his young disciples with a do-or-die spirit. The crusader, back on his native heath, was instantly poised on the attack and wrought a dramatic upturn in the county's fortunes. For the crowds flocking back to Lakenham, said Jim Swanton, Edrich's daring tactical approach struck a vein of reminiscence in accord with the exploits of his first county captain, Michael Falcon, in the great days between the wars.

Swanton's eulogy on the captaincy style of Edrich in Norfolk contrasted with the views of the young men, by now in their middle years, under his command at Lord's. Jack Robertson, one of the older Middlesex campaigners, said all other captains in his experience paled by comparison with the dynamic Walter Robins. Edrich, perhaps, suffered from the burden of succeeding Robins and another astute leader, George Mann. He was, at all times, a kindly guide; but there was a romanticism about his intentions which created a certain fallibility on the first-class scene.

John Murray, one of the improving Middlesex players under Edrich's command in the 1950s, remembered the honesty of his captain and how he would abide by his word in all circumstances. In one match against Kent at Dover, Edrich and his opposing captain, Jack Pettiford, the Australian leg-spinner, hatched a plot which nearly rebounded against Middlesex. They had each agreed before the start of the game to bowl five overs. Pettiford wisely delivered his quota on the first day. By the last afternoon the wicket was taking spin; Fred Titmus was bowling, and Middlesex were winning the match. There was, though, an increasing threat of rain, as a huge bank of dark clouds rose above the Kent hills.

At this point, Edrich was a man in a quandary. He had forgotten his pact with Pettiford. He prised the ball from Titmus's hands to the disbelief of his team. 'Hold on,' he said. 'I haven't bowled my five overs yet.' Murray recalled: 'Bill was going to bowl his overs, even if it meant that Middlesex failed to win the game.' Titmus resumed his place in the attack only just in time to seal the victory. 'Don Bennett raced forty yards round the boundary to take the winning catch off Titmus,' said Murray. 'The heavens opened as we left the field.'

In the unyielding terms of today, Edrich's ingenuous action at Dover might place him in the certifiable category. His cricket philosophy was old-fashioned but eminently cherishable. He gave another demonstration of this approach at Oxford in 1957. The university had not beaten a county eleven for seven years. In a dramatic finish, they were the winners by four wickets. What is not discernible from the records is the fact that Edrich insisted upon prolonging the match by ten minutes, so that Oxford could reach their target. Their victory had been well earned, and he did not think it fitting to deprive them of the honour by rigidly adhering to the playing regulations.

The conscientious ethic contrasted with the robust response when faced with intimidatory tactics. His anger was then something to be feared. One salutary example is related by Peter Parfitt, Donald Carr and Alan Moss, the latter one of the leading protagonists. It was a saga of two halves; the engagement a brace of matches, separated by a few days, between Middlesex and Derbyshire in 1956. In the first fixture at Lord's, Derbyshire had won by 88 runs. Les Jackson, with twelve wickets in the match, had shown the aggression which ought to have earned him more than a miserly two Test appearances for England. None of his opponents had relished his leaping deliveries at Lord's.

The wicket in the return match at Chesterfield was an 'absolute flier', in the words of Parfitt. Jackson – and his redoubtable partner, Cliff Gladwin – should have been even more fiercesome in these conditions. The problem arose when Jackson elected to bowl a beamer at a young batsman, Dennis Baldry. The thunderstruck Baldry hurriedly retreated and hit his wicket. He sprawled over the wreckage of his stumps. 'Bill, at the other end, was properly incensed,' said Parfitt. 'From eighty yards away in the pavilion, you could almost see him grit his teeth. He went on to hit 208 not out. It was a magnificent innings on a pig of a wicket.'

Edrich's double-century, mingling hooks and pulls of great power, included four sixes and 32 fours – 152 runs in boundaries. 'Bill got his old "cow" going that day,' said Alan Moss. 'He kept on hoisting Gladwin over mid-wicket, or into the trees at long-on.' Middlesex eventually totalled 408 for 4 declared and Moss took

11 wickets in a violent sequel, as Derbyshire lost by an innings.

Donald Carr, the Derbyshire captain, recalled that the vigour of the Middlesex bowling at Chesterfield was a riposte to the short-pitched deliveries directed by Jackson at the later home batsmen at Lord's. 'Wait until we get you at Chesterfield,' said Moss, one of the tailenders. At the time it did not seem the most sensible of comments, but it was Jackson, rather than Moss, who was called into batting action at Chesterfield. 'Middlesex made a lot of runs and we subsequently followed on after rain,' said Carr. 'We were still some way from saving the follow-on when Les came in at the fall of the ninth wicket. Mossie, only in fun, added eight yards to his normal run-up. His intention was to direct the ball some considerable distance outside Jackson's leg stump. He did this, but Les had retreated to exactly the same line before it arrived. It hit him straight on the point of the elbow. Les dropped his bat and tears were practically streaming down his face. He had had enough and retired hurt. Charlie Lee, our opening batsman, who had batted superbly to score 96 on a rain-affected wicket, was thus deprived of a deserved century.'

Jackson's nerves were already frayed before he was dealt the sickening blow. Edrich had not forgotten the events at Lord's, nor the discomfiture of young Baldry in the Middlesex innings. He instructed Moss to take the second new ball. 'It'll hurt them more,' he said in a voice loud enough for Jackson to hear.

Peter Parfitt was one of three Norfolk players – the others were John Edrich and Clive Radley – to gain England recognition and follow Bill Edrich on this proud journey to fame. John Edrich is the son of Fred, the youngest of Harry Edrich's family, and thus a direct cousin of Bill. Another cousin, Eric, bridged the generation gap as John's – and Peter Parfitt's – coach during their boyhood in Norfolk. Eric remembered how his uncle Fred, only nine years his senior, sought his assistance in providing tuition for John at his home at Blofield. The coaching lesson was held when Eric returned from Lancashire to resume his farming career in 1949. 'I had never seen a better thirteen-year-old in my life,' said Eric. 'I bowled at him one afternoon on a concrete path in the garden. I could hardly get one past him, let alone get him out. He had the best defence of any I'd seen, that boy.' John was as adhesively resistant as Bill Edrich in 77 Tests for England between 1963 and 1976. He lacked the exciting flair of Bill as a cricketer but he was a painstaking accumulator of runs. Their career batting aggregates, in John's case extending over an uninterrupted period and of a longer duration, were intriguingly similar. John scored 39,790 runs in 21 seasons and Bill, in five seasons fewer, trailed him by 2,825 runs.

Peter Parfitt, as another of the boys for whom Eric Edrich prophesied a bright future, was the beneficiary of Bill's encouragement at Lord's. He remembered the standards of discipline set by the Middlesex old guard. 'We were a happy side. Bill – and Denis Compton – had more effect on me and the way I approached life than anyone else I have ever encountered.'

One incident during his apprenticeship at Lord's is indelibly printed on his mind. It was a reflection of Edrich's deep-rooted aversion to cheating of any kind. It occurred in one of his early games for Middlesex against Gloucestershire at Lord's. George Lambert bowled a bouncer at Parfitt; he went to hook the ball, and it just flicked his glove as it darted into the hands of the wicket-keeper, Peter Rochford. 'All the Gloucestershire team went up for the catch,' said Parfitt. 'Emrys Davies, the Test umpire, and a good friend of the youngsters on the county circuit, sternly rebuked them and said: "Not out." '

The reprieve did not escape the notice of the Middlesex captain. At the interval there was a short but telling conversation between Edrich and Parfitt on the dressing-room balcony. Everyone else had gone upstairs for lunch. In answer to Bill's quiet inquiry about the rejected catch, Parfitt confessed that he had indeed gloved the bouncer from Lambert. 'Right,' said Edrich, 'in this side, if anyone touches the ball to the wicket-keeper, they don't require the umpire to make the decision. You are just as much out as if you had lobbed it to cover point. Now then, Peter, while you are in my team, if you hit the ball, you walk.' The conversation was never repeated; from that moment on Parfitt was an unreserved walker. Alan Moss has endorsed this respect for cricket etiquette. 'They were all straight men in the Middlesex team. We played in an era when you did walk. Those who did not were marked people.'

John Murray, along with other young players in Middlesex and Norfolk, has attested to the pleasures of playing under Edrich's leadership. Above all, as Murray remembered, he displayed a faith in your ability greater than your own belief. Murray was not a wicket-keeper when he first went to Lord's. The immaculate perfectionist of later years made his county debut as a seventeen-year-old, deputising for the injured Leslie Compton at Leicester in 1952. By the time Murray had completed his National Service Compton had retired and the wicket-keeping position was waiting to be filled.

Murray's ambition was to gain his county cap. Before the start of the 1956 season this bait was dangled enticingly before him by Edrich. Bill declared: 'Your target is fifty victims. Achieve that and I will give you

203

the cap.' Recalling this inspiring gesture, Murray said that the promise was made during the first game of the season. 'I was still an apprentice, unproven, but they'd read my potential correctly.' He duly completed the required aggregate by the middle of June and received the coveted award. By the end of this first full season with Middlesex he had assisted in 77 dismissals, more than anyone else in the country.

The young Middlesex players of Edrich's time were always heartened by his trust. There was, though – and at variance with the later testimonies in Norfolk – a more reserved view about his captaincy on the field. Alan Moss said: 'Bill would gamble on declarations and with attacking fields, sometimes costly in terms of gifted runs. But he had very set views on how you should bowl or place your field.' Edrich was a good organiser but not a great innovator as captain; he attempted to back winners and did not take long odds. Moss said there was little experimentation in field placings and, as a bowler, he could rely on timed spells of activity, perhaps five in a day. 'You could almost take your sweater off by the clock.' Edrich could be quite stubborn over economy in run-ups. 'Oh no, you've got to put it in, so as to get it out,' he would instruct his main strike bowlers.

The general view in the Middlesex ranks of Edrich as a captain was that he was inclined to be predictable and conservative; others, including his England colleague, Trevor Bailey, judged him a sound tactician but veering towards defensiveness. Another opponent, Doug Insole, said: 'Bill was prepared to accept captaincy challenges with the bat in circumstances which weren't over-propitious. But he wasn't terribly good in leaving targets with the ball.'

Edrich led Middlesex for five seasons from 1953 to 1957; before then he had shared the county captaincy with Denis Compton in what was considered a diplomatic and not entirely successful division of responsibilities. Insole, their Essex rival, wryly remarked: 'They knew who was skipper, but it wasn't obvious to anyone else.'

All of Edrich's 'boys' lay stress on the harmony which prevailed in the Middlesex dressing-room during their apprentice years. 'It was fun and if it was tough out there on the field, Bill would be right in the middle of the battle,' declared John Murray. 'If you were going over the top from the trenches, you would want to be following Bill,' enthused Peter Parfitt. Donald Carr and Jim Swanton have both stressed that no-one could quarrel with Edrich's cricket ethos. 'He had terrific stamina and enthusiasm for the game,' remembered Carr. 'It was all serious, positive cricket. He was absolutely straight and would never cheat anybody.'

Alan Moss wistfully returned to the romantic theme. The stories of Edrich's wild partygoing, he said, had to be placed in the harmless context. Bill was naturally ebullient; his drinking, while sometimes ill-advised since he couldn't really take it, was of the social variety. 'He didn't have to be legless to burst into song. All he needed were two halves of bitter and he was away. Everyone enjoyed themselves; there was no separation of seniors and juniors. Bill was very much with us as boys.' Amid this fellowship Edrich was always conscious of the welfare of the team. They were employees of a premier club and, as such, they stayed at the best hotels and enjoyed good food. As a corollary to this treatment, the players were expected to observe the disciplines of proper attire. It would have been unthinkable to arrive for duty at Lord's without wearing a jacket and tie.

Entertainment on tour, especially during Middlesex's

long absences in August, was pronounced in its lavishness. For someone of Edrich's temperament, it was an accessory in league with cricket. One of the regular August Bank Holiday venues was the then splendid Royal Albion Hotel, close by the Palace Pier in Brighton. One of the visits to the south coast in 1957 was a specially invigorating occasion, coinciding, as it did, with Bill's impending retirement from first-class cricket. Alan Moss, as the senior professional, was instructed by Edrich to draw £120 as expenses from the club coffers. 'All the wives and girlfriends came down with us to Brighton. We had champagne for breakfast, lunch and dinner. The bill for the weekend was horrendous,' recalled Moss.

The quality of Edrich's cricket rarely flagged during his final years at Lord's. In 1956, at the age of forty, he scored 1,831 runs and headed the county averages. *Wisden* reported: 'Edrich showed no decline in his ability. He increased his aggregate of runs and his captaincy brought the best out of the young members of the side.' A partnership between Edrich and Compton against Somerset at Glastonbury was touched with the glow of their youth. At The Oval, against Lock and Laker, Edrich lit another torch of remembrance in displaying his skills and concentration against the turning ball. His career was, however, drawing to a close. In 1958 he relinquished the Middlesex captaincy to John Warr, but he continued to play though his appearances were limited. There was just time for the lilt of adventure to surface once again and ennoble his performance for the MCC against Cambridge University in June. The MCC, having been set a target of 230 runs at 96 runs an hour, won by two wickets. The conclusive stroke came off the last ball of the match. Edrich, as always, led from the front. He hit 103 in under two hours, and the innings included seven sixes, all struck with disconcerting vigour.

Edrich's return to Minor Counties cricket in 1959 presaged a remarkable revival in the fortunes of Norfolk. It prompted Jim Swanton to wish that the old hero was a few years younger and able to show comparable daring as a leader at Lord's. Edrich's impact in Norfolk, despite his lack of knowledge of the players under his command, was immediately reassuring. The three preceding seasons had passed without a victory and the county had registered only twelve wins since the war. In 1959 Norfolk won four out of ten matches and rose to seventh place in the Minor Counties championship. Twice at Lakenham, having been set to make 220 in about two hours, they emerged as victors. Ted Witherden, a key batting stalwart, established a new county record of 1,031 runs. Five batsmen averaged over 40 and Norfolk's rate of scoring left the bowlers, who averaged around 22 overs an hour, ample time in which to dismiss the opposition. Edrich was irrepressible on his home ground, communicating the lessons of enterprise set by his Middlesex captain, Walter Robins.

'The whole approach to two-day cricket was transformed,' wrote David Armstrong, then the Norfolk secretary. 'No-one bothered very much with first-innings points, the emphasis being on an all-out result of one sort or another, and of Norfolk's ten games only two were drawn.'

One of Edrich's disciples, as he embarked on this new phase in his career, was Nigel Moore. Moore, an accomplished batsman who scored 5,000 runs for Norfolk, narrowly missed a blue at Cambridge during a time when the university fielded no fewer than five current and future Test players – Sheppard, May, Subba Row, Warr and Cuan McCarthy, the South African fast bowler. Moore recalled the benefits of Edrich's leadership, later to be linked to his personal skills. 'Bill was confident, positive, optimistic and inspiring. He left the players in no doubt as to what he wanted them to do, and our performances were enhanced as a result.'

There was, at first, a frailty in Edrich's batting. It was soon to be eliminated by abstemption from drink following his fourth marriage. Norfolk cricket had reason to be grateful for Valerie's support off the field. The 'shandy regime' lasted long enough to rejuvenate Bill and allow him to reveal his true qualities. 'One day, probably in his second season with Norfolk, I was batting with him,' recalled Moore. 'I suddenly realised that the man at the other end was showing a class I had not seen before.' Moore's verdict was confirmed by Bill himself, who said he had not seen the ball so well for years. 'From then onwards,' added Moore, 'his own personal performances made a huge difference to the side. The greater the challenge the more he was able to lift his game.'

An especially significant feature of Edrich's batting was his skill in countering the spin of former first-class cricketers, which usually had the other Norfolk players in difficulties. Very often the perplexing bowlers were left-handers. 'Bill played them very cautiously, normally scoring off them in ones and twos, with fast running between the wickets,' remembered Moore. 'He seldom went for them as he did against the off-spinners; these he murdered by hitting "with the tide".'

The duels between Johnny Wardle, the Cambridgeshire professional and former Yorkshire and England left-hander, and Edrich were constantly absorbing. Wardle spun the ball so much, said his Norfolk rivals, that it hinted at a full toss before it dipped fatally late in flight. One tailender, after he had played and missed throughout one over, was given the message by Wardle:

'Son, just keep your bat still. I'll hit it!' Edrich was a more worthy adversary. He always considered that he could 'read' Wardle. 'Watch his hand,' he told his hapless colleagues. It was unavailing for them but Bill played him superbly.

As a bowler, Edrich had long since reverted to his own mischievous brand of off-spin. He enjoyed great success in Minor Counties cricket, much to the surprise of many who considered his bowling fairly innocuous. His head would swivel inquisitively at umpires after each delivery to ensure that he had their full attention. He genuinely believed that his appeals for lbw carried conviction. The crown on his England sweater did tend to aid his authority. 'It just straightened nicely,' he explained after each dismissal. 'Two appeals and next was out,' said one fellow Norfolk bowler. His fieldsmen, occasionally less sure than their captain, were sternly instructed to be unsparing in their support. 'Why aren't you appealing?' was Bill's despairing cry.

Nigel Moore remembered Edrich's small hand and the fingers which prevented him from obtaining a firm grip of the ball. 'Bill bowled his little "off-rollers", usually round the wicket, and they sometimes turned on a helpful pitch,' he said. 'He did not seem to vary his pace a great deal, but dropped the ball unerringly on a good line and length. He was particularly good at throwing up the ball to give opposing batsmen an invitation to hit out and score quickly, or else get out. He always tried to keep our opponents in with a chance and was prepared to buy wickets.'

The policy of all-out attack is remembered by Edrich's Norfolk contemporaries. One county bowler, Billy Rose, was invariably given the best end and adjured to concede three runs an over. Any adjustment to the opposition's scoring rate was made by Edrich. 'If

209

they were going too slow, he would toss the ball up; too fast and he would ping it through,' said one colleague. On one occasion Edrich and Rose each bowled twenty overs in an unbroken spell to win a game.

One report in the *Eastern Daily Press* on Edrich's captaincy epitomised his challenging zeal. 'There was no room in his team for players who concentrated too much upon survival as opposed to run-scoring. If Edrich thought victory was possible, he would tell his batsmen to attack from the start. Once committed, whether batting or fielding, he did not change his tactics. If wickets were tumbling, he did not instruct the later batsmen to "put up the shutters". A welter of big hitting could turn the tide and batsmen were more likely to survive playing their normal game. Edrich was not prepared to close up a game, with the sole purpose of saving it.' Nigel Moore said the approach usually had the effect of enlivening the team. For some, less intrepid, it filled them with dread and reduced them to jelly. In one desperate run chase, the next man in asked: 'What do we do, skipper?' 'The rest of us knew what Bill's answer would be – "you run out there and win the game". He was almost chased down the steps!' In his anxiety the player said that he would prefer not to play again. He was overwhelmed by the tension of the frenetic scoring gallops.

Nigel Moore has stressed that Bill's captaincy, however daring, was never foolhardy. Past Norfolk teams had lost matches through over-optimistic declarations without having balanced adequately the respective abilities of themselves and their rivals. 'Under Bill in one year we won a number of matches by putting the opposition in first and chasing in the last innings ever more difficult targets. The time came when Bill would bat first because he felt that we might otherwise be set an absurd task, if we kept on winning in this way.'

Edrich, if an unappetising stalemate threatened, would respond with a lesson to ensure that it was not repeated. One season a rival county amassed a huge score in their first innings. Edrich said: 'If they want to ruin the game, we shall have to do the same by batting for the rest of the match.' Each side totalled around 500 runs in what was virtually a one-innings match. It was a precise rebuff; the indulgent occupation of the crease did not occur again in matches between the two teams.

The buoyancy of Edrich's captaincy captured the imagination of followers. It was the magnet for vast crowds at Norwich. The Norfolk revival was sealed in 1960 when they headed the Minor Counties table, and were paired with Lancashire II in the Challenge Match played at Lakenham. Edrich and Witherden each averaged 53 with the bat, and a formidable seam attack of Andrew Corran, the Oxford blue and a future Notts captain, Arthur Coomb and Peter Walmsley was backed by the off-spin of Edrich (43 wickets at 16.16) and two left-arm spinners.

In 1960 Lancashire, as challengers, were required to win to achieve their sixth title and first since 1949. Norfolk had only to avoid defeat to become champions for the first time. They were the first genuine Minor County, as opposed to the second teams of the first-class counties, to finish top of the table since Berkshire's triumph in 1953. Since then Devon, Northumberland (twice) and Oxfordshire had gained second places but had either lost or drawn their challenge matches.

Lancashire came to Lakenham in September with a team which boasted two Test bowlers and nine players with first-eleven experience. They included the captain, Malcolm Hilton, Colin Hilton (wicket-keeper), Geoff Clayton, Jack Bond, Brian Booth, Roy Collins,

211

Alan Bolton, Roy Tattersall (making his last appearance for Lancashire), and two aspiring teenagers, Peter Lever and Harry Pilling. It was a substantial force and yet, had it not been for one dropped catch at a crucial moment, Norfolk would surely have been proclaimed champions. Norfolk's first-innings total of 153 assumed menacing proportions when Lancashire lost six wickets for 44 runs. They had succumbed, perhaps irretrievably, to a combined spell of hostile and high-class bowling by Walmsley and Corran. Walmsley took four wickets for 25 runs in his first thirteen overs, and Corran, equally dauntless, secured the other two wickets.

Lancashire advanced their total to 66 before a missed catch by Thorne, at mid-on off Corran, erased their blushes and arrested the decline. Then followed a partnership of exasperating freedom between the seventeen-year-old Pilling and Collins. Collins hit 58 and the seventh-wicket pair added 68 runs. Lancashire slipped again to 131 for eight, but consolidated their position with 75 from the last two wickets. Pilling, the brave and resourceful little master, was unbeaten on 79 after two and a half hours. His innings was a key factor in his team's victory by nine wickets.

The last stages of the game presented the riveting spectacle of two England players in a personal duel. Roy Tattersall, who remembers the sheer tenacity of Bill Edrich in this contest, 'wheeled away with such nagging accuracy that there was only one scoring stroke in one series of eight overs,' reported the *Eastern Daily Press*. 'But Edrich did later find the opportunity on one or two occasions to sweep him to the long-leg boundary.' Edrich was Norfolk's top scorer with 43 before he lost his struggle and fell to a catch by Bond in Tattersall's leg trap. Tattersall was able to reflect on an extraordinary analysis in his farewell match: five wickets for 17 runs in 30 overs, 22 of which were maidens.

Edrich's enthusiasm did not wane in his golden twilight in Norfolk. David Armstrong watched him plot his schemes on the Lakenham field. 'Looking at Bill through my binoculars, I thought there was a man who was enjoying every second of his cricket.' Edrich's favourite pulled drive over wide mid-on regularly scattered the spectators in the Wanderers' tent. The urgency of a cricket champion was unfurled in a match of three declarations in 1961. Edrich, for the only time in his career, scored two centuries, each time undefeated, in an exciting victory by five wickets over Staffordshire. His reunion with Jack Ikin, the former Lancashire and England all-rounder and rival captain, stirred the brew of a fluctuating battle. Edrich and Ikin were kindred spirits in their approach to cricket.

Both of Edrich's centuries, placed alongside another from Ikin, were scored under heavy pressure. His first hundred came in the throes of a fight to save the follow-on; the second against the clock after Staffordshire had declared to leave Norfolk to score 262 to win in six minutes under three hours. For much of the game, Staffordshire, making their first visit to Lakenham for thirty-five years, were in the ascendancy. Ikin briskly led the way as they totalled 315 for seven declared at the rate of 85 runs an hour. Norfolk, in their reply, lost five wickets for 117. Edrich and Fiddler checked the collapse with an unbroken sixth-wicket partnership of 147 runs in two hours.

Staffordshire were the cheerful sporting accomplices, entering fully into the adventure of the game, after Edrich had made a challenging declaration before lunch. After their own second declaration, the visitors bowled 57 overs in less than three hours in Norfolk's second innings. More than half of the overs were

213

delivered by their quicker bowlers. The threat of rain loomed for a time, but the intermittent drizzle lacked the severity to halt an enthralling tussle. The finish was tight enough to provoke piping exclamations of dismay from the partisan small boys. The Staffordshire bowlers were besieged by an anxious chorus. They were told to get on with the game and not waste time drying the soaking ball, or make protracted field changes.

Blofeld and Hall, as the opening Norfolk batsmen, laid the foundations for the assault; the loss of Witherden gave pause for doubt before Fiddler and Coomb, in turn, securely helped Edrich to put on 128 runs in seventy-one minutes. Edrich went to his half-century in even time and hoisted his century in another forty-two minutes. He became the first Norfolk player to score two centuries in a match. It was altogether fitting that the winning runs – off the third ball of the last over – should come from Edrich's bat with his thirtieth boundary of the game.

Justin Edrich remembered another explosion of hitting in a match against Hertfordshire at Lakenham in 1970. Bill's lusty strokeplay enlivened a game drifting sleepily to a draw. Norfolk were set a target of 160 in fifteen minutes plus twenty overs. It was intended by Hertfordshire as a token declaration; but, as his son explained, Bill characteristically believed that it was within his striking compass. 'Father opened the innings and ended up with 93 not out. This was at a time when, at the age of fifty-four, he generally hit ones or fours. He was getting a little old to run twos.' The boundaries – two sixes and ten fours – did alleviate Edrich's exertions. It was a Bank Holiday act of derring-do to put to shame the tedious accumulation of runs on a firm and true wicket. Before Edrich's onslaught and the thrilling finale more than 650 runs had been scored in a profitless exercise in the broiling heat. Edrich's innings lasted just twenty-four overs and Norfolk raced to a scores-level draw.

The irony of the match was that the visitors gained three points for their first-innings lead. Norfolk's reward for Edrich's endeavours was a solitary point. Had Norfolk been all out, the match would have been classed as a tie and each side would have received five points.

The *Eastern Daily Press* reported on a match which suddenly 'boiled into a state of frenzied activity'. When the first of the last twenty overs was signalled, the Norfolk score was 29 for one and 131 runs were still needed at a rate of 6.5 runs an over. 'It was just the sort of challenge to spur Edrich. He has the quality of being able to mould his play to the situation in hand,' commented the Lakenham correspondent. The tempo never flagged in an exhilarating run quest. Eighteen runs were required at the start of the nineteenth over; a six-hit by Edrich sent the ball hurtling over long-on and two singles reduced the deficit to nine. Edrich scored two off the first ball of the last over and scampered a single off the second; his partner, David Pilch, ran a single off the third; and then Edrich took three runs off the fourth and fifth balls. The silence was now as tremblingly fearful as in any modern one-day final. The strike had, perhaps, passed to the wrong batsman. 'Pilch swung and missed; Edrich ran a bye to the wicket-keeper; and Pilch sprinted to the other end,' added the report. 'It was all-square in the book if not as regards points.'

Nigel Moore, along with other Norfolk players of the time, has commented upon the indestructibility of Edrich. 'He had a most remarkable constitution,' said Moore. 'He seldom seemed tired, or off colour. Even in his early fifties, he could bowl and field all day. Allied to this activity he could play commanding innings

215

involving scampering up and down the wicket almost like a young man.' Jack Borrett, a lifelong companion, described Edrich as a trusty competitor. 'I could not have wished for a better friend. The Norfolk boys, who played under Bill, would have lain down on a length if he had told them to do so.' Tracey Moore, one Norfolk bowler who prospered as a cricketing pupil, has endorsed the faith which Edrich engendered in the abilities of the young men at Lord's and Lakenham. 'I always thought that I was going to get wickets when Bill was skipper. He could instantly spot a batsman's weakness. If I bowled indifferently, I felt bad at letting him down. Bill was a great leader. We would have followed him to hell and back.'

Everyone marvelled at Edrich's undiminished appetite for cricket at a time when most men of his age and experience would have settled for slippered or deck-chair ease. It is highly unlikely that any other player of comparable stature has surpassed him in continuity of service. He had made his first-class debut for the Minor Counties against Oxford University at Oxford in 1934, having first represented Norfolk in 1932. Seventeen seasons with Middlesex were followed by another thirteen to complete a total of eighteen seasons with Norfolk. In his last Norfolk phase he scored 6,422 runs and took 300 wickets. In 1960, at the age of forty-four, he achieved his best Minor Counties aggregate of 852 runs, at an average of 53.25. Four years later he topped 700 runs and, if his contributions dwindled in the latter years, he could still be relied upon to rally his team in a crisis.

It was an impressive sequence; but the underlying keynote is that he loved cricket at any level, striving hard to win and yet magnanimous in defeat, provided all associated with him had done their best.

Bob Appleyard said that Bill would travel anywhere for a game of cricket. 'He didn't mind if he was a loser in contests with the younger generation. His attitude was to be always encouraging.' It was not in Edrich's nature, as might be true of other great cricketers, to be affronted by the temerity of a young colt bowling him out in a minor game. 'If it gives the boy some pleasure to do this, it must be good for the game,' was the response of an ageless gallant.

Appleyard, as a business associate of the Mackintosh chocolate manufacturing family, regularly visited their Norwich factory in the 1960s and 1970s. He was a guest of the then Hon. John Mackintosh, the president of the neighbouring Barford club. Appleyard was one of the many former first-class cricketers, including Edrich, who represented the President's XI in the annual matches against the village club. Nigel Moore was another member of the team. 'We could usually win the match as a result of our bowling strength on a very uncertain wicket,' he recalled. 'Batting, however, was a lottery and quite dangerous; most of us decided to have a slog before the inevitable shooter or lifter got us out. Not so Bill. He would bat as if his life depended upon it.' Moore remembered one match in which Edrich came in at tea, remarking that it was a 'very interesting wicket' and that it was necessary to watch the ball quite carefully. 'Bill took the knocks that came and ground out the runs with infinite patience,' added Moore.

Another facet of Edrich's personality was his total absence of mannerisms and nerves. As an illustration, Moore recalled one match at Lakenham. 'Most of the players needed to relax after a morning's bowl. They would shower and change at lunch-time. Bill never seemed to bother.' On this occasion, Bill had been bowling and the zip on his trousers had broken. Every

217

time he bent down, the zip slipped and he had to pull it up again and hold it in place while walking to the other end and directing the field. Moore said: 'On his return to the pavilion, Bill slipped on his England blazer as usual and went straight into lunch. He quite forgot to change his trousers and went out after lunch in the same state. He could not bowl again that afternoon.'

One of Edrich's last appearances for Norfolk was in the Gillette Cup first-round game against Middlesex in April 1970 at Lord's. It was a poignant occasion, befitting Bill's final match on the ground thirty-three years after first playing there. 'For one glorious hour he disdainfully rolled back the years and showed why he is part of the legend of Lord's,' wrote Alex Bannister. Middlesex were comfortable winners by 147 runs; but it was a day of overflowing sentiment and indisputably belonged to the returning hero. Edrich's day began with a telegram from Denis Compton. It read: 'Willing and able to run between the wickets for you!' Denis's services were not called upon as Bill, now with strands of greying hair denoting his years, proceeded to launch a fierce assault upon the Middlesex bowling.

Edrich came in to bat with the Norfolk score at 42 for three, his head thrust forward in the well-remembered gesture of antagonism. 'It is difficult for a small man to stride but Edrich still manages it,' reported John Woodcock. 'He arrived at the wicket at just after four o'clock and by quarter-past five he had got his pulled drive into working order. That, and the hook and the cut, always brought him his livelihood.' Bryan Stevens was also at Lord's to file a report for his Norfolk readers on a player he had watched and admired for a lifetime: 'Edrich, applauded all the way to the wicket, took some time to get off the mark. Gradually he moved into gear and brought the memories flooding back.'

The last six balls of Bill's innings yielded 22 runs.

They included two sixes, one struck high on to the Grandstand balcony, and another still higher on to the topmost tier. Keith Jones was the bowler in the firing line. Justin Edrich, as a later Suffolk opponent of Jones in a match against Bedfordshire, recalled being derided for not following his father's example. 'I feel sure that it was almost a pleasure for Keith to be struck hard and often in Bill's last game at Lord's.' Edrich was Norfolk's top scorer with 36 out of a total of 117. He was at the wicket for a little over the hour. He was bowled at last by the suffering Jones, attempting another steepling hit and quite clearly intent on dislodging Father Times from his pedestal.

Edrich's cricketing reign in Norfolk ended in 1971, thirty-nine years after he had walked out as a resolute schoolboy at Lakenham to face the mighty Mohammad Nissar. One other highlight was still in the offing, however, for, in August 1977, Norfolk's 150th anniversary was celebrated with a match against the MCC. Edrich, representing the visitors, did not neglect this important date. His presence was hailed by a large crowd at Lakenham.

David Armstrong wrote: 'They had, like me, come along to pay homage to a man who had been instrumental in giving the Norfolk cricketing public so much pleasure.'

CHAPTER 12

Farewell on
St George's Day

'Bill was a great sportsman, who contributed so much to cricket and provided everybody with all the good things about the game itself.' – *Denis Compton*

The assembly of diners at the Grosvenor House Hotel raised their voices yet again in another chorus of 'Land of Hope and Glory'. The band of the Blues and Royals blew strong on these chords of patriotism. The decibel count of the host of men singing their hearts out neared the volume of song at the last night of the Proms.

At the Sportsman's table at the St George's Day lunch in 1986, one emotional man was standing proudly to attention. Tears were streaming down his face. For Bill Edrich, the extraordinary patriot, this was his special day. He was having a wonderful time, beating out the rhythms of the music in a state of rapture. All were caught in the grip of his fervour as the band played on. 'Everything was so England,' recalled one of the diners, John Murray. 'Bill could not contain himself; before long he was among the bandsmen, still holding a glass of champagne; and marching with them on the ballroom floor.'

Among the guests at this gathering was Air Marshal Sir Ivor Broom. Sir Ivor and Edrich had both been involved in the low-level daylight attack on the power stations around Cologne in August 1941. It was the first meeting of two brave airmen. In his speech Sir Ivor singled out Edrich for special recognition. He praised the courage which had earned him the DFC. 'Bill was in a happy mood, surrounded by his many friends,' recalled Sir Ivor later. 'He was very touched that I should remind him of the great contribution he had made when he led his flight of six aircraft on a famous and historic raid.'

The champagne flowed to charge and recharge the merry reminiscences of the old wartime campaigners; and at six o'clock Bill Edrich was driven home in style in a company Rolls, ordered by one of the industrialist guests.

Nine hours later, John Murray was awakened by a telephone call from Bill's wife, Mary. She announced, to Murray's astonishment and sorrow, that Bill was dead. 'I couldn't believe what I was hearing. He had been in such marvellous spirits only a few hours earlier.' Edrich had belonged to a small élite of men who symbolised defiance in cricket and war. His unexpected downfall was both amazing and tragic. His reputation for indestructibility had reminded one writer of the death of the boxing champion, Rocky Marciano. 'If you stand over him and start to count to ten, I think you will find he will come round,' was the reaction of one friend at the news. It is certain that Bill's own friends prayed for a similar outcome.

Denis Compton, who had missed the St George's Day function for the first time in many years, especially mourned the loss. He later learned from Bill's widow that his old friend had arrived home safely after his happy day. Bill was in buoyant mood as he recounted the events at the lunch. He then excused himself to go upstairs for a rest. On the landing, he

221

overbalanced and fell heavily to strike his head at the foot of the stairs. He sustained a fracture at the base of the skull. He died on the stroke of midnight on the way to hospital. Denis has since recalled that, at the subsequent post-mortem examination, the doctor had described Edrich as a very fit man. He expressed the view that Bill was probably a teetotaller. 'So the old boy would have stayed with us for much longer but for his fall,' added Denis. Mary Edrich did not survive her husband by many months. She was killed in a car accident before she had time to recover from her distress at the bereavement.

Edrich's death came twenty-nine days after his seventieth birthday. Many people, mindful of his action-packed life, have commented that his final great achievement was to reach the biblical 'three score years and ten'. Bob Appleyard provided words of solace: 'Bill had enjoyed a splendid life,' he said. 'He had nothing to come back for to complete it.' The sadness in cricket circles was compounded by the death of another great player, Jim Laker, only twenty-four hours earlier. Laker, accounted the finest of England's off-spin bowlers, had died at his London home at the age of sixty-four. He had failed to recover from a recent gall-bladder operation.

The rivalry between Edrich and Laker – and their fiercely competitive duels – is enshrined in the folklore of the game. The ice was always broken off the field. Hostilities were suspended when they came together as England team-mates, notably as members of Leonard Hutton's eleven which regained the Ashes at The Oval in 1953. One of their contemporaries said: 'Bill used to rejoice in flogging Jim around. He will be delighted that Jim is going to have to bowl at him up there.'

The celebrations which had marked Edrich's seventieth birthday prompted one admirer, Ian Wooldridge,

"Now this is Heaven –
Laker bowling to Lethcn!"

to applaud the arrival at this milestone. He considered that any definitive profile of Bill would be more appropriate in *The Lancet* rather than *Wisden*. 'He played and fought with old-fashioned virtues; that you were never beaten until they'd battered the last breath out of your body. He was convinced that to be born English was to have drawn a winning ticket in life.' Wooldridge said that Edrich's birthday was the timeliest of reminders that cricket, in tight situations, demands the character that wins wars and does not get the peace out of perspective.

Ten of Edrich's closest friends were special guests among those invited to the birthday banquet at the Berkeley Hotel in London. It was sponsored and arranged by Raphael Djanogli, a Lord's Taverner, who had first watched Edrich from the eaves of the pavilion at Lord's in 1949. The tickets cost £100 a head and the dinner raised £3,000 for various charities. Arthur Morris, the former Australian captain and opening batsman, travelled to England to pay his tribute. He brought with him the congratulations of his compatriots, penned by Sir Donald Bradman, Keith Miller and Bill O'Reilly. They demonstrated their enduring respect for an indomitable rival and friend. Among other prized tokens of admiration, relayed by Morris, was a telegram from the Australian Prime Minister, Bob Hawke. It read: 'Bill is remembered with a great deal of affection as a determined and courageous batsman, who produced his best when the going was toughest. Ray Lindwall, Keith Miller and Bill Johnston led the Australian attack for much of Bill's Test career. His record against us was outstanding.'

Shortly before the age of sixty, in 1976, Edrich had embarked upon a new business career as a sales associate with Hambro Life (now Allied Dunbar). He combined this work with a key role on the Middlesex committee. John Murray remembered Edrich's studied guidance in club matters. 'Bill was very quiet in committee. He didn't rush to make points, but having considered them, he put his views across very forcibly.' Edrich's association with Hambro Life lasted until three months before his death. He brought an engaging zest to this activity; at his peak he was among the top ten per cent in the company's 2,000-strong sales force. Colin Webb, his former manager at the Oxford Circus branch in London, recalled Edrich's achievements: 'Bill was a very good door-opener, technically not brilliant, but admirable in spotting an opportunity. He could grasp the essentials very quickly before calling in the expert.' Bill had a host of influential contacts, who were ideally fitted as prospective clients for Hambro's range of financial services, including pensions, mortgages and investments.

Michael Denison, the stage and film actor, was one beneficiary of Edrich's acumen. Denison formerly lived at Regent's Park, within walking distance of Lord's, and he took every opportunity he could to watch Edrich and Compton in their great years. He and his wife, Dulcie Gray, were close neighbours of Edrich when his business commitments brought him back to live in the Buckinghamshire village of Chesham. 'Dulcie and I were never financial wizards,' said Denison. 'Our chief motive was not that we were on to a good thing, but to do something for Bill in appreciation of all the entertainment he had given us over the years.' He added: 'Our virtue was rewarded in enlisting his advice. We couldn't have done better with our investment.' The Denisons cherished their late flowering friendship with Edrich. In his flirtatious mode, said Michael, 'Bill did have a wicked gleam in his eye'; but it was friendly and never went beyond the bounds of courtesy. Dulcie adored Bill as, in another act of worship, she had become a convert to cricket after watching Keith Miller on television.

Edrich regained his stride and mobility after two hip joint operations in the latter years. He bounced back characteristically as if he had leapt over the smallest of hurdles. His elder brother, Eric, recalled an imperturbable man. Bill refused to allow one of the

operations to cause him to abandon a promise to visit
Eric at his home near Huntingdon. 'Bill said to me: "I'll
be seeing you, Friday week, 'Ric boy". He was as good
as his word. He came out of the station without a stick
and walked to our car. He had only had his operation
ten days before. My word, Bill was a determined lad.'
This may have been the time, as one correspondent
reported, when Edrich persuaded a business associate to smuggle in a bottle of whisky during his stay
in hospital.

Colin Webb has remarked upon Edrich's constitution, which did not weaken in the years leading
up to his death. 'Bill did get drunk very quickly;
he then continued slowly and had the capacity to
go on until five or six in the morning. He would
then present himself, bleary-eyed but still upright,
for a breakfast consultation with one of our clients
at the Ritz.' Webb said that, before lunch, Edrich was
'charming, very straightforward and an extremely nice
person'; afterwards, like Dr Jekyll after his potion, he
could be bullish and dogmatic and less amenable. One
constant frustration for the Hambro manager was that,
despite all his best attempts – and he was genuinely
concerned about the wasted opportunities – Bill would
not make provision for his own financial security. To
him it was an irrelevance; Edrich always lived for the
day. 'He was a man with a high income need and it was
necessary for him to sell at a reasonable rate in order to
live,' said Webb. Shortly before his retirement, Edrich
delegated some of his clients to a fellow sales associate;
under a split-commission arrangement, this enabled
him to receive part of the income generated under
the scheme. It was but a fraction of what he would
have gained by prudent investment in his best-selling
years. 'Bill ended up with virtually nothing in terms of
finance considering what he had earned,' said Webb.

In the evening of his life Edrich drew ever closer to his family. He was overjoyed to spend Christmas with his two sons, Jasper and Justin, in South Africa in 1982. 'Dad was desperately proud to be with us both for the first time,' recalled Justin. 'We would sit down and have long philosophical debates about the meaning of life. Dad hadn't got to grips with that too much, but he thought he had. Jasper would step back from arguing with the irrationality of some of his viewpoints. I couldn't do that. Bill would play "Plato" to my "Socrates" and we would be going at it hammer and tongs. Jasper was always the voice of reason, sensible and more grown-up than either of us.'

Bill and Justin were forged in the same mould; their verbal sparring, never malicious, was calculated, in the phrase of the son, to test his calibre, so that he could take over the mantle of his father. 'Dad would do this from the stance of acting the devil's advocate.'

Justin's last combat with Bill was fought just two weeks before his father's death. 'We went to a pub in Amersham for lunch,' he recalled. Over drinks, the exchange of words flourished and grew to the crescendo of a massive argument. It was a thoroughly entertaining interlude for them and others eavesdropping on the discussion. No quarter was given or lost in the contest. 'I drove Dad back to his flat at Chesham,' continued Justin. 'He opened the door, got out, and walked away.' Bill, as if sadly aware that their talks had drawn to a conclusion, looked back with a pensive glance. There were, however, words still left unsaid. He returned to the car and tapped on the window. Justin wound down the window. Bill said: 'You do know that I enjoy our little arguments together'. 'It was a lovely last memory of Dad,' Justin remembered.

Jasper Edrich, who now resides in Johannesburg, recalled the fluctuations of his father's increasingly frenetic life. Bill was beset by bouts of loneliness between his marital innings. He spent much time with his elder brother, Eric, in the 1980s. 'Dad tried very hard in late-night telephone calls to persuade me to return to Britain following the internal unrest in South Africa during this period. He would regularly phone, rather two sheets in the wind, and obviously in need of closer family contact.'

Following his fifth marriage to Buckinghamshire hairdresser, Mary Somerville, in 1983, Edrich swung back into a brighter state of mind. Cricket friends were always pleased that Bill was happy again. His nuptial excursions did cause amusement. John Warr once impishly declared that Edrich's favourite literary quotation was the words of the marriage ceremony. It was reported that at one of the weddings, when Warr was asked by the usher whether he wanted the bride's, or the groom's side of the church, he just said: 'Season!'

The flights of fun neglected the plight – the deeper worries – of a man who was compelled by nature to rush headlong and often heedlessly into romance. Bill clutched feverishly at the hems of happiness. He could not sustain his marriages because he was never fully at ease with the conventional mode of life. There was also, in the view of his sister, Ena, a determination not to lapse into enfeebled old age. Bill would have been a poor candidate for a wheelchair. In the latter days Ena had a firm conviction that her brother subconsciously wanted to die.

At her home in Western Australia she was constantly bombarded by telephone calls from Bill, at all hours of the morning. Ena remembered, with special vividness, their last conversation, two weeks before he died. On this particular day her husband, Philip, answered the call. Quite out of the blue, Bill remarked: 'Phil, you've been a good boy. I do thank you for looking after my sister so well'. Ena then came on to the line. Bill reminisced about the joys of his seventieth birthday celebrations. His following words made it clear that he thought Dinah – her pet family name from a 1930s song hit – could not 'have been finer'. At the close of their talk, he voiced his affection in an unaccustomed manner. 'Bill had never said it before – and I thought it was quite significant.' 'Dinah,' said Bill, 'I do love you very much,' was his parting shot. 'It was almost as if he had a sort of premonition of his impending death,' she said.

Ian Wooldridge in one telling tribute to a flawed but much-loved man, wrote: 'Edrich epitomised the particularly British breed of incurable scallywag. He may have cheated on a couple of his wives, but in the sports arena he never cheated in his life. It would have implied weakness, an admission that he wasn't good enough to survive within the rules.

'He loved life too much to harbour grudges, sustain feuds, or niggle opponents with whom, like as not, he'd be out on the tiles at the close of play. But there was a bottom line to all this roistering. You had to be there before the start of play, next day. Then, hungover or otherwise, you had to fight.'

The winning style and stamina were remembered by the gathering of cricketing personalities at Edrich's funeral service at St Mary's Parish Church, Chesham, in May 1986. They recalled the warmth of his personality and the good fellowship which was his trademark; and the uplifting effect he had upon people from many walks of life. The Rev. Robin Smith, Rector of Great Chesham, who conducted the service, said that for him, as a fellow native of Norfolk, Edrich had been the inspiration of his childhood. 'Bill had courage, skill and generosity, but beneath the public image there was a person who longed to be loved, appreciated and admired.' Edrich's ashes were later scattered at Lord's by his widow, a signal but very rare honour for a valiant servant of the game.

The following October a service of thanksgiving was held at St Clement Danes, the Central Church of the Royal Air Force in the Strand. George Mann, Edrich's former captain and Middlesex president, read one of the lessons; the other reading was by Brian Johnston; and the address was given by Denis Compton. 'We remember with gratitude his team-spirit and all-round skills,' said the Rev. R. N. Kenward, the Resident Chaplain of St Clement Danes. The minister praised Edrich's conscientious and positive contribution to Middlesex cricket and his support for the Lord's Taverners. 'Above all,' he said, 'we treasured the memories of the delight he would occasion through his great sense of fun and his ability to live life enthusiastically to the full.' The RAF Central Band played the 'Dam Busters March' and Anne Shelton, an evocative voice from the second world war, gave an encore of a song which had always charmed Bill – 'A Nightingale Sang in Berkeley Square'. Jessy Edrich was one of the returning wives, persuaded to attend by her son. She looked around nervously at her former cricket friends, surprised to find these veterans now greying at the temples and a little more portly, but still the affable companions of old. 'It was a fantastic occasion,' she said. 'You didn't come out feeling dreadful. Bill went out exactly as he would have wished.'

Bill Edrich was always a man of Lord's; he had a special empathy with a ground upon which he had taken his first dogged cricketing footsteps before decorating it with feats of grandeur. Gubby Allen, one of his influential mentors, had met Bill there during the war. Edrich was enjoying a few days' leave, as a break from his bombing operations. Gubby inquired as to the reason for the visit. Bill, with little expectation of surviving the war, replied: 'I'm just having my last look at Lord's, skipper.'

Happily Edrich did return to play upon the hallowed turf. He would have been proud to know that a stand at Lord's was to be named after him and dedicated to his memory, and that, next to it, was one similarly dedicated to Denis Compton. In 1991 two enclosures at the Nursery End, jointly celebrating the achievements of the two great cricketers, were opened during the lunch interval of a one-day international match. Justin Edrich, representing the family, walked alongside Denis Compton, Lord Griffiths, the MCC president, and Colonel John Stephenson, the club secretary, to take part in the opening ceremony. Justin remembered Denis's roguish comment on one serious omission in the new development. 'How could there be two such stands without a bar between them?' queried Denis.

As he walked out to the acclaim of the vast crowd at Lord's, Denis was besieged by recollections of his old friend. He did, perhaps, call to mind one expression of Bill's patriotism. 'His big thing was playing for England,' said Compton in an obituary tribute. 'He never got over that. "Playing for England, Denis!" he used to say. "Just think of all those other buggers who'll never play for England."'

Denis, who had raised his bat in salute on countless other major occasions at Lord's, was ill-at-ease before the beckoning spectators at the opening ceremony. He had fortified himself beforehand with a good measure of whisky. 'It was very touching to receive the ovation from the crowd. I did wish, though, that Bill had been there beside me. I thought how much he would have loved this day.' In his speech of thanks, Denis said: 'Bill, with a glass of champagne in his hand, will be looking down on us and enjoying every minute.'

The Edrich and Compton stands are side by side now, just as Bill and Denis were resplendently inseparable in their conquering years. They are sentinels of remembrance of a glorious era. Overlooking the illustrious field, they carry the message of a devoted sportsman. 'Cricket is a wonderful game,' said Bill Edrich. 'I hope I can still play it when I'm a really old man. Even if I have to walk out on to the village green, cricket will still be there, deep in my heart.'

APPENDIXES

BIBLIOGRAPHY

John Arlott: *Vintage Summer, 1947* (Eyre & Spottiswoode, 1967).

David Armstrong: *A Short History of Norfolk Cricket* (The Larks Press, 1990).

Trevor Bailey: *The Greatest of My Time* (Eyre & Spottiswoode, 1968)

Ralph Barker: *Ten Great Innings* (Chatto & Windus, 1964); *The Cricketing Family Edrich* (Pelham, 1976).

Sir Donald Bradman: *Farewell to Cricket* (Hodder & Stoughton, 1950).

Neville Cardus: *Close of Play* (Collins, 1956).

Dudley Carew: *England Over* (Chapman & Hall, 1930).

Denis Compton: *End of an Innings* (Oldbourne, 1958); with W. J. Edrich as co-author: *Cricket and All That* (Pelham, 1978).

W. J. Edrich: *Cricket Heritage* (Stanley Paul, 1948); *Round the Wicket* (Muller, 1959).

David Foot, *Beyond Bat and Ball* (Good Books, 1993).

Bill Frindall: *England Test Cricketers* (Collins Willow, 1989).

Alan Hill: *Hedley Verity* (Kingswood Press, 1986).

T. C. F. Prittie: *Cricket North and South* (Sportsman's Book Club, 1955).

Irving Rosenwater: *Sir Donald Bradman* (Batsford, 1978).

Alan Ross: *Australia 55 – A Journal of the MCC Tour* (Michael Joseph, 1955).

E. W. Swanton: *Denis Compton – A Cricket Sketch* (Sporting

Handbooks, 1948); *Sort of a Cricket Person* (Collins, 1972);
Swanton in Australia with MCC, 1946–75 (Collins, 1975).
*A Century of South Africa in Test and International Cricket –
1889–1989* (Jonathan Ball, Johannesburg, 1989).

Contemporary reports in the *Eastern Daily Press; The Bracondalian* (the Bracondale School Magazine); *Daily Telegraph, The
Times, News Chronicle, Daily Mail, Daily Express, Yorkshire Post,
Manchester Guardian, Sydney Morning Herald, Rand Daily Mail*
(Johannesburg); *Natal Mercury* (Durban); *Outspan Magazine;*
and *Everybody's* (containing articles by John Arlott, Louis
Duffus and Lindsay Tuckett); *The Cricketer;* and various
editions of *Wisden Cricketers' Almanack* have provided the
nucleus of printed sources in this book.

STATISTICAL APPENDIX

W. J. EDRICH IN FIRST-CLASS AND MINOR COUNTIES CRICKET

Born: Lingwood, Norfolk   Died: Whitehall Court, Chesham
26 March 1916   24 April 1986

COMPILED BY DAVID KENDIX

First-Class Debut: Minor Counties vs Oxford
University at Oxford
30 May 1934

Middlesex Debut: vs Northamptonshire at Lord's
8 May 1937

Capped by Middlesex: 9 June 1937

England Debut: vs Australia at Nottingham
10 June 1938

Final Match for England: vs Australia at Adelaide
28 January 1955

Final First-Class Match: Middlesex vs Surrey at Lord's
16 August 1958

ORDER OF SECTIONS

W. J. EDRICH IN FIRST-CLASS CRICKET
Season by season record
Summary of teams represented
List of centuries
Five wickets in an innings, ten wickets in a match
Double-century partnerships
Partnerships over 100 with D. C. S. Compton
Record on each UK ground
County Championship record for Middlesex
Record at Lord's
County record against each opponent
Test match record – series by series
Test match record against each country
Test match record – innings by innings

W.J. EDRICH IN MINOR COUNTIES
CHAMPIONSHIP
Norfolk record

A MISCELLANY OF FACTS AND
ACHIEVEMENTS

W. J. Edrich in first-class cricket

Season by season record

In England

Season	Matches	Inns.	N.O.	Runs	H.S.	Average	100s	Balls	Runs	Wkts	Average	B.B.	Ct/St
1934	2	3	1	130	63	65.00	0	354	169	1	169.00	1-110	0
1935	2	3	0	93	79	31.00	0	199	112	3	37.33	2-89	0
1936	5	9	1	440	114	55.00	3	270	160	3	53.33	1-1	4
1937	34	53	5	2154	175	44.87	3	1432	699	21	33.28	3-71	25
1938	30	51	6	2378	245	52.84	6	1054	587	15	39.13	4-15	27
1939	29	45	1	2186	161	49.68	7	1486	762	15	50.80	3-33	30
1945	9	16	3	602	78	46.30	0	648	354	6	59.00	1-19	7
1946	29	45	7	1890	222*	49.73	5	3086	1408	73	19.28	7-48	29
1947	30	52	8	3539	267*	80.43	12	3377	1513	67	22.58	6-28	35
1948	33	55	6	2428	168*	49.55	9	3042	1614	37	43.62	4-25	40
1949	35	62	5	2253	182	39.52	5	3379	1688	48	35.16	6-83	52
1950	27	45	5	1760	189	44.00	5	2231	1090	22	49.54	3-34	12
1951	37	58	4	2086	118	38.62	2	3183	1381	34	40.61	6-45	24
1952	34	63	4	2281	239	38.66	6	3176	1618	53	30.52	6-59	31
1953	32	60	6	2557	211	47.35	5	793	383	9	42.55	3-50	34
1954	31	50	5	1783	195	39.62	6	642	255	10	25.50	3-19	28
1955	33	63	5	1642	133	28.31	2	76	30	0			28
1956	34	58	3	1831	208*	33.29	2	161	84	5	16.80	1-4	30
1957	30	54	2	1192	77	22.92	0	458	173	5	34.60	2-84	34
1958	15	26	3	534	103	23.21	1						13/1
Total	511	871	80	33759	267*	42.67	79	29047	14080	427	32.97	7-48	483/1

Overseas

Overseas	Matches	Inns.	N.O.	Runs	H.S.	Average	100s	Balls	Runs	Wkts	Average	B.B.	Ct
1937/38	14	24	5	876	140*	46.10	2	587	318	13	24.46	4-25	11
1938/39	15	20	5	914	219	60.93	4	1144	458	13	35.23	4-10	12
1946/47	18	27	2	998	119	39.92	1	2072	1032	26	39.69	4-26	15
1954/55	11	18	0	293	88	16.27	0	64	53	0			5
1956/57	2	4	0	125	58	31.25	0	36	15	0			3
Total	60	93	12	3206	219	39.58	7	3903	1876	52	36.07	4-25	46

	Matches	Inns.	N.O.	Runs	H.S.	Average	100s	Balls	Runs	Wkts	Average	B.B.	Ct/St
First-Class	571	964	92	36965	267*	42.39	86	32950	15956	479	33.31	7-48	529/1

Summary of teams represented

In England

Team	Matches	Inns.	N.O.	Runs	H.S.	Average	100s	Balls	Runs	Wkts	Average	B.B.	Ct/St
Middlesex	389	658	65	25738	267*	43.40	62	21694	9975	328	30.41	7-48	382/1
M.C.C.	45	79	7	2720	135	37.77	8	2435	1303	28	46.53	3-37	32
England (Tests)	24	38	2	1516	191	42.11	4	1821	993	29	34.24	4-68	31
Gentlemen (v. Players)	14	28	0	1240	133	44.28	3	720	430	9	47.77	3-9	8
Other	39	68	6	2545	164*	41.04	2	2377	1379	33	41.78	6-83	30
Total	511	871	80	33759	267*	42.67	79	29047	14080	427	32.97	7-48	483/1

The 39 other matches were for the following teams:

13 – (All) England (XI); 8 – South (of England); 3 – Minor Counties, H.D.G. Leveson-Gower's XI, T.N. Pearce's XI;

2 – Gentlemen of England, Sir P.F. Warner's XI; 1 – Players, R.A.F., The Rest, Over 30, Under 30.

Overseas

The five overseas tours were with the following teams:

1937/38 – Lord Tennyson's Team to India; 1938/39 – M.C.C. to South Africa; 1946/47 – M.C.C. to Australia and New Zealand;
1954/55 – M.C.C. to Australia and New Zealand; 1956/57 – C.G. Howard's XI to India.

List of centuries: 86

No.	Score	For	Opponents	Venue	Season
1	114	M.C.C.	Surrey	Lord's	1936
2	114	M.C.C.	Oxford University	Lord's	1936
3	112	M.C.C.	Kent	Folkestone	1936
4	175	Middlesex	Lancashire	Lord's	1937
5	113	Middlesex	Somerset	Weston-super-Mare	1937
6	129	Middlesex	Somerset	Lord's	1937
7	140*	Lord Tennyson's XI	Sind	Karachi	1937/38
8	130*	Lord Tennyson's XI	Madras	Madras	1937/38
9	104	M.C.C.	Yorkshire	Lord's	1938
10	115	M.C.C.	Surrey	Lord's	1938
11	182	Middlesex	Gloucestershire	Lord's	1938
12	245	Middlesex	Nottinghamshire	Lord's	1938
13	118	Middlesex	Gloucestershire	Bristol	1938
14	159	Middlesex	Warwickshire	Birmingham	1938
15	109	M.C.C.	Griqualand West	Kimberley	1938/39
16	101*	M.C.C.	Rhodesia	Salisbury	1938/39
17	150	M.C.C.	Natal	Pietermaritzburg	1938/39
18	219	England	South Africa	Durban	1938/39
19	118	Middlesex	Hampshire	Newport (I.o.W.)	1939
20	102	Middlesex	Lancashire	Manchester	1939
21	125	Middlesex	Lancashire	Lord's	1939
22	160	Middlesex	Nottinghamshire	Nottingham	1939
23	161	Middlesex	Sussex	Hove	1939
24	110*	Middlesex	Surrey	Lord's	1939
25	101	Middlesex	Warwickshire	Lord's	1939
26	109	Middlesex	Sussex	Lord's	1946

27	111	Middlesex	Essex	Westcliff-on-Sea	1946
28	127*	Middlesex	Gloucestershire	Lord's	1946
29	222*	Middlesex	Northamptonshire	Northampton	1946
30	147	Middlesex	Surrey	Lord's	1946
31	119	England	Australia	Sydney	1946/47
32	102	Middlesex	Somerset	Lord's	1947
33	225	Middlesex	Warwickshire	Birmingham	1947
34	106	Middlesex	Sussex	Lord's	1947
35	133*	Middlesex	South Africans	Lord's	1947
36	189	England	South Africa	Lord's	1947
37	102	Middlesex	Yorkshire	Leeds	1947
38	191	England	South Africa	Manchester	1947
39	257	Middlesex	Leicestershire	Leicester	1947
40	267*	Middlesex	Northamptonshire	Northampton	1947
41	130	Middlesex	Kent	Canterbury	1947
42	157*	Middlesex	Surrey	Oval	1947
43	180	Middlesex	Rest of England	Oval	1947
44	128*	Middlesex	Sussex	Lord's	1948
45	168*	Middlesex	Somerset	Lord's	1948
46	112	Middlesex	Essex	Brentwood	1948
47	133	Middlesex	Derbyshire	Derby	1948
48	111	England	Australia	Leeds	1948
49	111	Middlesex	Glamorgan	Lord's	1948
50	128	Gentlemen of England	Australians	Lord's	1948
51	122	Middlesex	Warwickshire	Lord's	1948
52	164*	All England XI	Glamorgan	Cardiff	1948
53	134	Middlesex	Northamptonshire	Lord's	1949
54	114	Middlesex	Warwickshire	Lord's	1949
55	113	Middlesex	Leicestershire	Leicester	1949
56	182	Middlesex	Hampshire	Bournemouth	1949

No.	Team	Score	Opponent	Venue	Year
57	England	100	New Zealand	Oval	1949
58	M.C.C.	129	Yorkshire	Lord's	1950
59	Middlesex	189	Glamorgan	Lord's	1950
60	Middlesex	152*	Sussex	Lord's	1950
61	Middlesex	111	Kent	Lord's	1950
62	M.C.C.	135	Yorkshire	Scarborough	1950
63	Middlesex	101	Cambridge University	Cambridge	1951
64	Middlesex	118	Glamorgan	Swansea	1951
65	Middlesex	126	Kent	Lord's	1952
66	Middlesex	239	Oxford University	Oxford	1952
67	Middlesex	175*	Worcestershire	Dudley	1952
68	Middlesex	109	Essex	Colchester	1952
69	Middlesex	109	Lancashire	Manchester	1952
70	Middlesex	129	Indians	Lord's	1952
71	Middlesex	166	Essex	Westcliff-on-Sea	1953
72	Middlesex	127	Leicestershire	Lord's	1953
73	Middlesex	105	Lancashire	Manchester	1953
74	Middlesex	211	Essex	Lord's	1953
75	Gentlemen	133	Players	Scarborough	1953
76	Middlesex	105	Hampshire	Lord's	1954
77	Middlesex	141	Worcestershire	Lord's	1954
78	Middlesex	161*	Cambridge University	Cambridge	1954
79	Middlesex	105	Leicestershire	Lord's	1954
80	Middlesex	195	Warwickshire	Birmingham	1954
81	Middlesex	102	Northamptonshire	Northampton	1954
82	Middlesex	125*	Warwickshire	Birmingham	1955
83	Gentlemen	133	Players	Scarborough	1955
84	Middlesex	208*	Derbyshire	Chesterfield	1956
85	Gentlemen	133	Players	Scarborough	1956
86	M.C.C.	103	Cambridge University	Lord's	1958

Five wickets in an innings: 11

O	M	W	R	For	Opponents	Venue	Season
13	3	5	30	Middlesex	Kent	Maidstone	1946
26	6	7	69	Middlesex	Northamptonshire	Northampton	1946
29	7	5	74	Middlesex	Surrey	Oval	1946
16	1	7	48	Middlesex	Worcestershire	Worcester	1946
17	2	5	52	Middlesex	Surrey	Lord's	1946
12	2	6	28	Middlesex	Gloucestershire	Lord's	1947
25.1	6	5	61	Middlesex	Worcestershire	Lord's	1947
27	5	5	69	Middlesex	Worcestershire	Lord's	1947
21	1	6	83	Over 30	Under 30	Hastings	1949
22	5	6	45	Middlesex	Sussex	Hove	1951
23	7	6	59	Middlesex	Warwickshire	Lord's	1952

Ten wickets in a match: 3

O	M	W	R	For	Opponents	Venue	Season
38	6	10	121	Middlesex	Worcestershire	Worcester	1946
52.1	11	10	130	Middlesex	Worcestershire	Lord's	1947
43.5	10	10	133	Middlesex	Warwickshire	Lord's	1952

Double-century partnerships: 24

P'ship	Wkt	Edrich	Partner	Score	For	Opponents	Venue	Season
424*	3rd	168*	D.C.S. Compton	252*	Middlesex	Somerset	Lord's	1948
370	3rd	189	D.C.S. Compton	208	England	South Africa	Lord's	1947
324	2nd	195	S.M. Brown	148	Middlesex	Warwickshire	Birmingham	1954
315	2nd	175*	A.W. Thompson	158	Middlesex	Worcestershire	Dudley	1952
304	3rd	182	D.C.S. Compton	163	Middlesex	Gloucestershire	Lord's	1938
296	3rd	114	E.H. Hendren	202	M.C.C.	Surrey	Lord's	1936
296	3rd	147	D.C.S. Compton	235	Middlesex	Surrey	Lord's	1946
287*	3rd	157*	D.C.S. Compton	137*	Middlesex	Surrey	Oval	1947
280	2nd	219	P.A. Gibb	120	England	South Africa	Durban	1938/39
277	2nd	257	D.C.S. Compton	151	Middlesex	Leicestershire	Leicester	1947
267	3rd	239	S.M. Brown	99	Middlesex	Oxford University	Oxford	1952
263	1st	109	L. Hutton	149	M.C.C.	Griqualand West	Kimberley	1938/39
228	3rd	113	E.H. Hendren	138	Middlesex	Somerset	Weston-super-Mare	1937
228	3rd	191	D.C.S. Compton	115	England	South Africa	Manchester	1947
223	3rd	106	D.C.S. Compton	110	Middlesex	Sussex	Lord's	1947
223	4th	161	F.G. Mann	88	Middlesex	Sussex	Hove	1939
222	2nd	134	S.M. Brown	108	Middlesex	Northamptonshire	Lord's	1949
221	5th	222*	A.W. Thompson	77	Middlesex	Northamptonshire	Northampton	1946
218	2nd	100	L. Hutton	206	England	New Zealand	Oval	1949
211	3rd	267*	D.C.S. Compton	110	Middlesex	Northamptonshire	Northampton	1947
209	2nd	129	G.E. Hart	84	Middlesex	Somerset	Lord's	1937
207	1st	98	L. Hutton	108	M.C.C.	Natal	Durban	1938/39
204	2nd	182	J.D. Robertson	123	Middlesex	Hampshire	Bournemouth	1949
203	2nd	102	J.D. Robertson	101	Middlesex	Northamptonshire	Northampton	1954

Other partnerships over 100 with D. C. S. Compton: 35

P'ship	Wkt	Edrich	Compton	For	Opponents	Venue	Season
181	3rd	99	113	Middlesex	Leicestershire	Lord's	1951
179	3rd	84	94	Middlesex	Northamptonshire	Lord's	1939
169	3rd	72	202	Middlesex	Cambridge University	Cambridge	1946
169	3rd	84*	88	Middlesex	Kent	Canterbury	1949
163	3rd	159	58	Middlesex	Warwickshire	Birmingham	1938
156	3rd	67	101	Middlesex	Kent	Lord's	1956
148	3rd	71	172	Middlesex	Warwickshire	Lord's	1951
147	3rd	83	74	Middlesex	Sussex	Hove	1953
146	2nd	104	77	M.C.C.	Yorkshire	Lord's	1938
144	3rd	94	107	Middlesex	Northamptonshire	Lord's	1952
138*	3rd	180	246	Middlesex	Rest of England	Oval	1947+
137	3rd	101	86	Middlesex	Warwickshire	Lord's	1939
136	2nd	115	100	M.C.C.	Surrey	Lord's	1938
135	3rd	77*	82	Middlesex	Gloucestershire	Lord's	1954
134	3rd	129	70	Middlesex	Indians	Lord's	1952
127	4th	40	104	Middlesex	Lancashire	Manchester	1957
126	3rd	50	115	Middlesex	Hampshire	Bournemouth	1946
126	3rd	63	72	Middlesex	Kent	Canterbury	1953
125*	3rd	93*	55*	Middlesex	Hampshire	Bournemouth	1946
121	3rd	122	84	Middlesex	Warwickshire	Lord's	1948
121	3rd	64	71	Middlesex	Warwickshire	Birmingham	1949

119	3rd	67	154	Middlesex	South Africans	Lord's	1947
119	3rd	189	75	Middlesex	Glamorgan	Lord's	1950
118	3rd	48	112	Middlesex	Worcestershire	Lord's	1947
115	3rd	79	55	Middlesex	Essex	Colchester	1952
113	3rd	109	90	Middlesex	Essex	Colchester	1952
111	3rd	71	71	M.C.C.	South Australia	Adelaide	1946/47
111	3rd	50	100	Middlesex	Northamptonshire	Peterborough	1953
106	3rd	57	65	England	South Africa	Nottingham	1947
106	3rd	36	113	Middlesex	Surrey	Lord's	1953
104	3rd	64	100*	Middlesex	Derbyshire	Derby	1948
104	3rd	53	179	Middlesex	Lancashire	Lord's	1949
103	2nd	60	85	M.C.C.	Cambridge University	Lord's	1937
103	3rd	54	66	England	Australia	Leeds	1948
102	3rd	119	54	England	Australia	Sydney	1946/47

+ Compton retired hurt on 55. On his resumption the pair added a further 82 for the fifth wicket.

Record on each UK ground

Ground	Matches	Inns.	N.O.	Runs	H.S.	Average	100s	Balls	Runs	Wkts	Average	Ct/St
Lord's	264	456	42	16906	245	40.83	37	14765	7018	212	33.10	263
Scarborough	25	49	2	1529	135	32.53	4	1343	893	15	59.53	14
Oval	23	38	3	1112	180	31.77	3	875	466	15	31.06	23
Hove	15	22	2	1023	161	51.15	1	905	355	15	23.66	12/1
Manchester	15	26	4	1080	191	49.09	4	1072	531	13	40.84	13
Birmingham	12	16	2	1175	225	83.92	4	514	219	9	24.33	9
Nottingham	12	17	1	717	160	44.81	1	1134	571	14	40.78	8
Northampton	11	19	2	989	267*	58.17	3	1068	496	19	26.10	7
Leeds	10	17	0	741	111	43.58	2	396	185	9	20.55	14
Cambridge	7	12	2	597	161*	59.70	2	732	368	7	52.57	8
Canterbury	7	12	2	665	130	66.50	1	396	194	3	64.66	7
Oxford	7	11	1	462	239	46.20	1	482	201	6	33.50	4
Worcester	7	11	1	420	78	42.00	0	471	216	12	18.00	9
Hastings	6	11	0	419	79	38.09	0	330	209	9	23.22	5
Bristol	5	9	1	287	118	35.87	1	205	78	4	19.50	8
Derby	5	9	0	376	133	41.77	1	234	104	1	104.00	4
Folkestone	5	10	1	381	112	42.33	1	403	241	7	34.42	5
Sheffield	5	7	0	106	39	15.14	0	204	80	1	80.00	6
Gloucester	4	6	0	173	55	28.83	0	288	142	4	35.50	2
Leicester	4	8	1	568	257	81.14	2	270	119	3	39.66	2
Portsmouth	4	6	0	113	50	18.83	0	282	108	4	27.00	2
Swansea	4	6	1	332	118	66.40	1	228	93	3	31.00	9
Bath	3	6	1	82	57	16.40	0	189	50	5	10.00	2
Bournemouth	3	6	1	364	182	72.80	1	210	98	3	32.66	6
Bradford	3	3	0	150	69	50.00	0	164	93	1	93.00	4
Chelmsford	3	6	0	144	58	24.00	0	42	25	0	–	3

Cheltenham	3	5	0	81	50	16.20	0					
Chesterfield	3	4	2	236	208*	118.00	1					
Southampton	3	6	2	73	24*	18.25	0					
Westcliff-on-Sea	2	6	0	411	166	68.50	2	210	71	3	23.66	4
Cardiff	2	4	1	204	164*	68.00	1	48	29	3	9.66	2
Colchester	2	4	0	246	109	61.50	1	91	69	0	–	1
Dover	2	3	0	53	30	13.25	0	180	97	4	24.25	5
Maidstone	2	4	0	52	26	17.33	0	192	74	7	10.57	1
Taunton	2	2	1	65	39	16.25	1	186	108	2	54.00	–
Weston-super-Mare	1	2	0	128	113	128.00	0	12	17	0	–	0
Blackpool	1	2	0	40	31	20.00	1	42	27	1	27.00	2
Brentwood	1	1	1	117	112	58.50	0	66	25	0	–	1
Buxton	1	2	0	14	14*	–	1	113	48	3	16.00	1
Dudley	1	2	2	197	175*	35.50	0	56	41	0	–	2
Frome	1	2	0	71	71	69.50	0	120	39	2	19.50	0
Glastonbury	1	1	0	139	89	54.00	0	138	54	1	54.00	0
Hinckley	1	1	0	54	54	56.00	0	66	42	0	–	1
Kettering	1	2	0	56	56	1.00	0	24	4	0	–	1
Kidderminster	1	1	0	2	1	52.00	0	72	41	2	20.50	1
Kingston-upon-Thames	1	2	0	52	52	21.00	0	72	18	2	9.00	2
Liverpool	1	2	0	42	35	45.50	0	139	96	2	48.00	1
Loughborough	1	1	0	91	81	118.00	1	18	27	1	27.00	1
Newport (I.o.W)	1	2	0	118	118	52.50	0					0
Peterborough	1	2	0	105	55	87.00	0					1
Rushden	1	2	1	87	87*	14.50	0					2
Southend	1	2	0	29	26	42.50	0					3
Skegness	1	2	0	85	79	48.00	0					0
Tunbridge Wells	1	1	0	0	0	0.00	0					0
Total	511	871	80	33759	267*	42.67	79	29047	14080	427	32.97	483/1

County Championship record for Middlesex

Season	Matches	Inns.	N.O.	Runs	H.S.	Average	100s	Balls	Runs	Wkts	Average	B.B.	Ct/St
1937	24	36	4	1559	175	48.71	3	790	341	10	34.10	2-24	17
1938	17	29	3	1675	245	64.42	4	632	318	11	28.90	4-15	18
1939	25	38	1	1948	161	52.64	7	1422	718	14	51.28	3-33	29
1946	24	39	7	1739	222*	54.34	5	2826	1256	68	18.47	7-48	22
1947	20	34	5	2257	267*	77.82	8	2274	967	47	20.57	6-28	27
1948	17	25	3	1331	168*	60.50	6	1908	923	25	36.92	4-25	22
1949	22	38	3	1419	182	40.54	4	2348	1080	27	40.00	3-49	34
1950	17	27	4	1090	189	47.39	3	1430	676	16	42.25	3-34	8
1951	27	42	4	1733	118	45.60	1	2463	1052	26	40.46	6-45	21
1952	26	50	4	1689	175*	36.71	4	2436	1163	41	28.36	6-59	23
1953	22	41	4	1748	211	47.24	4	373	154	6	25.66	3-50	22
1954	23	37	3	1381	195	40.61	5	361	141	8	17.62	3-19	24
1955	28	54	5	1296	125*	26.44	1	64	21	0			24
1956	28	47	3	1427	208*	32.43	1	121	46	3	15.33	1-5	28
1957	26	46	2	1016	77	23.09	0	458	173	5	34.60	2-84	29
1958	13	22	3	335	63	17.63	0						10/1
Total	359	605	58	23643	267*	43.22	56	19906	9029	307	29.41	7-48	358/1

Record at Lord's

For:	Matches	Inns.	N.O.	Runs	H.S.	Average	100s	Balls	Runs	Wkts	Average	Ct
Middx (Championship)	191	330	31	12308	245	41.16	27	10859	4958	168	29.51	203
Middx (Other Matches)	15	27	3	866	133*	36.08	2	808	470	9	52.22	12
M.C.C.	35	59	7	2204	129	42.38	6	1764	905	22	41.13	27
England (Tests)	6	10	0	266	189	26.60	1	446	222	6	37.00	9
Other	17	30	1	1262	128	43.51	1	888	463	7	66.14	12
Total	264	456	42	16906	245	40.83	37	14765	7018	212	33.10	263

County Championship

Edrich's record in Middlesex matches against each opponent

County	Matches	Inns.	N.O.	Runs	H.S.	Average	100s	Balls	Runs	Wkts	Average	B.B.	Ct/St
Derbyshire	18	31	7	1150	208*	47.91	2	932	422	14	30.14	3-34	21
Essex	22	43	3	1858	211	46.45	5	1217	592	15	39.46	3-33	25
Glamorgan	12	20	2	736	189	40.88	3	588	254	9	28.22	3-21	12
Gloucestershire	22	39	4	1515	182	43.28	3	1181	520	23	22.60	6-28	27
Hampshire	24	42	4	1223	182	32.18	3	1375	546	22	24.81	4-25	24
Kent	26	45	2	1789	130	41.60	3	1263	655	27	24.25	5-30	20
Lancashire	24	43	3	1665	175	41.62	5	1183	559	10	55.90	3-19	22
Leicestershire	13	21	2	1191	257	62.68	4	642	295	7	42.14	2-37	11
Northamptonshire	27	45	3	2204	267*	52.47	4	2128	958	31	30.90	7-69	19
Nottinghamshire	20	31	2	1283	245	44.24	2	1172	590	15	39.33	4-25	19
Somerset	21	38	5	1408	168*	42.66	4	949	446	18	24.77	4-25	28
Surrey	31	56	3	1548	157*	29.20	3	1123	525	17	30.88	5-52	30
Sussex	31	48	7	1967	161	47.97	5	1731	778	24	32.41	6-45	30/1
Warwickshire	22	32	4	1900	225	67.85	7	1334	617	29	21.27	6-59	22
Worcestershire	19	29	3	1138	175*	43.76	2	1297	559	32	17.46	7-48	21
Yorkshire	27	42	4	1068	102	28.10	1	1791	713	14	50.92	2-13	27
Total	359	605	58	23643	267*	43.22	56	19906	9029	307	29.41	7-48	358/1

Other Matches

Opponent	Matches	Inns.	N.O.	Runs	H.S.	Average	100s	Balls	Runs	Wkts	Average	B.B.	Ct
Australians	4	7	1	222	84	37.00	0	120	59	0			4
New Zealanders	3	6	1	80	51	16.00	0	186	103	3	34.33	3-60	1
West Indians	3	6	0	173	58	28.83	0	58	43	1	43.00	1-24	3
South Africans	3	4	1	241	133*	80.33	1	288	165	4	41.25	2-91	3
Indians	1	2	0	150	129	75.00	1	42	40	1	40.00	1-40	0
Pakistanis	1	2	0	0	0	0.00	0	114	60	0			1
Cambridge University	7	12	2	597	161*	59.70	2	732	368	7	52.57	3-45	8
Oxford University	6	10	1	407	239	45.22	1	206	91	5	18.20	3-75	4
Yorkshire	1	2	0	32	19	16.00	0	42	17	0			0
Rest of England	1	2	1	193	180	193.00	1						0
Total	30	53	7	2095	239	45.54	6	1788	946	21	45.04		24

	Matches	Inns.	N.O.	Runs	H.S.	Average	100s	Balls	Runs	Wkts	Average	B.B.	Ct/St
All Middlesex Matches	389	658	65	25738	267*	43.40	62	21694	9975	328	30.41	7-48	382/1

W. J. Edrich – Test match record

Series by series

Season	Opponents	Tests	Inns.	N.O.	Runs	H.S.	Average	100s	Balls	Runs	Wkts	average	B.B.	Ct
1938	Australia	4	6	0	67	23	11.16	0	212	139	4	34.75	2-27	4
1938/39	South Africa	5	6	0	240	219	40.00	1	400	154	2	77.00	1-9	4
1946	India	1	0						116	68	4	17.00	4-68	0
1946/47	Australia	5	10	0	462	119	46.20	1	923	483	9	53.66	3-50	1
1946/47	New Zealand	1	1	0	42	42	42.00	0	66	35	1	35.00	1-35	0
1947	South Africa	4	6	1	552	191	110.40	2	809	370	16	23.12	4-77	5
1948	Australia	5	10	0	319	111	31.90	1	318	238	3	79.33	1-27	5
1949	New Zealand	4	6	0	324	100	54.00	1	162	97	2	48.50	2-18	9
1950	West Indies	2	4	0	94	71	23.50	0	204	81	0			1
1953	Australia	3	5	1	156	64	39.00	0						6
1954	Pakistan	1	1	0	4	4	4.00	0						1
1954/55	Australia	4	8	0	180	88	22.50	0	24	28	0			3
Total		39	63	2	2440	219	40.00	6	3234	1693	41	41.29	4-68	39

Record against each country

Opponents	Tests	Inns.	N.O.	Runs	H.S.	Average	100s	Balls	Runs	Wkts	Average	B.B.	Ct
Australia	21	39	1	1184	119	31.15	2	1477	888	16	55.50	3-50	19
South Africa	9	12	1	792	219	72.00	3	1209	524	18	29.11	4-77	9
New Zealand	5	7	0	366	100	52.28	1	228	132	3	44.00	2-18	9
West Indies	2	4	0	94	71	23.50	0	204	81	0			1
Pakistan	1	1	0	4	4	4.00	0						1
India	1	0						116	68	4	17.00	4-68	0
Total	39	63	2	2440	219	40.00	6	3234	1693	41	41.29	4-68	39

Test match record – innings by innings

Season	Opponents	Test	Ground	Position	Runs	How Out	Balls	Runs	Wkts	Cts
1938	Australia	1	Nottingham	3	5	b O'Reilly	78	39	1	
		2	Lord's	3	0	b McCormick	24	5	0	
				4	10	c McCabe b McCormick	32	27	2	
		4	Leeds	1	12	b O'Reilly	18	13	0	
				1	28	st Barnett b Fleetwood-Smith				1
		5	Oval	2	12	lbw b O'Reilly	60	55	1	1
1938/39	South Africa	1	Johannesburg	1	4	c Mitchell b Davies	72	44	0	1
				1	10	c Mitchell b Gordon	24	7	0	
		2	Cape Town	6	0	b Gordon	40	15	0	1
		3	Durban				24	5	0	
							32	9	1	
							56	16	1	
		4	Johannesburg	7	6	lbw b Langton	32	11	0	
		5	Durban	6	1	c Rowan b Langton	72	29	0	
				3	219	c Gordon b Langton	48	18	0	1
1946	India	3	Oval				116	68	4	
1946/47	Australia	1	Brisbane	3	16	c McCool b Miller	200	107	3	
				3	7	lbw b Toshack				
		2	Sydney	3	71	lbw b McCool	208	79	3	
				3	119	b McCool				
		3	Melbourne	3	89	lbw b Lindwall	83	50	3	
				3	13	lbw b McCool	144	86	0	
		4	Adelaide	3	17	c & b Dooland	160	88	0	
				3	46	c Bradman b Toshack	56	25	0	

Test	Season	Opponent	Venue	Pos	Score	How Out				
5	1946/47		Sydney	3	60	c Tallon b Lindwall	56	34	0	1
				3	24	st Tallon b McCool	16	14	0	
1		New Zealand	Christchurch	3	42	c Taylor b Scott	66	35	1	1
1	1947	South Africa	Nottingham	3	57	b Smith	120	56	1	1
				3	50	b Smith	24	8	0	3
2			Lord's	3	189	b Mann	54	22	0	
							78	31	3	
3			Manchester	3	191	b Tuckett	211	95	4	1
				3	22*		136	77	4	
4			Leeds	3	43	c Melville b Mann	102	46	3	1
							84	35	1	
1	1948	Australia	Nottingham	3	18	b Johnston	108	72	0	1
				3	13	c Tallon b Johnson	24	20	0	
2			Lord's	3	5	b Lindwall	48	43	1	
				3	2	c Johnson b Toshack	12	11	0	1
3			Manchester	3	32	c Tallon b Lindwall	42	27	1	
				3	53	run out	12	8	0	
4			Leeds	3	111	c Morris b Johnson	18	19	0	2
				3	54	lbw b Lindwall				
5			Oval	3	3	c Hassett b Johnston	54	38	1	1
				3	28	b Lindwall				
1	1949	New Zealand	Leeds	3	36	c Donnelly b Cowie	54	18	2	3
				3	70	b Cave	12	13	0	
2			Lord's	3	9	c Donnelly b Cowie	24	16	0	2
3			Manchester	3	31	c Hadlee b Burtt	24	8	0	
				3	78	c Rabone b Burtt	30	26	0	
4			Oval	3	100	c Cave b Cresswell	18	16	0	3
										1

Year	Opponent	Test	Venue	Inns	Score	Dismissal				
1950	West Indies	1	Manchester	3	7	c Gomez b Valentine	12	4	0	
		2	Lord's	2	71	c Weekes b Ramadhin	18	10	0	
				3	8	c Walcott b Ramadhin	96	30	0	
				3	8	c Jones b Ramadhin	78	37	0	1
1953	Australia	3	Manchester	2	6	c Hole b Hill				2
		4	Leeds	2	10	lbw b Miller				1
				2	64	c De Courcy b Lindwall				
		5	Oval	2	21	lbw b Lindwall				2
				2	55*					1
1954	Pakistan	1	Lord's	5	4	b Khan Mohammad				1
1954/55	Australia	1	Brisbane	3	15	c Langley b Archer	24	28	0	
				3	88	b Johnston				
		2	Sydney	6	10	c Benaud b Archer				1
				6	29	b Archer				
		3	Melbourne	2	4	c Lindwall b Miller				1
				2	13	b Johnston				
		4	Adelaide	2	21	b Johnson				1
				2	0	b Miller				

W. J. Edrich in Minor Counties Championship
Norfolk record

Debut for Norfolk: vs. All–India at Lakenham, 2 June 1932
Capped by Norfolk: 1933
Last Match: vs. Buckinghamshire at Lakenham, 22 July 1971

Minor Counties Championship – Season by season record

Season	Matches	Inns.	N.O.	Runs	H.S.	Average	Overs	Maidens	Runs	Wkts	Average
1932	7	12	0	181	50	15.08	87.0	17	176	11	16.00
1933	10	14	0	293	71	20.92	172.0	37	462	23	20.08
1934	9	11	0	527	138	47.90	213.0	46	515	40	12.87
1935	10	15	0	488	152	32.53	229.0	55	629	27	23.29
1936	10	11	2	397	101*	44.11	121.0	16	331	16	20.68
1959	10	17	7	468	65*	46.80	153.4	49	386	19	20.31
1960	11	20	4	852	102*	53.25	244.3	60	695	43	16.16
1961	8	12	5	558	127*	79.71	144.3	24	436	18	24.22
1962	9	16	2	587	99	41.92	226.5	74	528	39	13.53
1963	11	16	2	587	136*	41.92	306.1	75	750	45	16.66
1964	12	22	4	713	101*	39.61	299.2	87	700	28	25.00
1965	12	20	3	349	73*	20.52	113.3	29	313	10	31.30
1966	12	21	2	496	93	26.10	175.4	50	482	29	16.62
1967	10	17	3	300	62	21.42	189.0	66	428	16	26.75
1968	9	11	3	317	57*	39.62	116.0	45	242	12	20.16
1969	10	17	4	430	83*	33.07	151.0	55	321	14	22.92
1970	11	18	6	424	93*	35.33	238.1	69	487	25	19.48
1971	3	6	0	67	28	11.16	20.0	2	75	0	–
Total	174	276	47	8034	152	35.08	3200.2	856	7956	415	19.17

Including matches against touring sides and the friendly vs. Suffolk at Lowestoft in 1933, career record is

	Matches	Inns.	N.O.	Runs	H.S.	Average	Overs	Maidens	Runs	Wkts	Average
Norfolk Total	178	281	47	8308	152	35.50	3267.4	872	8161	417	19.57

Highest Score: 152 v. Hertfordshire at Broxbourne, 1935
Best Bowling: 7-45 v. Suffolk at Lakenham, 1962
He took 154 catches, including 16 in 1963

A miscellany of facts and achievements

W. J. Edrich achieved the following feats:

1000 runs by the end of May (all scored at Lord's)

In 1938: 9 Matches, 15 Innings, 3 Not Out, 1010 Runs, Average 84.16:
All 1010 runs were made at Lord's.

104	M.C.C.	v. Yorkshire
37 & 115	M.C.C.	v. Surrey
63 & 20*	Middlesex	v. Warwickshire
182 & 71	Middlesex	v. Gloucestershire
31 & 53*	M.C.C.	v. Australians
45 & 15	Middlesex	v. Lancashire
245	Middlesex	v. Nottinghamshire
0	Middlesex	v. Worcestershire
9 & 20*	Middlesex	v. Australians

1000 runs in a calendar month

In July 1947: 6 Matches, 11 Innings, 3 Not Out, 1047 Runs, Average
130.87:

191 & 22*	England	v. South Africa	at Manchester
257 & 29*	Middlesex	v. Leicestershire	at Leicester
79 & 5	Gentlemen	v. Players	at Lord's
44 & 83	Middlesex	v. Essex	at Lord's
267* & 27	Middlesex	v. Northamptonshire	at Northampton
43	England	v. South Africa	at Leeds

Carrying his bat

140* out of 303, for Lord Tennyson's XI v. Sind at Karachi in
1937/38

Century before lunch

104* at lunch on 3rd day, for Gentlemen of England v.
Australians at Lord's in 1948

260

75% of a completed innings total

127* out of 169, for Middlesex v. Gloucestershire at Lord's in 1946

6 Catches in a match

For Middlesex v. Surrey at Lord's in 1949

Partnership records

280 with P. A. Gibb, at Durban 1938/39:
England's highest 2nd wicket stand v. South Africa
370 with D. C. S. Compton, at Lord's 1947
England's highest Test 3rd wicket stand
(and was at the time the 3rd wicket record in all Test cricket)
424 with D. C. S. Compton v. Somerset, at Lord's 1948
Highest 3rd wicket stand in England, highest at Lord's, and Middlesex record

Season aggregates

1000 runs in a season 15 times, including 2000 runs nine times
His 1947 aggregate of 3539 beat T. W. Hayward's record of 3518 in 1906
It is second to Compton's 3816, also in 1947, during which season Edrich scored 870 runs and Compton 1187 runs against the South African tourists

200 runs and 8 wickets in a match

222*, 7-69 & 1-23 for Middlesex v. Northamptonshire at Northampton, 1946
191 & 22*, 4-95 & 4-77 for England v. South Africa at Manchester, 1947
(becoming the third player, after G. Giffen and G. A. Faulkner, to achieve this feat in a Test match)

261

INDEX

Close, D.B., 180
Collins, R., 211–12
Colman, J., 55
Compton, D.C.S., 20–4, 28–33, 42,
44, 46–7, 58, 65, 71, 75, 81, 85, 92,
94–9, 104, 108, 112–14, 117–18,
120, 122, 128–30, 137, 142–3,
146–7, 149–54, 156–8, 160–9,
170–1, 177, 180–1, 183–4, 186–9,
190–1, 193, 195, 202, 205–6, 218,
220–2, 225, 230–1
Compton, L.H., 20, 28, 102, 203
Coomb, A.G., 211, 214
Coope, M., 184
Corran, A.J., 211–12
Cowdrey, Sir Colin, 138, 193
Cranston, K., 165
Crapp, J.F., 188
Crisp, R.J., 25, 45, 60–1, 107

Dalton, E.L., 60–1, 66, 69
Davies, D.E., 202–3
Dawson, O.C., 156, 163
Delisle, G.P.S., 92
Denison, Michael, 143, 225
Dewes, J.G., 95, 151, 180–1
Djanogli, R., 224
Doggart, G.H.G., 153, 176
Douglas, James, 166
Douglas, J.W.H.T., 103
Duffus, Louis, 146, 150, 154–9
Duleepsinhji, K.S., 103
Duncan, A., 28
Durston, F.J., 28
Dyer, D.V., 163

Eagar, E.D.R., 23
Easterbrook, B., 145
Edrich, Alice (aunt of W.J.), 9
Edrich, Betty (first wife), 127
Edrich, Bill senior (father), 4–8, 18,
26, 54, 83
Edrich, Brian (brother), 2, 6, 10, 54,
77, 85, 89, 93, 101, 105, 107, 141
Edrich, Edith (mother), 8–9, 10, 18,
125, 127
Edrich, Elizabeth (grandmother), 4,
9
Edrich, Eric (brother), 6–8, 10,

16–17, 26, 47–8, 54–5, 65, 85, 130,
201–2, 225–6, 228
Edrich, Fred (uncle), 201–2
Edrich, Geoffrey (brother), 6, 16, 54
Edrich, George (uncle), 7
Edrich, Harriet (great-
grandmother), 9
Edrich, Harry (grandfather), 3–4, 9,
54, 201
Edrich, Jasper (son), 128, 130, 227–8
Edrich, Jessy (third wife), 127–8,
130, 132, 189, 230
Edrich, John (cousin), 201–2
Edrich, Justin (son), 126, 129,
130–1, 214, 219, 227, 231
Edrich, Marion (second wife), 127
Edrich, Mary (fifth wife), 125,
221–2, 228, 230
Edrich, Valerie (fourth wife), 129,
130–2, 208
Edrich, Bill (W.J.), passim
Evans, T.G., 101–2, 111–12, 114,
119, 132–3, 154, 172, 174, 176, 187,
192–3, 195–6
Evans, W., 26–8

Fagg, A.E., 51, 75
Falcon, M., 14, 16–17, 25, 54, 198
Farnes, K., 52, 59, 63, 101, 104
Fender, P.G.H., 103
Fenner, G.D., 213
Fiddler, G.G., 213
Findlay, W., 17, 28
Fingleton, J.H.W., 106, 155, 186
Fishlock, L.B., 108
Fleetwood-Smith, L.O'B., 49, 57
Foot, David, 106
Fortune, Charles, 160
Freer, F., 117, 120
Fry, C.B., 51

Garner, J., 94
Gibb, P.A., 37, 53, 57, 59–60, 66,
68–9, 111
Gimblett, H., 75
Gladwin, C., 163, 200
Goddard, T.W.J., 42–3, 168
Gomez, G.E., 176
Goodman, Tom, 121

266

Witherden, E.G., 207, 211, 214
Woodcock, J., 218
Wooldridge, I., 222–3, 229
Wooller, W., 178
Woolley, F.E., 31
Worthington, T.S., 37, 40
Wright, D.V.P., 60, 63, 96, 112, 159,
    168, 180

Wright, H., 140
Wyatt, R.E.S., 25, 88–9, 103, 138,
    173–5

Yardley, N.W.D., 37, 39, 51, 57, 99,
    110, 115 16, 154, 156–7, 173, 175,
    177–8, 187
Young, J.A., 105, 167–8

267